Libraries Designed for Users

A 21st Century Guide

NOLAN LUSHINGTON

Neal-Schuman Publishers, Inc.

New York   London

Published by Neal-Schuman Publishers, Inc.
100 Varick Street
New York, NY 10013

Table of Contents

PART IV
Library Design Source Box

List of Figures

Foreword

A handful of early career experiences sealed my interest in planning library facilities. The first of those experiences was sitting in on Walter Allen's buildings class at the University of Illinois Graduate School of Library and Information Science. Then came my first post-MLS job and the chance to participate in the endgame of a building project in progress under the direction of Marlene Deuel at the Popular Creek Public Library in Streamwood, Illinois. And a little while after that, as a library director "herding kittens" in a building project of my own, I discovered the first edition of Nolan Lushington's *Libraries Designed for Users.*

The first edition seemed to me to give a tacit endorsement to try new things, to take a new approach. I remember appreciating the first edition's focus on the patron's experience of the library's space. I appreciated the practical perspective Nolan brought to the discussion.

Later on, as I started doing seminars and workshops on library space planning, Nolan's book was always part of a select core of particularly useful resources listed on the inevitable bibliography prepared for the presentation at hand. Even as the first edition started to age a bit and people sometimes wondered about a 1980 publication date appearing in a workshop bibliography, I felt Nolan's book retained an essential relevance, and I recommended it gladly.

Now, a generation or so after its original publication, here's a new version of Nolan Lushington's classic *Libraries Designed for Users: a 21st Century Guide.* That's good news.

Library services have changed a lot. We've learned a lot in the last 20 years, and our buildings need to reflect current realities. Public library design today is shaped by a growing awareness of marketing and display strategies. Accessibility and humane design occupy our attention differently than was the case a generation ago. And then there's technology, which not only imposes its own demands on the library facility by bringing all those display screens and keyboards and plugs and wires into the building, but changes the library facility by changing the very nature of the service we offer.

At the same time our buildings need to reflect those current realities, they also need to anticipate, to the greatest degree possible, the changes that are still to come. There's no surprise in that observation; flexibility and adaptability have been the mantra of library design for many, many years now. But today, the impetus for change will come from a wider range of vectors and sources. The responsiveness of our buildings to future change has never been more important.

There is a tall order facing our libraries. With *Libraries Designed for Users: a 21st Century Guide,* we can look forward to more of Nolan's practical insights and counsel, reflecting the changes of the last 20 years and helping us keep ahead of the future as best we can. Nolan's clear thinking has benefited the many libraries he's consulted with over the years. Through his participation in ALA committees and other projects, and through publications like this one, we've all benefited. For my part, I'm also happy to have this update for those inevitable bibliographies.

Anders C. Dahlgren
President
Library Planning Associates, Inc.
Madison, Wisconsin

Preface

Libraries Designed for Users: a 21st Century Guide embraces and answers the critical questions asked by anyone presently thinking about constructing a new library or renovating an existing one. The library building of the twenty-first century is in many ways a new environment. Changes in demographics and users' needs have transformed library design in fresh, imaginative, and creative ways. Today a customer might walk through the front door of a library and see a coffeehouse, a computer lab, an electronic classroom, or an art gallery. Libraries in this new century need to be built or renovated not only to reflect the dynamics of an ever-changing world but to plan for ones we can now only imagine. Librarians and the people who design and plan new facilities are thinking outside the box to create blueprints that ingeniously address radically new demands. How can libraries better serve their communities? How will libraries offer multi-lingual services, late-night services, and remote-user services? How might libraries provide special services to youth, the aging, new parents, and full-time workers?

Librarians beginning to consider new, expanded, or renovated buildings need to be aware of trends and developments from two disparate areas. First, planners are using the research in other fields to best design or renovate library buildings. If research shows that customers entering department stores invariably turn right, it is quite likely that users will behave similarly in libraries. This research might translate into utilizing the right side of the front door as an ideal site for popular new materials. If studies reveal that customers find narrow store aisles unappealing, then wider book stack aisles are certain to be a better design plan. Collaboration is demonstrating that many of the winning customer service concepts popular in the private sector mirror the findings of successful library user surveys. For example, Joan Durrance's University of Michigan library school students' findings when they administered "Willingness to Return Surveys" in libraries is not dissimilar to a marketing study of customer service quality on the Internet showing that one must pay attention to customers' individual needs. This type of critical feedback can often turn into ideas for the design of libraries. If research shows that people respond better to longer individual reference interviews, then library reference desks that provide users with seats will be more popular than those that do not

Secondly, library architects and planners need to clearly understand the esthetic grandeur of these architectural library spaces and possess a clearer understanding of the functional virtue of the traditional library reading room and the grand book stack. Library spaces that lift the spirit of users and staff by using space and natural light in esthetically pleasing ways give the library building a lasting quality that great civic buildings deserve. Combining people, books, and computers in these spaces symbolizes the power of new and old ways of acquiring intellectual power. Both architects and planners need to understand twenty-first century opportunities to enhance traditional library designs and integrate electronic information delivery into the makeup of the library.

Libraries Designed for Users: a 21st Century Guide emphasizes the user's experience and how that should both inform and affect design decisions. The guide features numerous illustrations of library plans and equipment in order to demonstrate the variety of solutions to design issues.

The *Guide* is organized in four parts:

Part I, "Essential Background," examines in a single chapter the history of library design with an emphasis on new and future design concerns. *Libraries Designed for Users: a 21st Century Guide* describes the various trends and influences on library buildings during the twentieth century. The chapter summarizes new models for public libraries emerging in the twenty-first century and enumerates general principles for designing an ideal library now.

Part II focuses on the basics with "The Planning Process." Chapters outline the library building planning process, long-range planning, detailed space-needs analysis, and architectural design. Chapter 2 presents an introductory overview of the planning process. "The Needs Assessment" is examined in Chapter 3. Long-range planning is covered in Chapter 4, "The Library Program Document." Chapter 5 explores "The Architect and Architectural Work," emphasizing functional planning. Chapter 6 discusses "Site Selection and General Design Considerations." An essential yet often overlooked area ends Part II with "Review of Plans."

Part III, "The Planning of Specific Functional Areas," looks at general design principles, site selection, and each major functional area. Chapters 8–16 are devoted to describing design for the functional aspects of the library's individual parts. "Parking, Entry, and Circulation," "Browsing and Magazine Display Areas," "Reference Services," "Material Storage," "Special Spaces for Children and Teens," "Meeting Rooms," "Administrative and Staff Work Areas," "Climate Control, Staff Lounge, and Rest Rooms," and "Computer Areas," are examined. The final two chapters in Part III explore special design considerations. "Graphics, Lighting, and Chairs" are discussed in Chapter 17 while the last chapter offers a handy perspective on "Quick Improvements." In each of these chapters user behavior and convenience and staff productivity are the focus of the design suggestions.

Part IV is the "Library Design Source Box" where useful material is offered. This section includes criteria for post-occupancy evaluation, model templates for library specification—complete with sample spreadsheets and functional area design sheets. There is also a steel book stack specification, a list of library equipment suppliers, and the final source directs the reader to resources and further reading.

Helping librarians communicate their needs to architects as well as helping architects understand the needs of library users and staff are the overall goals of *Libraries Designed for Users: a 21st Century Guide*. It covers many critical topics and has been designed to be suitable both for the experienced librarian as well as for the beginner in planning. It is my hope that the book will be both a sequential guide to the planning process as well as a reference manual on library design specifications.

Ken Dowlin, a leader in encouraging library innovation in the 1990s, once said that managing a library today was like trying to fix a tire while a car was rolling down a hill. Engaging in a library improvement project often has that feeling. Librarians, consultants, and architects are trying to improve a building while the services in that building are changing on a daily basis. In addition, the detail and complexity of the service is affected by the different individuals we are trying to help and by the variety of resources with which we deliver our services.

Architects involved in planning the library come to the design process with their own criteria and experience about what constitutes a beautiful library. It is their expertise in designing the structure and fitting it into its site that will give life to the building and determine how users respond to the library. Architects violating many functional precepts may impart an enduring beauty in proportions and finishings that overcomes functional considerations. On the other hand, buildings that ignore function may result in such frustration to the staff and users that all the design attention cannot overcome the functional defects. Each design has its own set of experiential and esthetic responses.

For these practical reasons it is unlikely that we will ever get it all completely right. Even if you think your building is perfect, it's probably because you are not aware of the latest new ways to deliver library service. Still we engage in the quest to create buildings that will serve the best of our ambitions. Trying to design the best buildings to help people in pursuit of their individual aims is always the goal. We take comfort from the creativity, energy, and enjoyment of the effort. The librarians, users, staff, architects, and builders involved in library improvement projects are what make the journey worthwhile. *Libraries Designed for Users: a 21ˢᵗ Century Guide* is conceived as a valuable guide on the endless journey to beautiful and effective library design.

Acknowledgments

Acknowledgments are terrifying. I know I will probably forget my most formative contributor, so I apologize in advance.

The way I learned how to be a library consultant was to work on 197 small- to medium-sized libraries with librarians, trustees, architects, and volunteers. I am grateful to all of these hundreds of people over a 30-year span for giving me the opportunity to work on their libraries.

My wife Louise Blalock, *Library Journal's* 2001 Librarian of the Year, who is a constant inspiration, critic, and best friend.

My editor Virginia Mathews, who also worked on my two earlier books, has been an inspiration not only for her penetrating insights into the making of a useful book, but also for her comprehensive and wonderful view of how important libraries are to everyone.

Anders Dahlgren, an excellent expert reader, gave useful advice on improving the book.

My colleagues in the library consulting profession: Frank Hemphill, Robert Rohlf, Gloria Stockton, and Ray Holt.

My colleagues at Lushington Associates: Mary Beth Mahler, who helped put together this book and took several of the best photographs, Kevin McCarthy, David Hinkley, and Ed Stubbs who were helpful readers of the manuscript.

Mary Louise Jensen for her planning expertise and years of toil in trying to improve Connecticut's libraries.

Architects with whom I have worked:

Tony Tappe for inviting me to join him in teaching at The Harvard Graduate School of Design and thus giving me the opportunity to develop this book over the past ten years of teaching the summer workshop on public library design to dozens of librarians and architects. Jeff Hoover who worked extensively on the architectural work chapter and Michael Cohen who gave it an important critical read. Wills Mills, Jr. who was an excellent collaborator on the 1979 edition of this book. Charlie King, Rick Schoenhardt, Jay Clough, Robert Kelly, Robb Kinsley, Felix Drury, Peter Gisolfi, Michael Cohen, Peter Wells, and Bruce Tuthill—all inspirational architects who care about the design of public libraries.

Roz Levine, Jeff Hoover, and Bruce Tuthill who prepared many of the illustrations. Peter Wells who labored hard on the Isometrics small library drawing.

Dr. James Kusack who wrote the section on workstation design and who was a rigorous co-author of my 1991 book on the design and evaluation of public library buildings and introduced me to the Macintosh computer. Outstanding clients—Sandy Ruoff and Lana Ferguson, Barbara Gibson, Susan Bullock, Alan Benkert, Trish Calvani, Bill Schell, Lora Lynn Stevens, and many, many others.

My three children, Christopher, Nancy, and Michael, who shared a patient interest in libraries.

There is a Zen aphorism: "An enemy is better than a Buddha," which I take to mean that you learn best from your severest critics. I thank them all.

I

Essential Backgrounds

1

History, Trends, and Design Criteria for the Ideal Library

A brief history of public library planning and design, new models for the twenty-first century, and characteristics of the ideal library.

The Invention of the Public Library

The free public library idea captured the imagination of the public during the last half of the nineteenth century and public library buildings were designed in ever increasing numbers. Innovations in printing and paper making, as much as public education, created large new reading populations who understood the opportunity to better themselves through access to mass produced books and magazines. Foresighted library pioneers in Boston, Massachusetts, and Manchester, England, seized on the opportunity of the new market and the new availability of printed material to devise a plan to provide freely available library service to all citizens by taxing the entire community.

Architects and Librarians—the Professionals Clash

Architects produced a wide variety of designs in the rush to construct libraries. By the 1880s outspoken librarians such as Frederick Poole were critical of these early attempts. In 1879 Poole told an audience of his colleagues at the Fourth Annual American Library Association convention, "Avoid everything that pertains to the plan and arrangement of the conventional American library building."

Poole was referring to the alcoved book hall library such as the one Henry Hobson

Richardson designed for the Winn Library in Woburn, Massachusetts. The book stack was closed to the public so staff climbed a precarious spiral stair and clambered up ten-foot-high bookcases to retrieve books for users waiting at the delivery desk. It was next to impossible to heat the galleried book hall to a comfortable temperature without overheating its upper levels and damaging the books. The book stack capacity was minimal and much of the space was unusable for library purposes. Nonetheless, the Winn Library is a glorious cathedral-like space considered a monumental achievement by architects and much beloved by many library users. Monumental designs like the Winn Library pose similar problems for today's librarians. For example, in a recent post occupancy evaluation of the San Francisco Public Library design, librarians were critical of the interior space lost to the atrium.

However, there is something to be said for atrium designs. In addition to being a beautiful space bringing natural light into the heart of the building, an atrium orients users to the central circulating space in the library and affords intriguing glimpses of functions taking place in other parts of the building.

Function and Esthetics—Planning the Carnegie Libraries

The process of designing a beautiful and functional library has always depended on balancing the esthetic criteria of architects with the functional needs of librarians to achieve an architectural masterpiece that works well as a library.

In the early 1900s Andrew Carnegie made available funds for constructing libraries throughout the United States and Canada. Early designs were so dysfunctional they prompted Carnegie's library consultant, Richard Bertram, to issue one of the first codifications of useful library design. Bertram wanted "To obtain for the money the utmost amount of effective accommodation, consistent with good taste in building." His emphasis was on economy of space. He especially disliked wasted space at the entrance. "Too valuable space allotted to cloak rooms, toilets and stairs." Bertram liked the one story and basement rectangular plan subdivided by bookcases. The site should admit natural light and be large enough to allow for expansion. Although he actually supplied six sample floor plans, he steered away from suggesting designs for the exterior. He felt that it was useful to plan for future expansion by allowing for a rear wing to be added for expanded book storage. Since his basic plans called for very small book collections, book stack expansion plans became increasingly important.

The Great Book Stack

During the period from 1850–1920 there was an enormous boom in book publishing, consequently lower book prices appeared as well as a movement to open up the book stacks for browsing. In 1897 John Cotton Dana pointed out that the decreases in book costs made the concept of a library as a storehouse of treasures obsolete.

The new open library allowed readers to enjoy "the touch of the books themselves, the joy of their immediate presence." Dana felt that libraries were more like stores than museums. This changed the nature of design by requiring that libraries increase their book capacities and open their stacks so that anyone could browse the entire collection. Earlier designs that placed the book shelves around the walls of the reading rooms were replaced with free standing stacks requiring reinforced floors to support heavy seven-foot-high stacks to meet the new requirements for thousands of volumes.

Grand Schemes and Monumental Libraries— the People's University

Libraries designed from 1880–1920 fulfilled the promise that American institutions for the people would be designed as great monuments to the uplifting of all citizens. Whether they were funded by private money, as was the New York Public Library, or by city funds, as in Boston, the concept reflected the great civic pride of the time.

Architects in this period were conscious of the basics of library function in their designs. The great reading rooms flooded with light from tall windows contained useful chairs with ample study space. The great book stacks were orderly in their configuration for easy finding of a particular book among the thousands housed in closely spaced stacks and in multi-story layers with low ceilings and functional lighting.

While libraries celebrated people and books their ornamentation and art glorified the buildings. Many people including architects and municipal leaders loved these temples, but for the average person the design was formidable no matter what the incised stone letters above the Greek revival columns said about "the People's University."

There were problems with these libraries that librarians began to notice and call to the attention of architects. The pedestal steps were tiring to climb and excluded older and handicapped users. The great reading rooms were intimidating and inhuman in lining up readers at long tables like assembly lines. The closed, cramped, narrow aisle book stacks did not permit easy browsing by library users. Minimum provision for children's services discouraged potential new users. A conversation between two teenagers recently overheard at night outside one of these monumental libraries illustrates the problem. One boy asked his friend as they lounged outside the library at night, "What's that place?" The other answered, "I think it's the library but it's not for us, it's only for rich people."

One of the most visionary library thinkers was a stack manufacturer, Angus Snead McDonald, who wrote a book in the 1920s envisioning public libraries as the center for public learning for the entire community staffed by leading experts in engineering, science, and the humanities. The library would not only provide the materials but also the expertise for learning a wide array of useful professions—truly becoming the People's University.

During the depression of the 1930s public libraries became citizen learning centers despite limited resources. People desperately flocked to libraries to learn new trades and acquire competitive skills for the job market that was suddenly so limited. National per capita library circulation reached its all time peak in the depression.

Modular Libraries and the Flexibility Fallacy

Modular libraries were introduced in the 1950–60 period in an effort to design flexible open spaces for a variety of functions. Architects searched for the perfect column spacing module useful for all library functions. Structural steel frameworks without bearing walls allowed for easy changes within the structure.

These anonymous looking international style modern buildings have become highly criticized, bland, overcrowded spaces with little character and not as much flexibility as the planners intended. Converting a book stack into a reading room requires more than just moving furniture. It's often unpleasant for readers in these open spaces, a long way from the cozy reading alcoves of the 1880s.

The problem with flexible design is that specific library uses have different functional requirements. A bookstack to house books efficiently requires 150-pound floor loading to hold the weight of books. The seven-foot-tall stacks require column spacing that matches the aisle spacing so that columns do not end up in the middle of the aisles. The lighting must be designed to reach the bottom shelves. The ceiling height can be just above the top shelves. Heating and cooling is less important because users will not be seated for long periods.

On the other hand, in a reading room long-term comfort is more important for the seated readers, the load bearing capacity is only 75 pounds per square foot and lighting should be related to the user seated at tables. Natural light is much more important for the user but may actually be destructive for the books.

Library Standards—the American Library Association

In the 1950–70 period library planners began to agree on empirical standards for the size of public libraries based on population. These standards, supported by American Library Association planning guidelines, were useful planning guidelines with progressive library communities constructing buildings having one square foot of space per capita and five seats for every 1,000 people served.

As collections grew they occupied almost 50 percent of the usable space in the building. These newer libraries had book lifts and even high density storage for materials. Technical spaces were designed for efficient flow of materials.

ALA—the American Library Association

The Buildings and Equipment Section of the ALA in its programs in the 1980s encouraged librarians, consultants, and architects to look critically at library designs by offering annual ALA programs for critiquing new libraries. Tough minded library consultants, like Robert Rohlf of Hennepin County, Minnesota, showed how architects drifted away from function in their designs.

The Multi-Function Public Library

In the 1980s, the Public Library Association adopted eight specific library roles and the use of output measures for public libraries. This turned sharply away from the earlier traditional emphasis on the library as a warehouse for books and a research center for the well-educated elite. Instead, this new process examined the library as a multi-function service combining many different uses. The library was an information center for everyday needs—job hunting, fixing the plumbing, buying a car, health information. It was a community cultural center for music, lectures, and meetings of all kinds.

Recent Library Designs

The 1990s saw a remarkable period for library construction in big cities. Chicago, Los Angeles, San Francisco, San Antonio, Phoenix, Cleveland, Denver, Vancouver, and Toronto all built new or renovated main libraries.

Some of these designs focused on how people used libraries and on the comfort of library users. Phoenix, San Francisco, and San Antonio offered books together with computers and gave users a choice of study and reading spaces. Phoenix especially introduced lighting and comfort into many of the user spaces.

Chicago on the other hand is a parody of the monumental designs of late nineteenth century libraries. As in the addition to Boston Public, designed by Philip Johnson 20 years before, books are hidden away from users until they reach the second floor. The monumental spaces such as the Winter Garden in Chicago have little to do with library function, and the functional spaces are often bland.

Design ideas found in many of these libraries include:

ERGONOMIC DESIGN

Interior designers introduced new furniture designs shaped for the human body to let people sit comfortably for long periods of time.

THE POPULAR MATERIALS DISPLAY LIBRARY AND THE BOOKSTORE CONCEPT

The popular library movement of the 1980s changed the way libraries looked by emphasizing popular materials with multiple copies of best sellers and display shelving for front covers of videos and CDs. Frank Hemphill, the Library Facilities Coordinator at Baltimore County, Maryland, incorporated new display, lighting, and arrangement ideas. In the late 1980s, mega bookstores not only displayed front covers, but expanded their stores with thousands not just hundreds of books, becoming more like libraries in the process.

THE COMPUTER LIBRARY

Kenneth Dowlin burst on the library scene in the 1980s talking about the computer-centered information library with masses of terminals and community databases. The San Francisco Library designed by Pei and Freed in the 1990s incorporates computers and books on every floor in dramatically designed workstations for public use.

At the Science Industry and Business Library in New York a superb indirect lighting system provides glare-free lighting for the computers and a double floor was installed for ease in reconfiguring the computer arrangement. A central convenient maintenance center for keeping the computers running was planned. Computer instruction is offered in a variety of group and individual learning environments. The bulk of the book collection is in compact, high-density stacks inaccessible to the public and housed on floors above the computer areas.

The Twenty-First Century Public Library—New Models

In the twenty-first century, library architects and planners have an opportunity to create new facilities designed to recapture the elusive user by taking advantage of the libraries great resources and assets and offering them in new ways:

In the twenty-first century what are some of the forces changing public library design? What will these new library designs be like? What should we look for in plans and designs that acknowledge these changes? How should the library planning process be improved?

Changing Demographics and Library Needs

Emerging multi-ethnic populations and the increasingly urgent need for literacy and computer skills are new trends requiring changes in the design of library buildings. Materials and signage in many different foreign languages need to be clearly evident at the library entrance. In Hayward, California, an entrance display includes books in 11 different languages. A combination library and swimming pool in a South London neighborhood includes books in Urdu.

When the San Francisco Public Library opened it was a spectacular public success. The library use quadrupled in the first few months unlike many other new buildings, which experienced less rapid growth in use. The library celebrated the diversity of its population by encouraging ethnic communities in the city to create centers at the library to celebrate their cultures with beautiful showcases of books and displays.

Ergonomic Design

In one important respect, even San Francisco failed to reflect the advances made in designing workstations for the human body. Perhaps the most important element in ergonomic design is adjustability. People come in all shapes and sizes, and they need to be able to change their position frequently, to move around in their chairs. At San Francisco the workstations lifted the CRT too high for visual comfort and used expensive but non-adjustable hard wooden chairs. By contrast, at New York's Science, Industry and Business Library designed by Gwathmey and Siegel the expensive Herman Miller Aeron Chair, a fully adjustable and ergonomic design, was adopted as the standard seating accommodation. This will become standard seating in libraries since new inexpensive ergonomic chairs like Turnstone's UNO chair are now available.

Designs for Children

Librarians have recently begun to recognize the vital importance of library services to children. We know how important the preschool library experience can be for children striving to break free from the illiterate limitations of their parents. New children's libraries are twice the size they were ten years ago. They include tutorial rooms, collaborative electronic workstations, display bins for books and CDs.

Family Place children's facilities in Middle Country, Glens Falls, New York, and Hartford, Connecticut, encourage families to come to the library together to attend programs, read together, and learn parenting and computer skills together; children actually encourage parents to become literate.

At Dallas, after the original design had hidden children's sevices on an upper floor, a spectacular redesign and expansion made it a feature of the library's main entrance floor.

New Teen Libraries

For many years librarians have been fretting about the disappearance of their potential new customers just after they reach the sixth grade. At Phoenix, Arizona, and Los Angeles, California, new teen age centers have been designed featuring music, video, and study spaces including group study to try to recapture these users. Los Angeles' TeenScape Cyberzone includes a computer cafe. Anthony Bernier, the Oakland, California, consultant who worked on the Los Angeles design emphasizes the need for audio separation and a wide range of seating options, including a three-position chair.

The Multi-Function Library

People entering library buildings come for a wide variety of services. This multi-function concept needs to be at the heart of the design. The entrance experience should reveal the many functions that take place in the library, such as browsing, reference, computers, research, community center, self-education, and children's services. Atriums can make differing functions on each floor visible from the floor of the atrium, but all too often each floor looks like every other floor. At Chicago half of the arrival floor was actually subtracted from the entrance experience by using it for the upper part of the auditorium. Materials are often concealed from the entrance, or, as in the case of San Francisco, de-emphasized by lower lighting levels.

The Popular Library

The idea of the popular library and its similarity to bookstore design has been around for decades, but only recently have public libraries begun to adopt such features of this model as the coffee shop and extensive front cover display of materials. In the twenty-first century multimedia display units such as those introduced by the innovative Austrian company LIFT will integrate lighting with display units designed to attract users to CDs videos, magazines, and books in a single modular unit. LIFT has recently introduced a listening unit offering users brief previews of thousands of CDs in a single station.

Many people still come to browse in the latest books, videos, and CDs. Library users spend ten times the amount of time reading books, viewing videos at home, and listening to CDs than they do using computers in the library building. Yet in many libraries a person arriving in the building doesn't actually see any materials to borrow. Philip Johnson in designing the addition to the Boston Public Library eliminated any hint of books from the library entrance or the atrium. In many libraries the front covers are hidden in cased shelves with the spine out and subjected to dim lighting. At San Francisco on one memorable visit I witnessed a grandson helping his grandfather select a CD by reading to him the tiny lettering on the spines of the jewel boxes. Other library users were sitting on the floor to see the low shelves. A library building should celebrate the beauty and excitement of its new materials with dramatic lighting and display fixtures.

Displays in the Stacks

Book stack design has remained relatively unchanged for decades and libraries have focused on capacity rather than on customer service.

The new book stack will have wide four-foot aisles, no lower shelves, and integrated lighting and display opportunities for front cover display on each eye-height shelf in the stacks. A single book would be selected for display with cover out, so that users walking through the stacks would be encouraged to pick up books serendipitously. Recently Bill Schell's York, Pennsylvania, library experienced a 20 percent increase in circulation using this methodology.

The stacks will have overhead line of sight subject signs in the aisles so users know exactly what subject section they are in at all times without having to swivel their heads to see the tiny shelf signs. Libraries need to help users find information by showing physical pathways to materials.

In many libraries, computers are lined up in separate areas from materials, but in new model libraries E-panels incorporating flat screens would be installed as end panels in the book stack. Users can search not only for books but for information related to book searches. For example, the user searching for a book on the French Revolution finds a dozen titles on the shelf and determines which one to borrow by consulting brief reviews on the computer. Screen savers could be programmed to display reviews of the most recently returned titles in each range of stacks. As books are checked out, a new title review would be displayed.

The Electronic Library

Computers will be everywhere in the library, not just grouped at the entrance like the old card catalogs. Flat screens and keyboards will be mounted on stack end panels. Wireless networks will make it possible for users to bring their own laptops and hand-held computers and link them with the library's databases. Electronic workstations will be adjustable for sitdown or standup use. Embedded terminals will make it possible for a reading table to become an electronic workstation at the flip of a switch.

Computers will access not only the library's collections but remote databases and reference materials. Library home pages will point users to useful Internet Web sites. Web rings will link library collections on similar subjects. Jeff Bezos, founder of Amazon.com, has revolutionized the concept of a book catalog. By combining listing with reviews even soliciting reader reviews he has shown the way to libraries. Library OPACs (online public access catalogs) should display user and professional reviews for each book and video. We should adopt Amazon's methodology for relating book subject and readers' preferences. We need to encourage readers by identifying similar topics and author styles identified by tracking other readers' preferences.

PLA—the Public Library Association—a New Planning Process

Both the 1987 edition of the Public Library Association planning manual entitled *Planning and Role Setting for Public Libraries* and the 1999 *Planning for Results* emphasized the community role in planning with efforts to communicate with community groups during the strategic planning process. A structure of mission statements, goals, and objectives are part of this process and building objectives are related to service responses.

Strategic planning emphasizes user outcomes rather than output measures. User outcomes focus on how users are changed by library services. Output measures focus on quantitative measures of library use that can be easily counted. With the need for libraries to focus on community problems such as literacy and family services we will need to develop more sophisticated outcome measures. This in turn may affect library space planning by placing an emphasis on collaborative tutorial and group study spaces especially for children and young adults.

To build a library designed for users librarians need to look at how people actually use libraries. In this regard an interesting model might be Paco Underhill's tracking process as explained in *Why We Buy*. Underhill employs trackers to follow users around stores and describe their actions and preferences. Do people prefer to select CDs and videos from bins rather than conventional spine-out shelves? Do people need help in navigating a library? Where should this help occur and in what form? Signs? Holograms? Librarians? Do library users want to ask their questions standing or sitting?

We also need to understand at the outset of planning what staff and users see as the defects of the existing library. The evaluation process that is one of the first steps in planning should include:

- A staff evaluation to reveal the daily problems that prevent service response.
- A user focus group to show how users experience the library's problems.
- A consultant/architect evaluation to compare with other libraries.

This preconstruction evaluation should then be followed by a postconstruction evaluation after the library has been completed and occupied long enough for flaws to become evident. Funds need to be available to correct these flaws.

Alternating Environments

Coffee—Book Sales—Computers—Conversation

Alternating quiet and noisy areas in libraries provide the user with a useful choice of environments and act as a relief valve for noisy library users. Coffee service in libraries has been available in England for decades and in the United States for at least the last ten years. These library areas should also incorporate the following features:

- Embedded terminals under tables provide opportunities to search while sipping a beverage.
- The sale of library selected best sellers in a small library bookstore will bring in

revenue while reducing the pressure to buy new titles. However, book sales of donated books often pose a dilemma for libraries, because sale books are not selected with the same criteria applied to the development of the library collections. If these sale books are displayed prominently their display suggests a recommendation by the staff.

CHILDREN

Children are particularly susceptible to quickly changing needs. This will often mean space to roam and things to climb on such as a low platform or a tree nook for reading. Equally important is a stimulus shelter or refuge where a child can get away from activity and read quietly or even nap. Lighting, color, and furnishings can suggest behaviors with low-key lighting and gray and brown upholstery on large cozy egg shaped shelter chairs suggesting quiet, while bright colors, intense light, mobile toys, and open space suggest movement. Parents and other caregivers come to the library with children. They need a family place to share the library experience with the child; a space with oversize chairs so parent and child can read together, collaborative electronic workstations for sharing a computer experience and for easy instruction by the librarians, and group study rooms for projects.

TEENAGERS

Teenagers need to have recreational areas to listen to music and meet other teenagers. They also need homework and project space to work with librarians, teachers, and other students and individual study carrels for quiet concentration. Alternating these functions gives young people choices that symbolize what libraries are all about. Anthony Bernier's work at Los Angeles provides a good example of design for teenagers.

Topical Feature Library Mobile Modules

Libraries could take advantage of major topics of interest by a flexible arrangement of spaces, furnishings, and staffing. This model envisions small teams of staff who would be assigned responsibility to reconfigure spaces on a quarterly basis. Each space would contain:

- Linked mobile displayers to display materials cover out on the top shelf and spine out below.
- Dedicated two-wheeled wireless mobile electronicwork stations programmed to list relevant library materials, magazine articles, and Web sites on the topic.
- A centralized reference desk staffed to monitor and service all topical areas.
- Mobile chairs and tables.
- Discussion area to encourage public and staff discussion of topics with coffee.

Quick Delivery

Amazon claims it will deliver a book in four days. Libraries could do it in two. Libraries could mail books to users with return envelopes. An ambitious and well-organized library could do it in two hours by bicycle delivery. Business delivery of non-copyrighted materials by fax or E-mail could be provided in minutes.

Rotating Split Collections Based on Changing Frequency of Use

Several decades ago libraries began to experiment with split collections in which they selected the most popular materials to house in a smaller conveniently accessible book stack and housed the remainder in more efficient compact stacks. The system was not widely adopted except in very large libraries, because it was difficult to determine which books were most frequently used and because librarians felt that users should have access to more materials.

Since that time, book stacks in libraries have grown and many small libraries are now housing tens of thousands of books in overcrowded shelves with narrow aisles. Today's computerized systems can more easily identify the most frequently used materials. Busy library users need more convenient access to smaller preselected collections that afford an easier browsing experience.

A new model for popular collections would house the most popular 30,000 books in a book stack with wider aisles and higher bottom shelves for convenient access. Less frequently used books might be housed in closer spaced conventional stacks, high-density stacks, or in electronic or hard copy delivery systems.

As books were borrowed from the older stack they would be returned to the popular collection. Each month books not recently used would be reshelved with the older materials. For the library user this would mean an up-to-date constantly changing collection of materials voted popular by the user community.

The H.W. Wilson company has been publishing for years lists of books constantly revised to select the most useful titles in a particular category. Categories include: *Books for Public Libraries*, *The Fiction Catalog*, and the *Children's Catalog*. Taken together these lists would include about 30,000 titles.

The Ideal Library

An ideal library design is an effective combination of many related functions. The building gives people a wide range of choices and services, and accommodates many different needs.

Orientation and communication among users and staff requires an intricate combination of signs, lighting, furnishings, and spatial zoning to suggest opportunities for alternative behaviors. These include:

- An open coffee area for conversation
- Acoustically separated group and individual study rooms
- Computers and books distributed throughout the library, at the entrance, in the book stacks, near reading places, and at public service points
- A variety of computer configurations—ergonomically designed electronic work-stations, stand-up E panels in the stacks, embedded terminals, and wireless mobile lap top stations
- Quiet click-free zones without computers or cell phones.

Whether constructing a new library, renovating an existing one, or simply seeking to improve your facilities as time and budget allow, you can improve your services by employing some of the following ideas.

Choosing a Site

Libraries need to be located where people go in their everyday activities. Unlike museums, which are usually visited only once or twice a year, people use libraries frequently for a wide variety of functions:

- Reading a daily paper or weekly magazine
- Sharing opinions and ideas with others
- Selecting a good read
- Asking a question about health, business, investing, or an important purchase
- Conducting research
- Finding a job
- Taking kids to the daily story hour
- Doing homework

For these reasons a library should be nearby other daily activities such as retail stores or town centers. It should be on a heavily traveled road. It should have sufficient and convenient parking and easy access to mass transportation

Finding the Building

People should find the library easily; park in a well-lighted parking lot convenient to the entrance; and enter easily carrying their materials, pushing a baby carriage, or managing a wheelchair.

Displaying New Materials

The display of materials should emulate a good bookstore. People select a recent video, CD, an interesting book or book-on-tape from an attractive display of new materials with covers well lighted for easy browsing. However, unlike some bookstores, users can always find a particular title because materials are sequenced.

Offering Choices

A public library is a multi-functional community center. The variety of services and activities need to be seen at the library entrance. The building should help to explain how different users find and use these functions and how these functions relate to one another.

Finding a Book

Public libraries are fundamentally self-service institutions. Most users never contact a staff member except to check out materials. People select a book on a particular subject from a large collection of materials on a wide variety of subjects. Users can locate a particular book in a collection of thousands because the library's collections are uniformly arranged by subject in an easy-to-find sequence. The great book stack containing tens of thousands of books is carefully laid out for easy user orientation to the book sequence as the user approaches the stack. End panels with flat screen computers face the user and line of sight signage in the aisles constantly orients the user to the subject sequence. Computers are available throughout the stack for easy searching and database access.

Getting Help—Advice to Readers

Experienced, well-trained librarians assist users to select a useful book, get an answer to a question, find homework assistance, or learn how to search the Internet. A prominently located, well lighted, and easily identified information, reference, and readers advisory desk staffed with a well-trained professional librarian is easily accessible. The area includes computers, reference books, and file storage as well as cordless telephones to communicate while in the stacks. Nearby are oversized collaborative electronic workstations with two chairs each so that staff can assist users with their searches.

A Place for Quiet Study—Click-Free Zones Without Cell Phones

Students can find a quiet place in the library to read a book or study reference materials. The library provides acoustically separated study locations with glare-free lighting and ergonomically designed mobile seating.

A Place to Meet

The library offers the community a range of meeting spaces for small groups and large programs. A coffee service area for casual meetings and book discussions is open during library hours. The program meeting area has a sound system, video and electronic projection, and comfortable stacking chairs. Restrooms, kitchen facilities, and storage areas are nearby.

A Place for Children

An interesting, exciting, and calming place for children where they can listen to stories, look at puppet shows, browse materials with a parent, get help from a librarian, study quietly, or conduct research on the Internet. Different sized chairs and tables, open activity areas, and quiet study locations are provided. Chairs for parents to read to children and browsing bins for easy access to the colorful front covers of picture books are also available.

Teenscape

Teenscape is an exciting area designed by and for teenagers with music listening opportunities, video viewing, cyber zones with computers, group study opportunities, and a food service area divided into acoustically separated zones visible to library staff.

A Productive and Pleasant Place to Work

Library staff are able to:

- Help users find materials and suggest optional and alternative sources
- Answer users' questions
- Monitor the behavior of users with clear sight lines to all parts of the area
- Control the checkout of materials with a staff desk close to the exit
- Order, process, and catalog a large volume of materials in a work flow designed area with natural light convenient to the delivery entrance
- Work in a climate that they can control easily and consistently

Objectives for Effective Library Building Design

- Convenient and prominent location to encourage library use.
- Convenient access to all materials for the physically challenged, elderly, and temporarily disabled. Make it easy to find, park, and enter.
- Display of the newest and best library materials throughout the building.
- Storage on easily accessible, well-lighted shelves sequenced to make it easy to find materials.
- Comfortable, quiet, easily supervised, and adequately heated, cooled, and lighted single and group study areas for long-term use.
- Efficient materials circulation designed for convenient public service and self service.
- Efficient staff and technical services work areas to assure good productivity.
- Children's facilities zoned for programs, materials, electronic access, staff work, and quiet study. Places for children and caregivers to work together.
- Young adult area with a choice of quiet areas or group study, sound-dampened areas with musical listening, video viewing, and computer opportunities.
- Adequate natural and artificial light levels and reduced glare.
- A community meeting room for library programs with access during times when other library services are not in operation. Equipped for electronic services.
- Flexibility for future changes/expansion such as:
  - additional electronic workstations with local and remote access
  - internal and external communications technology
  - additional seating and material storage.

The need for flexibility must be balanced against the need for specific functional design requirements. Converting book storage spaces into electronic workstation locations requires planning for the differing environmental requirements of these differing functions. Air conditioning, natural light, structural floor loads, and column spacing need to be analyzed for conversion scenarios during the planning of the building.

Order and Choice in Library Design

The democratic idea that an individual is free to choose any book and find a place to sit and read is still at the heart of the public library. Organizing the library so that the user, on his own, can find a subject or a book among the thousands available demands a rigorous order that is a paradoxical challenge for librarians and designers.

Library staff help users get answers to their questions and give advice on good books to read. Electronic resources and user convenience require detailed design coordination to effectively deliver this combination of services.

In the twenty-first century, over a hundred years since Richardson's great book hall, the public library has not only become a more open, accessible, and democratic institution, but recent developments in technology have emphasized the multiple service nature of the library. The symbolic idea of offering users a great choice in materials has now been extended to a great choice not only in materials but in the modes of delivery.

Designers now seek to make the library a more open and welcoming community institution. Glass facades showing what is going on in the library, a wide choice of seating and electronic workstations, computer screens, and collaborative staff/public workstations combine to make the public library an intricate design exercise blending enormous choice with user friendly customer service accessibility. In a hundred years, designers have sought to glorify books and create monumental celebrations of learning while making the library open, accessible, and human scaled.

This continues to be a fascinating journey in function and design.

II

The Planning Process

2

An Overview of the Planning Process

This chapter describes the first part of the planning process in which the community analysis, mission, and service responses are developed to shape the needs assessment.

The Long Range Planning Process

In this chapter we show how building planning fits into the long range planning process. In any planning process the first step is to understand the community by collecting factual information about the community and by observing and talking to people who live and work there. Only then can a mission for the library be devised to serve as the organizing force in determining objectives to improve library services. Finally, the library facilities role in accomplishing these objectives can be translated into a building program with quantities and costs.

The Planning Team

The several members of the planning team will become part of the planning process at different stages and their roles will change as the process moves forward. Members of the team may include:

- Library staff who initiate the process and serve as the client.
- Town planning group who determine the overall mission.
- Library consultant who is familiar with the planning process.
- Architect who translates the program into a structure.
- Interior designer who selects and coordinates furnishings and equipment.
- Construction manager or general contractor who supervises the construction.

Complex Changing Relationships

In a library building process that may last three to five years the relationships among the library building consultant, architect, and librarian are crucial to the success of the project. This relationship inevitably and appropriately changes throughout the planning process. In a complex process with several interrelated participants it is most useful for all participants to be involved early in the project although the extent of involvement of each team member will change as the project proceeds.

Team Members and Their Roles

LIBRARY STAFF

The library staff often initiate the library improvement process by perceiving that the physical facility is beginning to limit the quality of service. This will result from observation, public complaints, and comparisons with other similar libraries. The staff may then involve the library board and members of the community funding authority. Throughout the project the staff will work closely with consultant and architect to shape the planning process and building design.

TOWN PLANNING GROUP

The board of trustees or town building committee will be active in determining the mission and objectives for the project and working on the library's long range plan for service improvement. They also serve as communicators and liaison with the community. They may work on selecting the architect. The staff, consultant, and architect will keep them informed of the progress of the project by monthly informational meetings.

The day-to-day planning and construction will be performed by the staff, consultant, and architect working together as a team.

THE LIBRARY CONSULTANT

A library consultant to help with planning may be retained because of the need for experience with the process. A consultant is an experienced coach familiar with the process who knows about the alternatives. A consultant will teach about users and buildings, frame the process, supply knowledge of the details, improve the product, and save the client money.

The consultant's role in the process will vary from library to library. Building programs are often written by the consultant although some libraries with experienced staff may be able to write their own building programs with guidance and coaching from a consultant. The consultant's most important role is in the review of plans at the schematic phase of design to assure that library program requirements have been met.

Identifying a consultant can be accomplished by:

- Talking with other colleagues who have been through the process
- Getting lists of consultants from library organizations such as state library agencies or the American Library Association LAMA division

The process of selecting and retaining a consultant often begins with a request for proposals for consultants, which should include:

- Description of the project
- Long range plan
- Request for consultant qualifications, which should include:
    - M.L.S.
    - Experience as a library director and public service librarian
    - Experience as a building consultant
- Fee and expense parameters

Interview consultants by touring the library with them and listening to their questions and comments about the building. Does the consultant listen to you and respond with thoughtful comments about the library and its services? In addition to the library tour and interview, selection should be based on:

- Experience
- Comments of former clients

The consulting fee will not exceed 1 percent of the construction cost or 10 percent of the architects fee and a good consultant will save the library twice the consulting fee.

THE ARCHITECT

The architect designs the library based on the building program. His work will be discussed in Chapter 5.

INTERIOR DESIGNER

The interior designer works with the architect to select and install furnishings required by the program.

CONSTRUCTION MANAGER OR GENERAL CONTRACTOR

The construction manager or general contractor builds the library based on the architectural plans.

Major Phases of the Library Planning Process

The following phases are explored in greater detail later in this chapter and in the next two chapters. A sample timeline for planning and construction is given in figure 2–1.

Demographic and Community Analysis and Input

Demographic statistics document existing status and future population changes in the community. Some communities will have an updated development plan that will provide an important context for library planning.

Community input into the process is encouraged by:

- Interviewing community leaders
- Conducting focus groups
- Community meetings
- Community surveys by telephone or by distributing questionnaires

Support for the project is developed as a by-product of these activities.

Mission and Objectives

With community input the library board determines the library mission and sets overall objectives to improve services.

Library Service Analysis and Service Responses

The consultant and staff analyze changes in library use since the last time facilities were built, added onto, or renovated. Book circulation, reference use, program attendance, and in-library use are considered. A chart is prepared indicating use changes to justify additional space needs. Service responses are prioritized.

Library Facility Review

Staff and the consultant review the existing library facility from the staff and user points of view.

Needs Assessment

The consultant analyses facility needs developed from service responses to facility evaluation. An outline building program in spreadsheet format comparing present and future space needs is created in this step. The board/building committee, consultant, and staff are the primary movers with review by the board/building committee.

Building Program

This document has three parts:

Part 1 includes the community and library service description and the building evaluation described above.

Part 2 describes the space needed to carry out the program and how the major service areas should be functionally designed.

Part 3 includes functional area sheets that list all furniture and equipment needed in each part of the library. The consultant and staff work together on the program.

Architectural Work— Design-Schematic-Development-Construction Documents

The architect develops plans that are reviewed by staff and the consultant to verify that plan capacities for seating and materials meet program requirements. The chapter on architectural work explores this in greater depth.

Furnishings and Equipment

Architect selects furnishings guided by the staff and consultant.

Figure 2-1	
Time Line for Planning and Construction of a Small Library	
Planning	**Months**
Demographic and community analysis and input	1
Mission and service responses	1
Service analysis, needs assessment, outline program	2
Building program	3
Design	
Schematic design (overlaps building program completion)	3 and 4
Design development	5–7
Construction documents	8–14
Construction	15–27
Furnishings and equipment (during design construction)	5–27

Post Occupancy Evaluation

A year after the building opens the planning team and additional experts evaluate how the plan was carried out and make changes to reflect new uses of the library.

Demographic Analysis

A demographic analysis should focus on those factors that most affect library use. Basic population growth will have the most effect on library use, and, if possible, this should be estimated for the future twenty-year period.

Educational attainment is the best predictor of library use for populations of the same size. Better educated people will use the library more often thus requiring a larger facility. Census reports report the percentage of people over the age of 25 who have completed high school or college. Comparing this percentage with similar state or national statistics may be useful in determining library capacity and size.

With staff assistance compile a brief demographic profile and projections of the growth direction of the town and its census districts including at minimum:

- Percentage of adults 25 years and older who have completed high school compared with the state average (an excellent predictor of potential library use).
- Population projections for the next twenty years from a variety of sources such as school statistics, utility statistics, regional planning, or state planning.
- Median family income levels and percentage of employment. If unemployment is high it may affect library space and service needs because people come to the library for employment information and job skills.

These indicators should be compared with state averages over the past decade. The library staff may obtain this information from:

- Town or city planning departments
- Regional planning agencies
- State planning agencies

- School districts
- Utility companies

More than one estimate allows comparison. It may be helpful to investigate the prior accuracy of predictions by asking for predictions for the past ten years and comparing them with the actual figure.

The most useful statistics compare demographics and library use over time within the town itself. For example, a library with a new building in 1980 and a population of 20,000 may have grown in population by 10 percent by the year 2000 but library use may have increased by 50 percent and the educational attainment may have changed from 75 percent to 85 percent high school graduates. These changes may signal an increased need for expanded facilities than that of a town with more consistent population and library use.

Collecting and interpreting this information should be done by the library staff with the consultant because the staff may know about specific local changes that may affect particular space needs such as small new immigrant groups requiring literacy training.

Library statistics have evolved considerably in the past twenty years. Now libraries routinely measure not just library circulation but attendance, program attendance, reference questions, and in-library use. Use of computers in the library is of primary importance in needs assessment. Success in obtaining needed materials and answering questions is also measured.

How do these statistics affect library space planning? A demonstrated increase in library use can be a powerful argument for the need for more space.

In collection size the responsiveness of the collection to user needs is more relevant than sheer numbers of materials. Use of the Internet and electronic periodical databases may reduce the need for reference books and magazines but require more electronic workstations.

Community Analysis

This process is at the heart of long range or strategic planning. It shows how the community looks and works. Understanding how the community works and how the library responds to special community needs will affect the success of the improvement project.

Walking around, driving around, and observing people may provide some useful clues. Is there pedestrian traffic past the library? Does the foot traffic increase during the lunch hour? What can the library do to attract pedestrians. Large display widows with special spot lighting and front cover display of materials? Sidewalk or front plaza design for library outdoor activity during the busy lunch period?

Suburban libraries far from pedestrian traffic might instead give more thought to the relationship of library to drive-up service or to making the library more attractive from the parking lot side.

In looking at the community, library improvement clues might come from competing establishments such as bookstores, record stores, or display strategies in other retail outlets.

Interviewing Community Leaders

Leaders to be interviewed should include:

- Government and financial planners
- Major employers
- Potential fund contributors
- Communication leaders
- Organization leaders
- Political leaders

One-on-one meetings with community leaders provide an opportunity to discover their attitude towards the library. The meetings may result in suggestions for improving library services, as well as assessments of fundraising potential. They inform community leaders that the library is planning to improve and solicit their support for library plans.

Community Meetings

Meetings with community organizations and community government agencies, especially fiscal authorities, are useful not only in planning but more importantly in building community support by actively involving community groups in the library planning process and getting a "buzz" going in the community about the library.

Community organizations are important in library improvement efforts to identify library needs in the populations they include or serve and to develop support for library capital funding. The best way to create community support is to involve representatives of groups and agencies early in the planning and to make their needs part of the facility improvement program. Coming to community organizations to ask for support after the library is planned will lead to lukewarm interest compared to involving them early in the planning process.

The library staff can be helpful in relating community characteristics to planning:

- Determine how the library can assist with early childhood education by working with Headstart, daycare facilities, family groups, and care givers needing information on child development
- Identify unique diverse cultural elements in the community:
  - Ethnic groups
  - Language needs
- How are needs met by the library?
  - Ethnic programs
  - Foreign language collections
  - Literacy tutorials
- Identify community problems and aspirations that the library can satisfy such as:

- ◆ Increased computer literacy
- ◆ Job preparation
- ◆ Medical information needs
- ◆ Local history
- ◆ Early learning for infants and preschool children
- Identify recent changes in the community such as:
  - ◆ New immigrant groups
  - ◆ Economic problems and their solutions
- Library trustees and friends may also have useful information on the community:
  - ◆ The history of library improvement efforts
  - ◆ Analysis of constraints in library improvement activities
  - ◆ Identify movers and shakers in the community
  - ◆ Identify community organizations for collaborative efforts

Headstart and other preschool caregivers for children can be strong advocates for the expansion of children's facilities to include children's meeting and program space and tutorial facilities.

Ethnic organizations will support the library's need for literacy tutorial space, and foreign language collections including music and videos.

The Chamber of Commerce will support the library's efforts to introduce potential new businesses to library information resources.

Health agencies will support the library's efforts to inform the community about health information topics. Libraries can partner with health agencies to help train mothers to give their babies a physically, mentally, and emotionally healthy start.

Realtors will support an improved library because such efforts enhance the quality of life by encouraging and stimulating the intellectual and cultural community.

Educational institutions will support the expansion of the library's facilities to support their students' work. However, beware of the potential competition with the Board of Education for capital expenditures, and be prepared to fight for the library's fair share of long-term, capital expenditures.

The community governing body and fiscal authorities should also be involved in preliminary planning so that the library can be assured of financial resources.

Focus Groups

Convening focus groups of staff or library users will be helpful in determining perceptions or attitudes. Focus groups should be selected from library users. Zealots and extremists who might dominate or inhibit an open exchange of ideas should not be encouraged. Trustees, town employees, taxpayer groups, and relatives of staff and trustees have strong biases that may inhibit discussion. A trained discussion facilitator will encourage open discussion.

Staff focus groups often concentrate on staff facilities, complaints about temperature fluctuations, and working conditions. They should be encouraged to also discuss library public service needs and improvement objectives. Staff might know about common questions asked by the public relating to the building design. Do people seem confused about basic service locations? Locations of elevators or stairs or restrooms? Can library users easily find the children's and program rooms? Are there frequent complaints about noise or temperature?

Too often, library users are tolerant of poor conditions. This may be a function of the library's poor response to complaints. The staff should be encouraged to welcome complaints as useful guides for improvement. Staff sometimes take complaints as personal criticisms or pass them off as examples of administrative failure on the part of the bosses. Complaints should be recorded in writing by the staff and a written response forwarded by the administration. If complaint books or slips are used the response to the complaint should appear in the book.

Beware of assuming that the focus group accurately represents the community. Focus groups suggest ideas that can then be tested with a survey. To measure community opinion, a random sample telephone survey will be more accurate than a focus group.

Mission

The library mission is based on community and library expectations for services. It should reflect not only the history and traditions of the library, but look forward to opportunities to improve and increase the use of library services. It should be reviewed every five years but may remain unchanged for some time if it continues to be relevant. A broad and concise mission statement will allow more specific service responses to be built on this mission foundation. Some late nineteenth-century mission statements have survived well into the twenty-first century. For example, the mission of the Greenwich, Connecticut, library for 100 years was "The Promotion of Useful Knowledge." In this mission the library's role is to encourage use, not just provide materials. The library has a broad concern with knowledge rather than a narrow focus on information or materials.

Knowledge Not Just Information

People sometimes confuse information bytes with knowledge.

The Internet provides access to data and information but seldom has the impact that comes from spending ten hours reading a book. Experiencing a period of history, an extended journey to a foreign country, or a real or fictional life story are products of the library experience more powerful than acquiring a byte of information.

If every seat in the library was an Internet terminal used all the time the library was open, this use would only amount to a tenth of the time spent reading books borrowed from the library, acquiring knowledge not just information.

Library Service Analysis

The library staff and consultant look at changes in library services:

• Analyze library use statistics and output measures for past years especially for the year of the last time facilities were improved. Compare with state or regional averages.

- Interview library staff to determine the extent and rhythm of staff activity and space needs and to reveal staff attitudes to new technological options for service delivery.
- Conduct a library survey to determine community perceptions or attitudes towards the library.
- Observe library services and staff activities to verify user and staff perceptions.
- Interview non-users to determine the potential for increased use by assessing non-user attitudes and perceptions.

Service Responses

The Public Library Association planning manual called "Planning for Results" outlines and discusses a long range planning process for libraries. This process emphasizes community planning similar to the process we have discussed earlier in this chapter. It also lists public library service responses that may be useful for defining the library's mission and goals. The library may select several responses resulting from an analysis of community needs and may prioritize them for emphasis, or the library may choose to modify or draft their own service responses. Many of these service responses have space planning implications. Here are some selected service responses:

Current Topics and Titles

The library will provide a current collection with sufficient copies of titles in high demand to ensure that customer requests are met quickly. Materials will be offered in the formats and in the languages people want and will be selected primarily on the basis of local demand. The library's collections will be organized in ways that make items easy to find and will be merchandised to the public through the use of displays and display shelving. Space for display and appropriate display fixtures and lighting will be required for this service.

General Information

The library will offer print, non-print, and electronic reference resources that cover a wide variety of topics.

The library will provide staff skillful in determining users' needs and in locating relevant information that satisfies those needs including Internet searching, The location, organization, and equipment for accessible and easy-to-use reference and information services will be essential to deliver this service.

Information Literacy

The library will provide training and instruction in skills related to locating, evaluating, and using information resources of all types. Teaching the public to find and evaluate information will be stressed over simply providing answers to questions. The library will provide access to information in a variety of formats and will offer public Internet training and access. Library staff will be knowledgeable about how people seek information and learn. Tutorial rooms will be very helpful in satisfying this need.

Formal Learning Support

The library will provide informational resources, personal assistance, and educational tools, such as computers, that further the educational progress of students. Library activities and materials will support the curricular objectives of a teaching institution or institutions. The library will also provide physical facilities conducive to learning. Quiet study carrels and long-term group study facilities may be helpful for this service.

Lifelong Learning

The library will provide and maintain an extensive collection of circulating materials on a wide variety of topics in which the general public has a sustained interest. Collections will be easily accessible and organized to encourage public browsing by subject area. Staff knowledgeable in subjects and topics of interest to the general public will provide expert assistance in locating materials of all types and in all formats. The library will develop lists of services, materials, and Web sites or other finding tools to assist library users in learning about specific subjects or topics for which there are frequent requests. Well-trained readers advisory staff located in an accessible and communicative setting with seating for users to discuss their needs will help to accomplish this service.

Commons

The library will provide public space for meeting and gathering that is recognized as inviting, neutral, and safe by all individuals and groups in the community.

The library may provide a variety of meeting and gathering spaces including large meeting rooms, small group meeting and study rooms, and open public spaces that invite conversation and discussion. A casual coffee setting for users will encourage this activity.

Cultural Awareness

The library will provide in-depth collections of materials and resources in many formats and will offer programs and special displays that reflect the cultural heritage of populations in the library service area. Well-designed meeting room spaces to accommodate programs of varying sizes will be needed for this service.

Local History and Genealogy

The library will provide a significant collection of materials and other resources that chronicle the history of the community or region in which the library is located. Family histories and genealogical research tools are provided. The library will provide the equipment required to read, print, and copy all formats in which information is supplied. A designated local history room with study facilities in a quiet setting will help accomplish this objective.

Community Referral

The library will establish ongoing relationships with community organizations and local governmental agencies. The library will develop and maintain or will facilitate the development and maintenance of a database of available services and the qualifications for receiving those services. The library will provide easy, convenient, confidential access to the information in a wide variety of ways such as walk-in service, toll-free telephone service, or Internet access. The library will provide contact assistance for those who don't know how to make contact with agencies. A private referral setting for this service will encourage users to respond to this service.

Consumer Information

The library will provide expert assistance and specialized electronic and print resources to individuals who are interested in becoming more knowledgeable consumers and to individuals who need to make important consumer decisions. The library will offer resources that include critical reviews of products and services and wholesale price guides for durable goods. The library will also offer access to information on maintaining and repairing consumer goods. This activity may be part of the information services area.

Business Employment and Consumer Information

The library will provide expert personal assistance, specialized electronic and print resources, and services of interest to the business community, to investors, to individuals who are seeking employment or who are dealing with a changing work environment, and to individuals who are contemplating a career move or change. Library users will be able to access a significant amount of information without visiting the library by using the telephone, fax, e-mail, or other electronic delivery systems. This activity may be part of the information services area.

Government Information

The library will provide access to a wide selection of information by and about governmental agencies in print and electronic form. The staff will have full Internet access, and Internet access may be provided for public use as well. The library will provide staff knowledgeable in using government documents, searching the Internet, determining users' needs, and locating relevant information that satisfies those needs. This activity may be part of the information services area.

Basic Literacy

The library will provide a learning environment, specialized materials, and access to trained tutors to help people reach their personal literacy goals. The library may provide specially designed facilities and access to instructional technologies that enhance the effectiveness of tutoring efforts. Tutorial rooms and group program rooms will be helpful for this service.

A notable lack in this list of service responses is a response directed specifically at services to children. The library association feels that children's services are included in the other responses but many librarians feel that services to children are so specialized that it is important to direct a service response uniquely for them.

Early Foundations of Literacy and Language

According to Virginia Mathews, "The library is the only free, non means-tested accessible learning center that provides materials and programming for preschool children and their care giving adults." Children are welcome from birth to school age, the prime years of brain development that governs not only cognitive skills such as language and emerging literacy but also emotional stability, positive self expression, self control, and associated social skills such as sharing and learning to live with others. This service is not one of the basic Public Library Association Service Responses.

In addition to selecting many of these service responses, William Schell and the staff of the York Pennsylvania Library decided to create topical service modules that would relate books, media, Internet sites, and specific articles on topics of current community interest in several small mobile locations in the library.

The planning team may select several of these service responses and may designate some to be major improvement priorities. These decisions should be based on the community analysis and on the library service analysis.

Examining how the library is actually used may suggest service response priorities:

- Has children's program attendance increased?
- Are there more magazine readers?
- Are there complaints about overcrowding in computer area?
- Does the noise and activity level interfere with quiet reading?

The Long Range Plan

Building improvement is only one part of a library long range plan, which may include:

- Brief history of the library
- Demographic and community analysis and input
- Mission and service responses
- Library service analysis
- Community activities and programs
- Staff development
- Customer service improvement
- Collection development
- Budget and resource development
- Marketing and public relations
- Library facility evaluation
- Needs assessment

- Building program including needs assessment, major service area descriptions, and functional area sheets
- Executive summary of the library improvement plan

The long range plan may develop a list of service objectives with evaluation criteria and quantitative measures for meeting objectives. Be mindful about user outcomes as well as quantifiable objectives. Think about users not just numbers.

A Streamlined Approach to Planning for Small Libraries

Small libraries may find it useful to use the following condensed steps in planning:

- Form a committee to plan
  - ◆ Include community members
    - —Town government
    - —Finance body of town
    - —Potential contributors
    - —Local organizations
    - —Friends of the library
- Develop fact sheet about the community and the library
  - ◆ Population projection for 20 years
  - ◆ Library activity for past ten years
  - ◆ Library history
- Orientation of planning committee (who, what, why, when, who)
  - ◆ Timeline for process
- Determine community vision
  - ◆ Define current conditions in the community and the library
    - —Strengths, weaknesses, opportunities, threats
- Select library service responses—link to community needs
- Write mission statement
- Determine goals and objectives—specific objectives for services and building
- Identify activities—needs assessment, building program, architect, construction
- Determine resources required—budget, staff
- Write plan/obtain approval

As we have discussed, these community and library concerns serve as the basis for developing the library building program that delineates specific space needs, describes space relationships, and specifies furniture and equipment needed for these objectives.

The next part of the book focuses on the Library Building Program part of the long range plan.

3

The Needs Assessment

In this chapter library service analysis and facility evaluation are used to develop objectives and create an outline spreadsheet of space needs.

In Chapter 2 we emphasized the need to engage in long range strategic planning with considerable community involvement before beginning to develop a space needs assessment. In this chapter we show how the space needs assessment itself is developed based on the earlier community planning process.

Consultants work with the staff to determine specific space needs:

- Analyze community library service needs as in Chapter 2
- Observe library users
- Evaluate existing facilities
- Compare with other communities
- Set objectives

The librarian should take the lead in this phase with the consultant coaching the librarian by suggesting the framework for the process:

- Demographic and statistical analysis of community and library history
- Evaluation of facilities by staff interviews, observation of users by consultant, focus groups, and surveys
- Comparison with past and with other libraries

The librarian often initiates the improvement planning process by becoming aware of a need. Too many books crowding the shelves, users waiting to use a terminal, complaints about not enough space for story hours may be reasons for action.

State grants, private donors, or budget surpluses may be opportunities for action. Collaboration with other agencies may suggest space needs and opportunities.

A library building consultant will be useful in analyzing needs and preparing a library building program.

Facility Evaluation

Facility evaluation should begin with a staff focus group and a user focus group to discuss what is good and bad about the present library facility.

In addition, the following techniques may be used to evaluate facility use:

Behavior Mapping

Behavior mapping studies determine the kinds and frequencies of use of the variety of library services. This technique records the relative use of various library furnishings and equipment. A map is prepared showing the location of tables, lounge chairs, study carrels, electronic workstations, standup work desks, computers, listening or viewing stations, bookstacks, and staff service desks.

Date and time are recorded at the top of the map and at each hour the number of users at each location is recorded on the hourly map. At the end of a week the hourly maps are studied to compare the use of tables versus lounge chairs versus carrels at various times.

Relative overall activity in each area of the library can be used to move staff to the busiest locations. Equipment type and quantities can be reorganized.

Tracking Studies by Trained Observers

A trained observer is characterized by knowing alternatives and by creative thinking about libraries. Observers must be both experienced about libraries and creative about solutions. Trained observers in libraries can spot the favored study locations and consider the combinations of ambiance, furnishings, lighting, and spatial relationships that affect these favored locations. Trained observers have seen users in different libraries and understand how library space problems can be solved.

Tracking studies determine how people respond to the building:

- How do people travel through the building? Where do they stop? What do they do?
- Will children borrow more picture books from face-out bins or from spine-out divider shelves?
- Observing library users clustered around terminals with printers suggests that more printers or a more efficient method of delivering copies to users are needed.

For observation to yield useful results the library must provide choices in its existing facility and observers must be experienced with potential patterns of library user behavior and alternative responses to that behavior:

- A choice of seating may yield the need for more table or lounge seats.
- Offering users a choice of computers on tables or embedded terminals will show which they prefer.

Paco Underhill's decades of research into retail shoppers' behavior in his 1999 book *Why We Buy* is an example of how observation of user behavior can improve interior design.

THE INVARIABLE RIGHT

Shoppers invariably turn to the right when entering stores. Major bookstores place their most attractive browsing sections to the right and tuck away the cash counters to the left of the entrance where they are easily visible to the right of shoppers when they are leaving the store. Libraries should locate their most attractive books and not the checkout desk to the right of the entrance.

FAST LIGHTING OR SLOW LIGHTING

Lighting can affect behavior. Trained observers know that bright glaring lighting in fast food stores makes people leave the store quickly, while low-glare, softer light encourages people to stay. In libraries, quiet study areas for long-term use need low-glare lighting while the checkout desk lighting needs to be brighter for quicker response to waiting customers.

In addition there are several other techniques that may be helpful in evaluating how the library performs:

- Maximum use studies determine times when there is a maximum use of library facilities. Chart specific times and determine percentage of maximum use compared with total open hours.
- Compare with library standards. This involves comparing existing library facilities with library standards for communities serving the same population.
- There are few national standards, but many states have building standards.
- Compare services, capacities, and holdings of similar libraries.
- Analyze the relationship of use of various segments of the collections with the amount of materials and the annual expenditures in these segments.
- Document the inadequacies of the building for handicapped accessibility, materials storage, public service, staff work space, and public safety. This is accomplished by detailed measurement of the physical plant and observation of safety features.

Objectives

Once mission and role priorities are established the library staff may develop specific objectives to improve services to users. Library users should be able to:

- Browse through new materials easily, quickly, and comfortably
- Find a book quickly and easily by author, subject, or title
- Study comfortably and quietly for a long period of time

- Get professional library assistance quickly and easily
- Provide security for materials, patrons, and staff
- Easily find the building, park, and enter it even with a handicap

Space Needs Assessment in Public Libraries

A basic preliminary space estimate may be made by looking at the sizes of the major parts of the public library building. This estimate is then further refined by a careful analysis of each functional area.

The Major Functions

There are several major activities in a public library

- Collection space to store materials for public use (often 50 percent of the library)
- People space to read, use computers
- Meeting space for programs, tutorials, or group study
- Staff areas for public service or staff support services (often 25 percent of library space)

The size of each of these areas is affected by a variety of factors.

Non Assignable Space

In addition to space for library functions all buildings must include space for the building infrastructure. This varies from 25–40 percent of the total area depending on the architectural design.

It includes space for:

- Entrance and vestibule
- Walls
- Restrooms
- Stairs, elevators, and hallways
- Heating, ventilating, and air conditioning equipment
- Custodial, cleaning, and maintenance equipment
- Deliveries and general storage

TRADITIONAL POPULATION STANDARDS

In the past, public libraries were often sized according to population served. These standards, based on the democratic assumption that similar sized towns should have access to similar sized educational resources, are still a useful starting point for assessing library space needs. For smaller libraries serving from 10,000 to 50,000 people a standard of one square foot of building space for each person served by a library was often used.

Three to five books per capita and five seats per thousand population were also used. However, in addition a wide variety of other factors need to be considered:

Collection Space—
Estimating Space Requirements for the Collections

Guidelines and Space Standards for Material Storage
The American Library Association book *Building Blocks* details space standards for various library functions. In addition, Connecticut and Wisconsin publish planning guidelines that are useful in determining size and capacity standards. Variations will occur in different libraries because of different shelving policies and mixes of materials. It is impossible to predict 20-year material storage requirements with hairline accuracy for these reasons:

- Thickness of books varies from library to library and from time to time
- Percentage of various media in the collection varies
- Percentage of materials in circulation varies
- Introduction of new material types is difficult to predict
- Electronic delivery and use of materials will change

However a variety of estimates can be made based on current collections and shelving practices and future projections.

QUICK PRELIMINARY ESTIMATE—TEN ITEMS PER SQUARE FOOT
The preliminary rough estimate may use ten items per square foot of floor space as a useful conservative estimate of space requirements in a stack storage area.

TRADITIONAL BOOK STACKS
Ninety-inch-tall, seven-shelf standard double-faced bookstacks with stack ranges spaced five feet on centers will accommodate ten to fifteen books per square foot depending on the thickness of volumes. Tall books will not fit on these shelves and must be housed separately out of sequence with other books on the same subject.

BROWSABLE BOOK STACKS
An aging population needing more convenient browsing may lead libraries to increase aisle width to six feet on centers and reduce the number of shelves from seven to six or even five, eliminating bottom shelves that are seldom used. This shelving may house only eight to ten books per square foot. Tall books will fit on all these shelves and will be in sequence with other books on the same subject. See Figures 3-1 and 3-2 for calculations and dimensions for various book stacks.

FLEXIBLE THIRTY-FOOT COLUMN SPACING
Library stacks with thirty foot spacing between support columns will accommodate five feet on center traditional range spacing as well as the more browsable six feet on center spacing. Libraries may decide to start spacing ranges six feet on centers and later convert to five foot spacing when additional capacity is needed. Lighting should accommodate this change easily.

CHILDREN'S STACKS
Children's materials are thinner than adult books so more will fit on each shelf. However, they are often taller than adult books and children's stacks are often lower,

Type of Material	Vols/Items per Square Foot of floor space	Vols/Items per Linear Foot of shelf space
Adult fiction and nonfiction	15	8
Adult reference	10	6
Adult special	10	8
Children	10	15
Children reference	10	6
Video tapes, DVDs, and compact discs	10	8
Talking books and cassettes	10	10
Periodicals displayed (title)	1.5	1

A quick approximation for a public library assumes ten books per square foot of space. These are preliminary calculations based on tall eighty-four inch high stacks with seven shelves and minimum handicapped access aisles. Variations in height and aisle width will affect capacity.

A stack spacing six feet on center and only five or six rather than seven shelves high would better accommodate older and handicapped users. These stacks will hold about eight books per square foot of floor space.

60-inches high or less with only four or five shelves. For these reasons children's stacks will often hold a similar ten to fifteen items per square foot of floor space.

NON-BOOK MEDIA

Media such as CDs, DVDs, and videos are often uniform in dimension so that it is easier to predict shelf requirements. Although they require less shelf space than books, their thin spines with small type may require that they be housed in low bins for easy browsing, so they may require a similar amount of floor space. These collections may also have a larger percentage of items in circulation than books and so require less storage space. However this may become less true as collections grow in size.

RESHELVING SPACE

Space for reshelving needs to remain open on each shelf so that items do not have to be rearranged to make room for returned materials.

CALCULATION EXAMPLES

A library serving 20,000 people may own 100,000 items or five per capita.

- Existing collections, and withdrawals—The size of existing collections plus annual—*net* acquisitions for a given planning period, often 20 years, should be considered. The library acquires 3,000 items per year and discards 1,000 for a net gain of 2,000 items per year. Over a 20 year planning period it will need space for 40,000 additional items.
- Quick Estimate—The present collection may take up 5,000 square feet of floor space crowded onto closely spaced five feet on center seven shelf high stacks. For the future a quick calculation might require that the library plan to house a total of 140,000 items in browsable stacks spaced six feet on centers with five shelves. This may require 14,000 square feet of space to house the entire collection of 140,000 items.

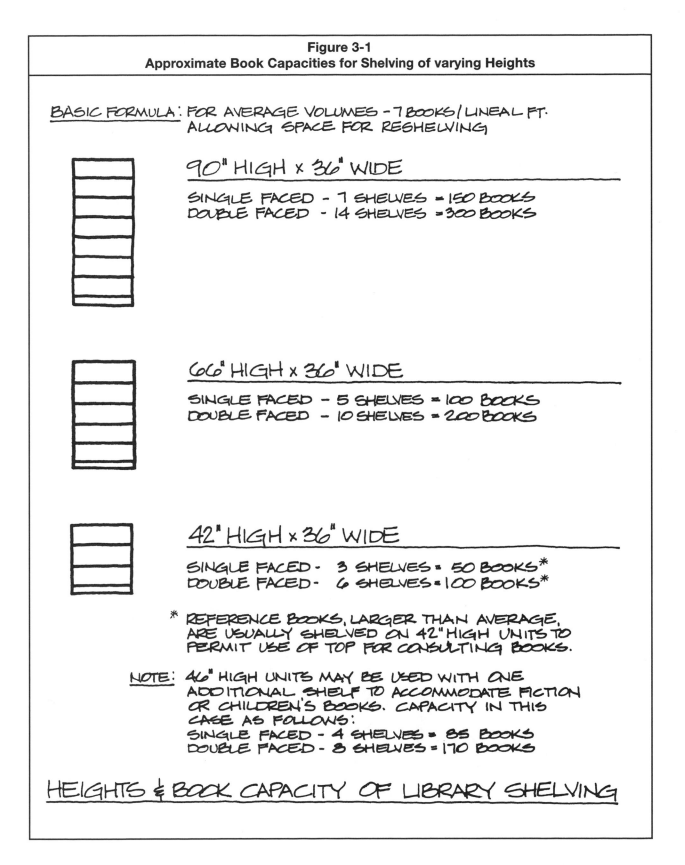

Figure 3-1
Approximate Book Capacities for Shelving of varying Heights

<u>BASIC FORMULA</u>: FOR AVERAGE VOLUMES – 7 BOOKS/LINEAL FT.
ALLOWING SPACE FOR RESHELVING

90" HIGH x 36" WIDE

SINGLE FACED – 7 SHELVES = 150 BOOKS
DOUBLE FACED – 14 SHELVES = 300 BOOKS

66" HIGH x 36" WIDE

SINGLE FACED – 5 SHELVES = 100 BOOKS
DOUBLE FACED – 10 SHELVES = 200 BOOKS

42" HIGH x 36" WIDE

SINGLE FACED – 3 SHELVES = 50 BOOKS*
DOUBLE FACED – 6 SHELVES = 100 BOOKS*

* REFERENCE BOOKS, LARGER THAN AVERAGE,
ARE USUALLY SHELVED ON 42" HIGH UNITS TO
PERMIT USE OF TOP FOR CONSULTING BOOKS.

<u>NOTE</u>: 46" HIGH UNITS MAY BE USED WITH ONE
ADDITIONAL SHELF TO ACCOMMODATE FICTION
OR CHILDREN'S BOOKS. CAPACITY IN THIS
CASE AS FOLLOWS:
SINGLE FACED – 4 SHELVES = 85 BOOKS
DOUBLE FACED – 8 SHELVES = 170 BOOKS

<u>HEIGHTS & BOOK CAPACITY OF LIBRARY SHELVING</u>

Figure 3-2
Dimensions of Standard Book Stack Sections

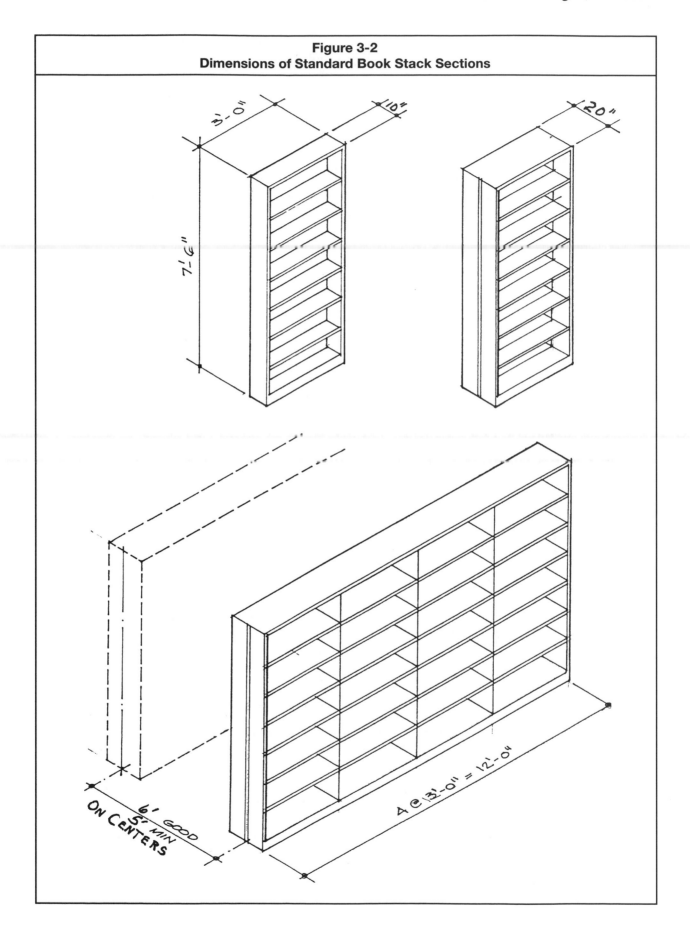

- More Complex Estimate—Materials in circulation should be considered in predicting the need for additional space. Circulation differs from month to month so there may be plenty of shelf space in January and crowded shelves in June. Improved facilities and more easily accessible shelves can increase circulation reducing shelving needs. Shortening the loan period may increase the circulation. The library may now have 20 percent of its items in circulation so it is actually housing only 80,000 items in 5,000 square feet. For the future, if 20 percent of its collections remain out in circulation it will need to house only 112,000 items and thus will require only 11,200 square feet of space. If items in circulation increase it may need to house only 100,000 items in 10,000 square feet.
- Frequency of use—Determining the actual percentage of the circulating collection that has been borrowed over a specified period of time, often two years, may suggest that an inordinate percentage of books are being retained that are not needed by the community. The Internet now makes it easy to find materials in other libraries and regional networks and delivery systems make Interlibrary Loan faster. Some planners believe that very large bookstacks actually discourage use. Older collections may also begin to look time worn and give the impression that most of the library's materials are out of date.

Libraries must balance the need for large in-depth resources against the need to look interesting and up to date. The nature of populations change and their response to a large bookstack full of older materials may differ from the response several years ago.

If the existing collection contains 20,000 items that are seldom used and can be discarded the collection space may be further reduced to 8,000 square feet. The changing mix of collections with more media requiring less space may further reduce this space requirement.

PEOPLE SPACE FOR SEATS AND ELECTRONIC WORKSTATIONS

Five seats per 1,000 residents for communities with a population of 10,000 or more has been a library standard for fifty years.

Table seats—25 square feet per seat,

Carrel seats—30 square feet per carrel

Lounge chairs—40 square feet per lounge chair

Electronic Workstations—40–60 square feet per work station

MEETING SPACE

Space for programs, tutorials, and group study vary widely depending on mission and service priorities, but there is a trend towards an increase in these areas. Generally even the smallest libraries will try to provide a 50-seat program room and these rooms will seldom be larger than 300 seats.

STAFF SERVICE AND SUPPORT AREAS

These will often require 25 percent of the library service area. They include: Service desks for circulating materials and answering reference questions, staff offices and lounges, and technical service areas for ordering and processing materials and maintaining electronic services.

NON ASSIGNABLE SPACE
Varies from 25–40 percent of the total area depending on the architectural design.

- Predicting future use—major improvements in a library facility will result in changes in use. This will affect space needs in different ways:
  Borrowing—As borrowing increases, fewer shelf spaces will be needed for materials in the building
  In-library use—As more people use electronic access to information, more space will be needed for workstations
- Budgetary considerations—maintenance and custodial care—a larger library may require more maintenance.
  Increased use—A more attractive library may increase cost for increased services. Consolidation of public service points—Fewer staff service points in a more efficient layout may result in more efficient deployment of staff and lower cost.
- Library use—libraries differ widely in how intensively they are used. A library that has 500 people a day entering the building will have markedly different space requirements than a library with 800 people a day. Intensity of use measures have an effect on space needs for example:
  In-Library use measures the extent of use of library materials *in* the library building which in turn may affect the need for additional seating.
  Behavior mapping can be used to determine how frequently seating and other facilities are in use thereby indicating how many additional seats may be needed.

PRELIMINARY ESTIMATE OF SPACE NEEDS FOR A LIBRARY
SERVING 20,000 PEOPLE

100 seats @ 40 sq. ft per seat	4,000 square feet
80,000 items @ 8 items per square foot	10,000
Service and staff accommodations (25 percent)	5,000
Community meeting space for 75 people	1,000
Total library space	20,000
Non-assignable space (30 percent of total)	9,000
	TOTAL 29,000 square feet

SUCCESSIVE APPROXIMATIONS
This first preliminary estimate of space needs will seldom be the actual size of the finished building. Later stages in planning will include a more accurate listing of all items of equipment and architectural design will further refine space needs.

However this first rough estimate will be useful to discuss size and costs with funding authorities to determine needed resources. In this estimate round the numbers off to a slightly larger rather than smaller amount than the actual needs because the various groups that review the plan will be more likely to decrease the size than to increase it.

Figure 3-3
Spreadsheet Showing Preliminary Space Needs

	A	B	C	D
1		Areas	Materials	Seats
2	Functional area			
3	Entry	300		
4	Administrative offices	200		
5	Circulation desk and work area	500		
6	Adult services			
7	browsing and magazines	340	500	8
8	reference desk and workroom	300	500	
9	reference	530	500	12
10	book stacks	3870	30000	4
11	non print	1000	8000	
12	local history Room	260	1000	4
13	Adult services total	6300	40500	28
14	Young Adult services	490	2000	6
15	Children's' room			
16	desk and office	300	500	
17	reference and reading	430	300	10
18	non-fiction and fiction	920	8000	4
19	easy reader, pi and ABC'S	480	3000	6
20	parents	200	300	4
21	story area	500		*30
22	storage	300		
23	Children's total	3130	12100	24
24	Program room	800		*75
25	Small meeting rooms	300		*20
26	Technical service area	300		
27	Staff room	200		
28	Maintenance area	200		
29	Total library function	12720	54600	58
30	Non-assignable area	3816		
31	Total area of library	16536		

It is often useful to compare present and future capacities and sizes
Non-assignable area is for toilets, walls, stairs, elevator, and HVAC
*Seats in bold are not included in library seating total since they are not for library study

PRELIMINARY SPREADSHEETS

Starting with the rough estimates based on the number of seats and materials together with staff and program space it is possible to construct a breakdown into smaller functional areas. This spreadsheet breakdown should be based on discussions with the library staff as to the specific functional area requirements. This is still only an approximation which will be further refined by a detailed analysis of specific furniture and equipment requirements and architectural layouts.

PRELIMINARY OUTLINE LIBRARY BUILDING PROGRAM PREPARATION

Using the quantities and standards on the preceding pages prepare an outline program delineating major functional areas and capacities in spread sheet format.

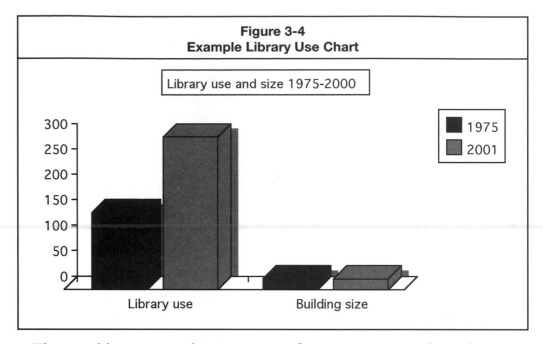

Figure 3-4
Example Library Use Chart

Library use and size 1975-2000

The spreadsheet presented in Figure 3-3 is for a 10,000 projected population size library with high use statistics.

PROGRAM PRESENTATION—OUTLINE PROGRAM REVIEW WITH FUNDING AUTHORITY

In the planning process it is important to pause and assure that funding is available before proceeding with the detailed facility planning required for the library program. Discuss this preliminary outline program spreadsheet with the library governing authority and town fiscal representatives. The funding authority should be informed of the project and input from them should be welcomed. During the presentation to the funding authority charts are helpful in showing how increased citizen use of the library is driving the need for library expansion. The chart presented in Figure 3-4 emphasizes the changes driving the library's need for expansion.

ROUGH PROJECT COST ESTIMATES

At this point it is possible to begin discussing facility cost. Since the time from this preliminary program until the library bids come in will be at least a year, no accurate cost estimate can be made since the bidding climate, overall economy, and changes in the final detailed plans will affect cost. Accurate cost estimates are not possible until the building has been designed but broad parameters of cost can be discussed by using square foot project costs of similar library projects in the same part of the country. Project cost includes architectural fees, site acquisition, construction, furnishings and equipment. Always use total project cost estimates NOT construction costs only.

At this moment in time it is essential to overestimate project costs because once a number is discussed this tends to remain as a cost estimate. Library buildings are furniture intensive compared to other building types so be careful to include a generous furniture allowance, up to 20 percent of construction cost, depending on how much electronic equipment is included.

4

The Library Program Document

This chapter describes the completion of the library programming process including the writing of functional area sheets and the program narrative.

Major Service Area Narratives

After the outline program is approved by the funding authority major library service areas should be described by the consultant. In this section of the building program the staff and consultant explain to the architect important considerations for the design of each major service area in the library. This document will also include information on general design concepts and flexible design features.

A sample narrative related to the design of staff work areas is:

Staff Work Areas, Technical Services

These areas house the functions behind the scenes that are necessary to support successful and efficient public services. The Technical Service work area will be adjacent to the delivery entrance.

Safety and security of staff personnel materials and equipment should be a primary consideration in locating work areas. Work areas should not be dead-ended, enclosed space where staff may be confined or isolated with library users.

The arrangement of work spaces, the location of machinery, and, most importantly in the design stage, color scheme and lighting, should promote productivity and attention to detail over relatively long periods of time.

Workstations

Space for individual expression, such as areas for green plants, wall space for posters, and decorations is necessary where work is unrelieved by the variety and the immediate satisfaction of public contact. Cork bulletin boards or a tackable surface should be placed at workstations so that staff can easily refer to schedules, procedural memos, and other temporary notes. All work areas will have coat closets and individual half- or box-lockers for employees' personal possessions.

Lighting

Natural lighting from windows is important for the morale of the staff. Natural light should be augmented by task-oriented lighting from lamps and fixtures. These should have flexible switching patterns. Under-shelf lighting should be avoided. While glare can be a major problem, dim lighting can cause the operator to strain to read a CRT screen or paper documents on the desk. Adequate lighting during the day may be completely inadequate in the evening. Because proper lighting is relative, adjustability in task lighting at the workstation is important. Workers are more productive when they can adjust the intensity, location, and the angle of light in their work area.

Comfort

The seating, work surfaces, and other furnishings must be comfortable and provide good support, especially to the sacro-lumbar area for staff who must sit at the workstations for long periods of time. Climate control is essential for staff who spend long hours at workstations. Insofar as possible, staff should be able to control their own climate.

Adjustability

All aspects of the workstation should be adjustable. This flexibility is critical because staff differ in size, bodily configuration, and work preferences.

Seating

The staff member should be able to adjust the height of the seat and the backrest. All adjustment levers must be readily accessible and easy to use.

Desks and Work Surfaces

Ideally, library workers should have desks and work surfaces that can be adjusted from 22 inches to 45 inches from the floor. At minimum, the work area must include an adjustable keyboard pan that enables a sitting worker to maintain upper and lower arms at a 90-degree angle (upper arm vertical, forearm horizontal) and their wrists at 10 to 20 degrees from horizontal.

The ideal work area is 60 inches wide but should be at least 30 inches wide to permit opening books or use of documents or other media. Leg clearance should be at least 24 inches wide and 16 inches deep. Space for book trucks at each workstation is imperative.

COMPUTER EQUIPMENT

Local Area Networks (LANS) and connectivity are important aspects of a library's use of this technology. Design features must reflect the need to power and connect equipment in each workstation as well as between the different departments. J-channels, ramps, grommeted openings for bundled cables, and power poles will be important design features. Plugs should be above work surfaces.

SCREENS

Placement of the CRT or VDT screen is also a primary concern. The screen should be approximately 18 inches from the worker's eyes and adjustable in height. Visual fatigue can be minimized by correct lighting. VDTs should not be placed next to windows but when this is necessary, the screen should be at a right angle to the plane of the window.

Technical Services

Location of the area is important to efficient operation. The area should be close to other library departments yet acoustically and visually separate. Traffic from other departments or to frequently used areas should not be routed through work areas.

This area should be one large, flexible open area subdivided by movable office landscaping into the following functions: receiving, shipping, acquisition, and processing functions for library materials in both print and non-print format including receiving and processing periodicals.

There should be an outside entrance for deliveries and mail. Two long counters for receiving, shipping, and distributing materials will be provided. A work counter in the center of the area will serve as a book processing location for jacketing, stamping, and other routine work. Ample electrical outlets will be provided at mid-wall height. Book truck space for maneuvering heavily loaded trucks should be left beside each workstation.

Functional Area Sheet Preparation

After discussing the design of major service areas, the consultant and staff work together to prepare detailed descriptions of each library functional area including all equipment necessary for each area. This will include:

- Name of the area
- Dimensions—size of the area in square feet
- Activities, functions performed—public and staff activities in the area
- Major design features and ambiance—the general nature of the area; special acoustical, lighting, graphics, technical, and environmental needs
- Occupants—maximum number of staff and public that will occupy the space at a given time
- Furnishings and equipment—quantity and dimensions of each piece of equipment

Figure 4-1
Functional Area Sheet Sample

Name of Area	Circulation Desk	Dimensions 288 Sq. ft.

Activities Staff operates terminals to check out and check in up to 500 items daily, place reserves, register users for library cards. Staff answers telephone, makes change for patrons, answers related questions,operates terminals, and contacts information services staff and pages to help users.

Occupancy

Public 5–10	Staff 1–3	Daily uses: 200–400

Major design features and ambience of area
Area must be inviting to first time library users.
Graphics should define functions for the public such as checkout and return of materials.
Desk should be visible from entrances and at a comfortable height for both staff and library users. Acoustical dampening, glare-free lighting, thermostatic control, adequate ventilation and protection from cold drafts are important design considerations for staff at this location. The floor should be anti-static with extra padding under the carpet.Traffic flow of staff and users into and out of this area will require space and careful planning. Disabled, elderly, children and parents with children in strollers all must be accommodated here with their varying physical requirements.

Furnishings & equipment
A U-shaped counter 15'–20' long, 37' high and 24–30" wide constructed as a "shell" desk with modular units independent of the structure to be flexibly configured for files, shelves, drawers, as required for changing electronic systems and library processes. The counter should be open at each end to allow staff to exit easily to assist users.
The book return area will include a terminal, a slot for returns and two adjustable book bins on wheels. In addition there will be space for 8 book trucks for returned materials that have been checked in.
The checkout area will include two terminals with printers.
The Information Registration area will have staff facing entrance area/lobby, visible to all public areas.

Seating   3 total staff seats

Materials Materials: 200 reserves plus 300 returns

Proximity
In sight of the entrance, and information desk, adjacent to circulation work area. Near the external book drop. Locate away from quiet area.

Information provided by Dr. Albert Knowitall   **Date**   Dec. 8, 2001

- Material storage capacity—kind and quantity of materials and type of storage
- Seating capacity—types and quantities of seats and total public seating capacity
- Area relationships—proximities and distances from other functions
- Information provided by—the person who was interviewed for this particular functional area sheet
- Date—the last date on which this sheet was written or modified

These sheets will form the basis for pre-schematic sketching of each area by the architect to verify area sizes and most importantly to determine the optimum shape

| Figure 4-2 |
| Functional Area Sheet Form |

Name of area   **Dimensions**

Activities

Occupancy
  Public   Staff   Daily uses:

Major design features and ambience of area

Furnishings & equipment

Materials

Seating

Proximity to

Information provided by   **Date**

of the area. This pre-schematic sketching should be done prior to schematic design so that the architect understands how each part of the library works and how their interdependence affects the size and shape of the library building. See Figure 4-1 for an example functional area sheet and Figure 4-2 for a blank form.

Functional area sheets should be reviewed with staff and architect. Architects can sketch furniture and equipment layouts for each functional area sheet right on the sheet so that staff can verify the efficiency of the layout and the size and shape of the room can be determined. A sample drawn by Michael Cohen is presented in Figure 4-3.

Figure 4-3
Sample Functional Area Sheet with a Sketch of the Layout and Size of the Room

Name of area   Children's Reference area   **Dimensions**   1,600 sq. ft.

Activities

Reference work and study

Occupancy
     Public   Staff   Daily uses:

Major design features and ambience of area

Carpeted
Good lighting
2- group study rooms each seating six
Outside entrance separate from adult areas

Furnishings & equipment

 2- Workstations with chairs and room for two book trucks for librarians
9- Sections of 39" high x 3' wide shelving for 800 books
2- Tables each seating 6 with 12 chairs in study rooms
3- 4-drawer vertical file cabinets
4- Tables each seating 4 with 16 chairs
6- Carrels with chairs

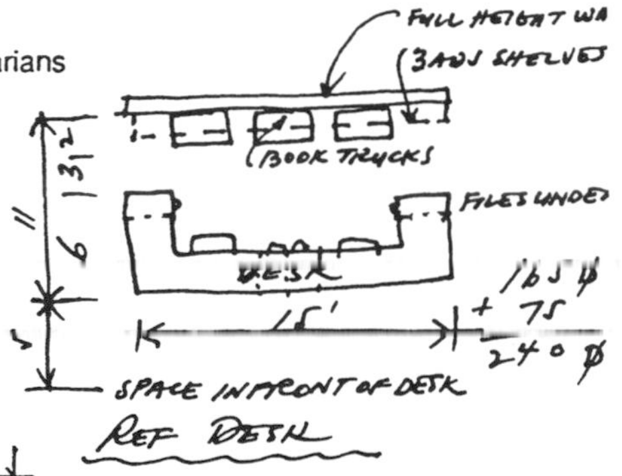

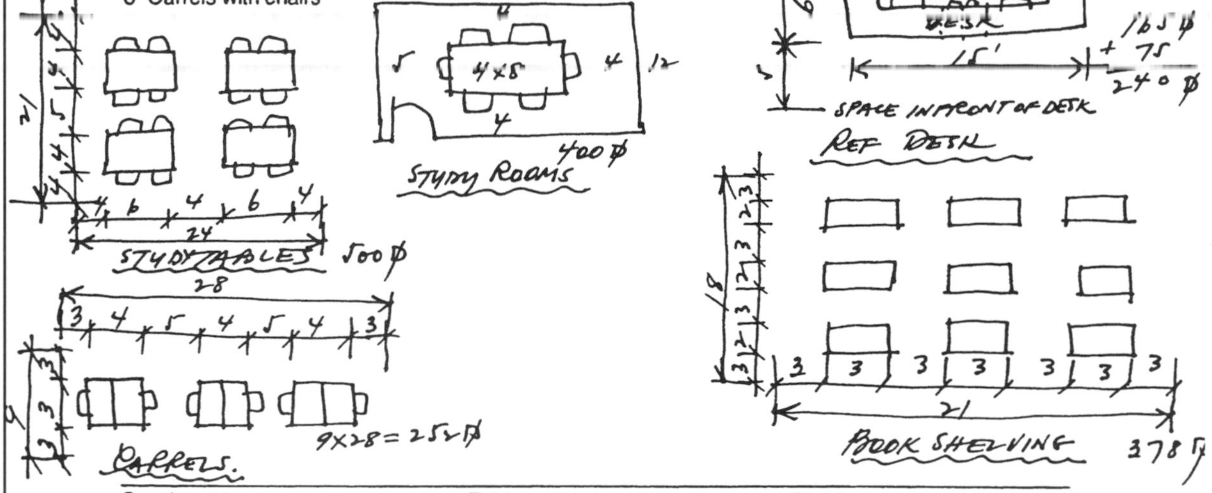

Seating 34	Tables 28	Carrels 6
Lounge	Staff 2	

Materials
     Books   800   Non-books

Proximity to

Other areas serving children's services

Information provided by   **Date**   6/8/89

Marketing the Project

To gain acceptance for the project it will be immensely important to meet with a wide variety of community organizations to get their input before going to the town governing authority with your program.

These presentations should be to small groups of 20 people or less to give opportunities for input into the process. The meeting should start with a 5-minute outline of your needs then ask participants what they think about your project. How will it help their organization? What are their special library needs?

Program Presentation

Present the final document to the funding authority. The final presentation should include an executive summary of the program mailed to the audience at least a week in advance of the meeting. The complete document often running to 60–80 pages is much too long for lay people to read. Also, giving out the complete program may result in detailed questions that obscure the main objective of obtaining approval for the project. The complete program is enormously useful to the architect for designing the project and ultimately it should be the document for reviewing the architectural plans to assure that they conform to the program.

At a public meeting emphasize the long-term benefits to the community, especially to children.

Show how economical libraries can be by saving taxpayers having to purchase expensive books. Compare the cost of running the library to the expense of buying books. If people in the community bought 100,000 books a year it would cost them $2,000,000. Yet the library checks out 100,000 books a year for much lower cost, and at the end of that time all those books are still available.

Show how the library emphasizes long-term quality in building collections selected for their value for the community.

Point out that the library is customer oriented not product sales oriented. We treat each individual customer as having a special need.

Also, remind them that libraries serve everyone from every walk of life: citizen education; pre-school literacy; adult literacy; computer literacy.

In responding to negative questions at a public presentation do not repeat the question; instead, answer as if you were responding to a positive question.

5

The Architect and Architectural Work

This chapter includes the architect selection process, a sample request for proposals, and a summary of the architectural phases necessary to complete the project.

Architectural Work

The work of the architect begins to be part of the library improvement process just after the space needs assessment is made. An architect should be retained after the outline program but before the final program is completed so that program requirements can be analyzed architecturally and adjustments made to take advantage of design opportunities.

The Architect Selection Process

Preselect a small number of architects (no more than five).
Sources for preselection might include:

- Recommendations from library colleagues
- Visits to other libraries
- Library building consultant recommendations
- State Library listings of library architects
- Library journal annual listing of library buildings and architects
- State or regional architectural organizations
- American Library Association/American Institute of Architects joint awards program
- Local chapter American Institute of Architects (AIA)

Figure 5-1
Request for Architectural Proposals (Sample)

We intend to renovate the existing library and build an addition.

We are inviting proposals from architects to accomplish the following work:

1. Based on the enclosed outline program prepare several alternative schematic plans for a renovation of the existing library with an addition. The floor plans will include furniture and equipment.
2. Review these design options with the library consultant, librarian, and library board.
3. Select an option or combine several of the options and prepare revised drawings with a complete furniture and equipment layout.
4. Estimate the total cost of the renovation and addition including electrical, heating, ventilation and air conditioning, and furniture and equipment.
5. Develop the design in detail with several staff/consultant reviews.
6. Prepare a perspective colored presentation drawing and fundraising brochure for the project.
7. Prepare furniture and equipment specifications.
8. Prepare construction documents.
9. Administer the bidding and assist in analyzing the bids.
10. Monitor the construction of the renovation and addition including furniture installation.

A walk through of the existing building for interested architects is scheduled for (Date). Please phone to register for this walk through.

Submit a written proposal outlining how you would proceed with each phase of this work, and include fee proposals with a range of costs for the following three sets of steps:

    Phase I   Steps 1–4
    Phase II   Steps 5–6
    Phase III   Steps 7–10

Please include information on library additions and interior renovations in which you were involved. Information should include the nature of your involvement in the project (i.e., were you the principal architect?), extent in square feet, photographs, date, cost as estimated and cost as built, and telephone number of reference.

Send proposals and bids to: Public Library Building Committee

Proposals should be postmarked no later than (two weeks after walk through)

Interviews will take place during the week of _____ (one month after proposals)

Architects will be evaluated on the basis of:

    Library design experience of the architectural team
    Architectural expertise
    Cost control
    Clarity
    Creativity

Selection will be made on the basis of library visits as well as on the interview.

Final fee will be negotiated with the selected firm.

No more than five finalists will be selected for interviews. Interviews will be one hour. Initial presentations will be limited to 25 minutes and should emphasize library and renovation experience, and cost control. The final 35 minutes will be reserved for questions from the committee and discussion.

Architects will be informed of the selection within two months.

Appendix to RFP

Project Description (an example)

• Development of an expanded children's facility to provide:
    Expanded story hour and craft area
    Increased material storage
    Increased reader seating with provision for electronic workstations

Figure 5-1
Continued

- Expansion of material storage capacity to accommodate continued growth especially in the audio visual area
- Expansion of electronic workstations
- Design of an electronic learning center
- Renovation of staff work areas for productive work

Mission Statement
library seeks to provide free and equal access to ideas and information to all members of the community. The library will:

    Provide open, non-judgemental service to all library users

    Provide a balanced collection of materials that reflect the diversity of ideas in our democratic society

    Advocate and support First Amendment rights and the Library Bill of Rights, and protect library materials and the public from censorship

    Create an environment that encourages learning, the free communication of ideas and information, and nurtures the joy of reading

Goals of the Library

1. Provide collections and services to meet the community's needs and interests, including children and adults of all ages.
2. Employ a staff of highest quality whose skills and knowledge ensure maximum use of library resources.
3. Promote library materials and services throughout the community including links to schools, other agencies, and other towns.
4. Participate in regional and statewide library cooperative programs that expand and enrich our local services including staff development.

Library Facility Evaluation (an example)

The library's mission statement states, "Create an environment that encourages learning, the free communication of ideas and information, and nurtures the joy of reading."

This is a library of nooks and crannies. It is comfortable and homelike for the public, but difficult for the staff to supervise and control. Built around an open court, there is ample sunlight in all the interiors and a feeling of openness which people find pleasing. There are many small, defined areas in which to read; the fireplace in a living room setting was mentioned by staff as one of the attractions in the building. But the present overcrowded facility has problems that prevent "efficient service in a nurturing atmosphere."

The interior of the building looks worn, the wallpaper is torn, the paint chipping off, carpets and upholstery in shabby condition. Aside from cosmetic needs, the overall look of the library is messy and disorganized. Much of this disorder is due to dire overcrowding, lack of space for books, storage, staff work areas, and study. The stack aisles are too narrow for patrons to navigate comfortably, books are piled everywhere. Most staff members objected to the feeling of clutter and the lack of space that interferes with their work and makes it difficult to be of full assistance to patrons.

There are entrances on two levels, which makes it necessary to maintain dual circulation and theft detection, and so adds to operating costs. No library activities are visible from the most used and constricted parking lot entrance. Instead people enter the library as if through the delivery and refuse door. The elevator is difficult to find, placed off to one side of the passage instead of directly in the line of sight.

Library Building Issues Summarized
Site—Although the location of the library is convenient on a heavily trafficked road centrally located near other retail activities, its sign is not sufficiently large and well lighted to be easily visible to vehicular traffic. Heavy traffic sometimes makes it difficult to exit or enter turning left.

Parking—The present parking facilities are inadequate for programs while other library activities are in operation.

Figure 5-1
Continued

Entrance—There are entrances on two levels requiring dual circulation desks and theft detection devices. People entering on each level are often unaware of services on the other level. Entering on the lower level is very confusing. As you pass through the arched opening, your natural inclination is to try to enter the building through the door next to the highly visible glass stair. However, this door has an "exit only" sign. There is no sign revealing that the entrance is to your right. When you finally find that entrance, there is no clear indication of what services are on each floor or how to reach them.

Building Capacities—During the years since the library opened, seats have been added to the adult area for computer services. The young adult and children's areas have lost seats. Thus the adult area feels overcrowded and the children's area has increasingly added materials while losing seats.

There are a variety of needs for additional space for children's services, computers, quiet study, programs, and staff work.

This is a library of nooks and crannies. There are lots of places for the public to snuggle into but these are difficult to supervise and control.

Detailed redesign of the circulation, technical services, and reference areas are needed.

Central Open Court—Provides sunlight in all the interiors but breaks up spaces. The nice, small, defined areas for reading are difficult to control and it is time consuming for staff to run around the courtyard for materials on the other side.

Narrow Stack Aisles—In some areas aisles are too narrow for handicapped access.

Building Consultant's Recommendations

It is apparent from the preceding evaluation that the existing facility needs to be renovated and expanded in order to fulfill the library mission. Population growth in various age groups during the next 20 years will require flexible expansion space and floors that can be easily redesigned for varying functions.

Recommendations include:

- Develop an expanded children's facility to provide:
    - Expanded story hour and craft area
    - Increased material storage
    - Increased reader seating with provision for electronic workstations
    - Increased staff work area
- Expand material storage capacity to accommodate continued growth especially in the audio visual area
- Install network center for technical networking equipment storage
- Expand reference area to increase the number of electronic workstations
- Expand meeting room facilities
- Redesign the courtyard entry to allow users to walk directly into the stairwell or elevator to get to the children's room or upper adult level
- Create new electronic learning center for teaching and individual use
- Improve staff productivity by expanding and redesigning staff and volunteer work areas including the director's office
- Renovate building furnishings including carpeting, wall treatments, upholstery, and theft detection systems
- Improve landscape with new plantings and new lawn sprinkler system
- Improve heating, ventilating, and air conditioning system to provide more consistent temperature and humidity control, protect computer equipment, and conserve energy
- Improve building infrastructure to comply with ADA, Life Safety, and current building codes
- Renovate carpeting, upholstery, furnishings, and equipment

CONSTRAINTS

Finding sufficient space onsite without reducing parking may be difficult. Enclosing the courtyard and the overhangs would not yield sufficient space and might compromise the original design integrity.

An addition on the side away from the road would be unobtrusive and would yield more space.

Figure 5-1
Continued

Preliminary outline building program

	A	B	C	D
	Functional area	Areas	Materials	Seats
1	Functional area	Areas	Materials	Seats
2	Entry	420		
3	Administrative offices	600		
4	Circulation desk	500		
5	Circulation work area	450		
6	Adult services			
7	browsing and magazines	700	1300	20
8	reference desk and workroom	500	200	
9	reference	4300	10500	74
10	book stacks	7667	115000	
11	non print	1000	10000	
12	Local History Room	500	3000	13
13	Adult services total	14667	140000	107
14				
15	Young Adult services	1500	5000	24
16				
17	Children's room			
18	desk and office	500	500	
19	reference and reading	1200	4200	36
20	non-fiction and fiction	2000	30000	
21	easy reader, pic and ABC'S	1100	7600	4
22	parents	200	300	3
23	media and viewing	300	2000	4
24	story area	500		*30
25	storage and bathrooms	300		
26	Children's total	5100	44600	47
27				
28	Friends store	1500		
29	Older Periodicals and books	2985		
30	Program room	1200		*100
31	Small meeting rooms	360		*24
32	Technical service area	1600		
33	Staff room	368		
34	Maintenance area	400		
35				
36	Total library function	31650	189600	178
37	Non-assignable area	9495		
38	Total area of library	41145		

Seating totals include only library seating, not meeting or program room seats.

REQUEST FOR PROPOSALS—RFPs

Send a Request for Proposals including evaluation, objectives, and a building program to the preselected architects. For renovation or addition projects send basic plan of the existing library. A sample RFP is included in Figure 5-1.

Verify the architects' professional credentials with AIA and state licensing authority.

Walk-through

If the project is an addition to an existing library it may be useful to arrange a walk-through of the building for the architects. This may be a single walk-through for all candidates, or a scheduled walk-through for each firm. Scheduled walk-throughs provide the selection committee with an opportunity to discuss the project and gain an understanding of how the firm feels about the existing building and how they would work on an addition. It can thus be an important part of the selection process.

Proposals

Evaluate proposals by comparing them with the Request for Proposals. Often proposals from architects merely state their qualifications for the job and do not demonstrate that they really understand this particular job. Does the proposal show that the architect understands the nature of the project? Does the proposal show exactly how the architect would proceed with the work? Select from among proposals by visiting libraries and interviewing library directors and staff. Discuss with them the good and bad aspects of their library project. When evaluating library designs you may want to use the criteria for an ideal library discussed in Chapter 1.

Examine architectural portfolios with a view to assessing the sensitivity of the architect to local community needs and esthetics as well as to functional library concerns.

Compare proposals as to:

- Understanding of your particular requirements
- Does the proposal show that the architect understands your objectives?
- Library experience—What similar libraries has the architect designed?
- Functionality—Are these libraries functional?
- Cost control—Does the architect show concern for cost in the proposal?
- Creativity—Are the designs attractive and distinctive?
- Esthetic results—Are the libraries handsome and appropriate for their setting?
- Comprehension of the scope and diversity of library uses

Interviews

At the interview judge the architect's presentation on the basis of:

- Understanding of your particular requirements
- Library experience and functionality
- Cost control
- Creativity and esthetics

Library Visits

Before and after proposals are received the committee should visit library projects so that selection can be made on the basis of the library designs as well as on the interview.

NEGOTIATE THE ARCHITECTURAL CONTRACT

Architectural fees are usually a percentage of the total construction cost, often 8–12 percent. They are often divided into the following phases:

Schematic design—In which the architect lays out the building on the site with several general alternatives and together with the owner and the library consultant a single design or combination of alternatives is selected that best meets the program requirements. This phase is often accomplished for a fixed lump sum fee or 15 percent of the total architectural fee.

Design development—In this phase the architect further develops a selected alternative including site work, HVAC, and structural system. Usually 20 percent of fee. Construction drawings require a lot of time and are 40 percent of fee.

Bidding—The architect works with contractors to bid the job. Usually 5 percent of fee.

Construction administration—The architect monitors the construction work of the selected bidder. Usually 20 percent of the architectural fee.

If the architect is responsible for furniture and equipment specification, bidding, and installation supervision, the fee will be 10 percent of the furniture and equipment cost in addition to the above architectural fees.

It may be useful to include a clause in the architect's contract to the effect that if the bids come in over the estimate the architect will be responsible for revising the drawings at no extra charge to the client.

Architectural Design Phases

Building design begins with the architect's analysis, understanding, and response to the base of data, intentions, and impressions collected in the process of discovering what there is to know about the project. The combination of all this into a unified solution is the synthesis that is the core of initial conceptual design.

PRE-SCHEMATIC DESIGN AND PROGRAM REVIEW

With extensive staff and consultant participation the architect prepares interactive sketches of each individual functional area. Ideally this is done in the presence of the staff members who will work in that space to allow for maximum staff participation. Pre-schematic sketching helps the architect to understand how the library works and to verify sizes, shapes, and spatial relationships within each space and from space to space. This should take place before the floor plan and building shape are determined. See Figures 5-2 and 5-3 for sample sketches.

With this understanding the architect can begin conceptual organization of the design that will be very helpful in site selection.

SITE SELECTION

The architect can evaluate sites as to the conceptual organization of the design. The cost of site work can be estimated with due regard to environmental impact, traffic, and access issues. The esthetics of siting a particular size building on a particular

Figure 5-2
Graphic Analysis of Program (program and meeting spaces not shown)

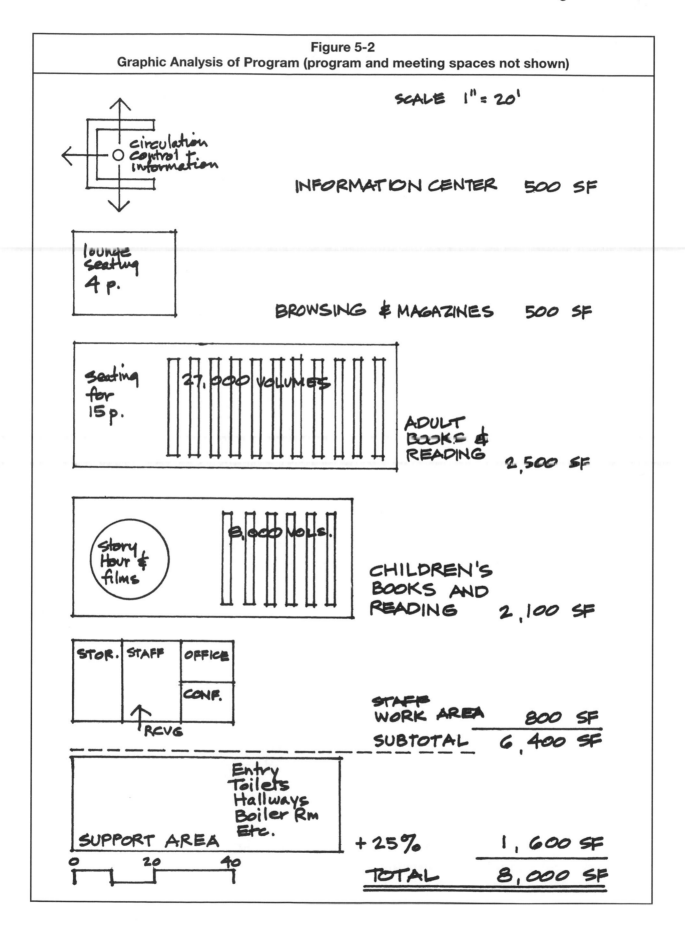

SCALE 1" = 20'

circulation control + information

INFORMATION CENTER   500 SF

lounge seating 4 p.

BROWSING & MAGAZINES   500 SF

Seating for 15 p.   27,000 VOLUMES

ADULT BOOKS & READING   2,500 SF

story Hour & films   8,000 VOLS.

CHILDREN'S BOOKS AND READING   2,100 SF

STOR. | STAFF | OFFICE
CONF.
RCVG

STAFF WORK AREA   800 SF
SUBTOTAL   6,400 SF

Entry Toilets Hallways Boiler Rm Etc.

SUPPORT AREA   +25%   1,600 SF

0   20   40

TOTAL   8,000 SF

Figure 5-3
Pre-Schematic Sketching and Program Verification (drawing by Michael Cohen)

Name of area   Magazine/newspaper reading area   **Dimensions**   1,000 sq. ft.

Activities

Reading and study area for patrons

Occupancy
          Public   30   Staff   Daily uses:

Major design features and ambience of area

This area is between reference and popular library areas and near compact storage of back issues.
Good lighting
Carpeted

Furnishings & equipment   5 SHELVES @ 4 MAGS/SHELF = 20 / SFS = 33 SFS = 99'-0"
                                                                      or 17 DFS

Shelving for 650 magazines:
650 magazines displayed on tilt and store double-faced shelving 60" high (8 sections) with approximately
one year's back issues kept at the display rack (100 linear feet).

5- 4' x 6' tables each seating 4 with 20 chairs
6- Lounge chairs

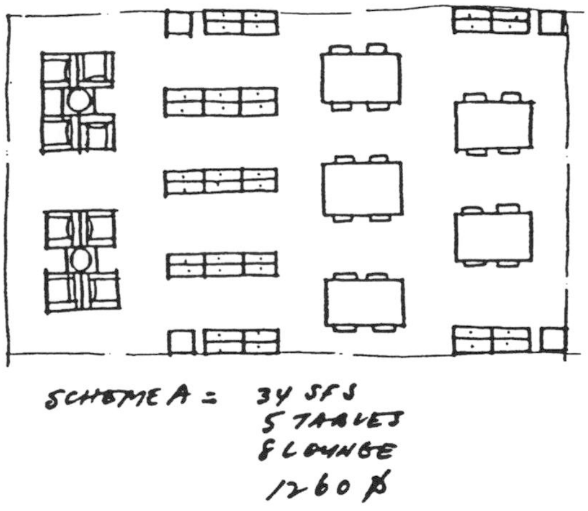

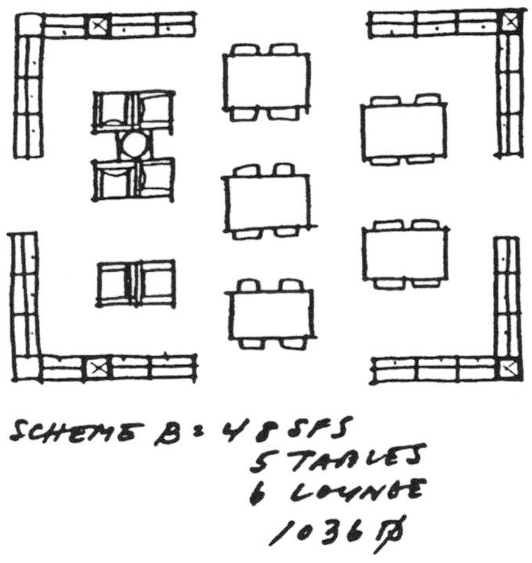

SCHEME A =   34 SFS
             5 TABLES
             8 LOUNGE
             1260 ß

SCHEME B = 48 SFS
           5 TABLES
           6 LOUNGE
           1036 ß

Seating 26
Table seats   20   Carrels   Lounge   6   Staff

Materials
          Books   650 magazines   Non-books

Proximity to
          Reference and popular library

Information provided by   **Date**   10/91

site can then be considered. A listing of site criteria is included later in this book.

A site is acquired and designated for the library.

The sketches in Figures 5-2 and 5-3 illustrate how the architect begins to turn the library program into an architectural plan.

SCHEMATIC DESIGN

For the library staff this is the most important design phase for a careful review of the plans to be certain that the seating and material storage capacities meet the program requirements and to determine how the building can be staffed and operated. These plans will show all the furniture and equipment in place.

The architect begins to visualize how the building may be designed. This phase establishes the general scope, conceptual design, and scale and relationships among components of the building. The primary objective is to arrive at a clearly defined, feasible concept. The secondary objectives are to clarify the program, explore the most promising alternative design solutions, and provide a reasonable basis for preliminary budgetary analysis of the construction cost of the project. The pre-schematic sketches of the functional areas are reshaped into a coherent plan of the building.

An important element of the schematic design is an understanding of the building context, including:

- The historic context
- The built context (adjacent buildings, utilities, roads, etc.)
- The natural context—landscape, topography and subsurface conditions (test borings and survey), and climate

Generally, the architect uses information provided by the owner to develop this understanding.

Several alternative plans are prepared to show how the building fits on the site. Alternative design solutions are explored with the staff and library consultant and evaluated from the users' point of view. This is the last opportunity to explore alternatives since the end of schematic design is often reached when a particular alternative is selected or several alternatives are combined. What can be expected by the end of schematic design typically includes the following:

- Schematic site plan
- Schematic plans (including furniture and equipment layout for each level); these plans should show a detailed comparison of program requirements with plan capacities for seating and materials
- Schematic elevation drawings
- Schematic building sections
- Schematic outline of building materials and systems
- Statistical summary of the design in comparison to the program
- Budget review
- Illustrative materials needed to present the concept adequately
- Models and sketches of the exterior design

Figure 5-4
Basic Site Plan (by Rick Schoenhardt)

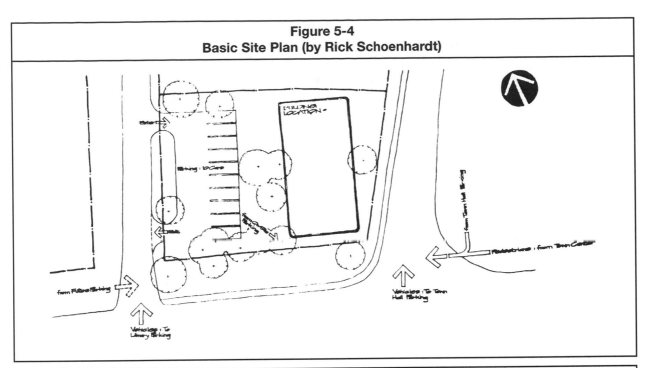

Figure 5-5
Major Functional Areas Showing Comparative Size

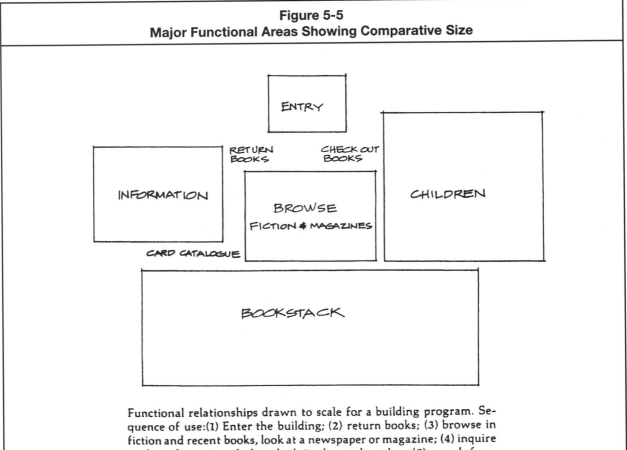

Functional relationships drawn to scale for a building program. Sequence of use:(1) Enter the building; (2) return books; (3) browse in fiction and recent books, look at a newspaper or magazine; (4) inquire at the information desk or look in the card catalog; (5) search for a particular book in the bookstack; (6) check-out a book, leave the building.

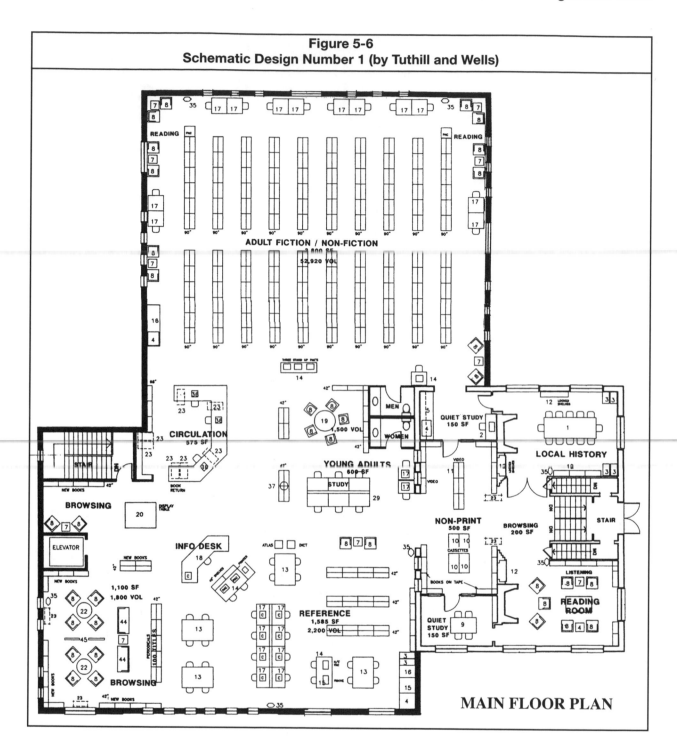

Figure 5-6
Schematic Design Number 1 (by Tuthill and Wells)

MAIN FLOOR PLAN

It will often conclude with a cost estimate by an independent estimator, a local contractor, or construction management firm. The level of detail in the budget estimate produced at the conclusion of this phase is still very general. The estimate will be broken down by major trades or systems (for example, foundations, structure, exterior closure, interior partitions and finishes, plumbing, mechanical, electrical, etc.), taking into consideration construction type and the general materials palette, but without attempting precise materials takeoffs.

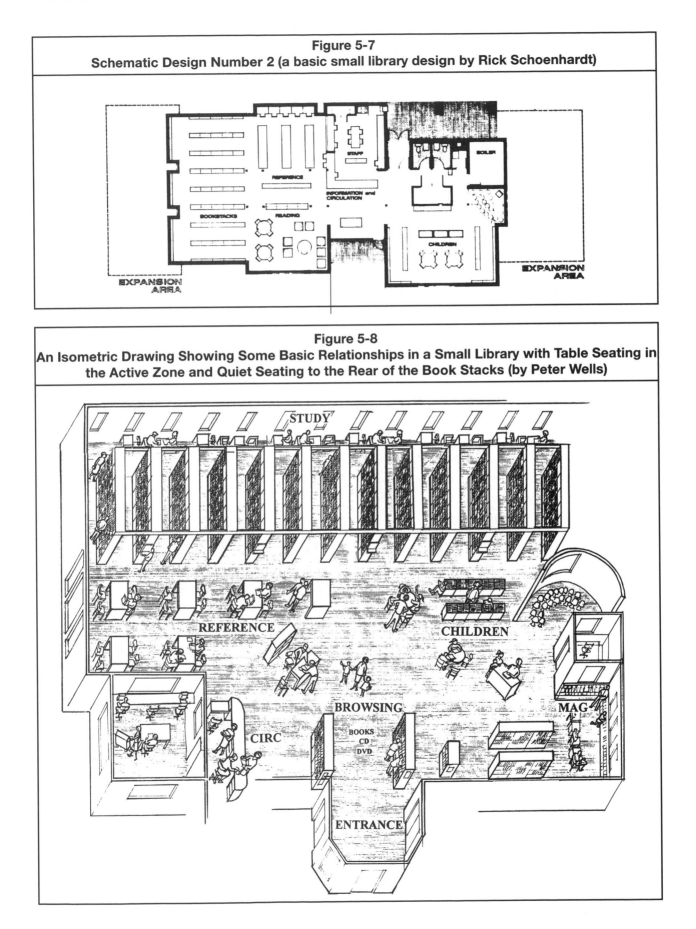

Figure 5-7
Schematic Design Number 2 (a basic small library design by Rick Schoenhardt)

Figure 5-8
An Isometric Drawing Showing Some Basic Relationships in a Small Library with Table Seating in the Active Zone and Quiet Seating to the Rear of the Book Stacks (by Peter Wells)

Schematic design may cost 15 percent of the architectural fee and take one to three months to complete. Figures 5-4 through 5-8 present examples of various components that comprise the schematic design.

DESIGN DEVELOPMENT

At the end of schematic design a particular plan is selected for further development. As planning proceeds it becomes more difficult to make major design changes so the development of a design should not change basically during this phase. The decisions that are made in schematic design are worked out at a scale that minimizes the possibility of major modifications during the construction contract documents phase. The primary purpose of design development is to further define and describe all aspects of the project so that what remains is the formal documentation of the construction contract documents.

Design development is the period in which the design itself achieves the refinement and coordination necessary for a piece of architecture. The architect creates more detailed plans including structural drawings on how the structure will be supported and mechanical drawings on how the building will be heated and cooled.

In coordination with the architectural drawings, the drawings of the other members of the design team are developed by the consulting engineers. Preliminary drawings from these engineers are included in the design development package to describe the basic building systems including:

- Structural
- HVAC (heating, ventilating, and air conditioning)
- Electrical
- Plumbing
- Fire protection

Also developed at this time is an outline specification that provides a narrative description of all the significant materials and manufactured products for the building. It will be costly to make extensive changes in the design after this phase so there should be several detailed reviews of the plans with the staff and library consultant.

Lighting, graphics, and furniture may begin to be planned at this phase. Coordination of lighting and signage is exceedingly important at this time, otherwise signs may be poorly lighted or may even be masked by lighting glare.

During design development, the design team works out a clear, coordinated description of the design. This typically includes more developed:

- Site plan
- Floor plans
- Building sections
- Exterior elevations
- Reflected ceiling plans
- Wall sections

At the conclusion of design development another more accurate cost estimate is made. Combining the information from the outline specification with the more detailed drawings, the budget estimate prepared at the end of the design development phase will incorporate a greater level of detail, making preliminary quantity surveys, determining unit costs, and extensions to identify the costs of the various assemblies within each trade. Still preliminary, the budget estimate will include a contingency for design details to be worked out in the next phase.

Design development may represent an additional 20 percent of the architectural fee and take several months to complete.

PRE-BID VALUE ENGINEERING AND PEER PLAN REVIEW

Near the end of design development it may be helpful to assemble a team of architects, engineers, and construction specialists to examine the project and make recommendations for design improvements and cost conserving changes.

GREEN DESIGN

This may also be a useful time to examine plans for green design and for staff productivity. Green design is an effort to conserve energy and create a safe and healthy work environment that complies with life safety codes that in turn may affect staff productivity.

Construction Documents

The architect prepares detailed drawings of all aspects of the project so that contractors can build from these plans. It is the purpose of this phase to document the building in sufficient detail for a contractor to price the execution of the building. Considerable time is invested to describe in detail a large range of surface configurations, material interfaces, and building systems components. This is the longest and most time consuming architectural phase.

Construction documentation may take six to nine months and cost 40 percent of the total architectural fee.

Bidding and Negotiation

Architectural services for the bidding and negotiation phase can include:
  Assisting in contractor pre-qualification
  Documents distribution
  Bid analysis review and recommendations
There are several options for getting the building constructed:

GENERAL CONTRACTOR

Bidding the building consists of encouraging general contractors to enter bids for construction. The general contractors will pick up plans and share them with specialist sub-contractors such as electrical, masonry, carpentry, heating, ventilating, and air conditioning. The general contractor will usually choose the lowest bid from the sub-contracting firms then add something for the supervisory work, obtain a required bid bond, and submit a sealed bid on the bid opening day.

CONSTRUCTION MANAGEMENT

Retaining a construction management firm to construct the building by selecting subcontractors to perform the required work is essential. The construction management firm often has detailed knowledge of how each sub-contractor will perform. In some cases this method may not be permitted by municipal- or state-mandated low bidder requirements. Some construction management firms also supply architectural services and are hired at the beginning of the project to manage costs.

DESIGN-BUILD

In this alternative the architect and construction firm are hired as a team to design and construct the library. This is often done as a fixed-fee contract after the program establishes the building size.

Once a construction option is selected, the need to make design decisions continues. The negotiation process inevitably leads to proposed substitutions or modifications to details to achieve cost savings or to simplify the construction process. Bidding services may cost 5 percent of the architectural fee.

Construction Administration

The architect's representative will meet with the contractor to discuss the work weekly or when required by the contractor. The library may also hire a clerk to represent the library/owner in observing how the work is progressing. There may be a construction management project manager who supervises the work of sub-contractors instead of a general contractor. The architect will approve payments to the contractor as the work progresses.

Change Orders

If changes in the work become necessary because of new requirements by the owner, omissions from the contract plans, or unforeseen circumstances, a change order will be initiated by the architect and submitted to the library for approval before the change is accomplished.

Construction Administration Services

Construction contract administration services assure the owner that the building will be constructed as it was designed. The architect:

- Observes the construction work for its compliance with drawings and specifications
- Approves materials and product samples
- Reviews the results of construction tests and inspections
- Evaluates contractor requests for payment
- Initiates requests for design changes during construction
- Administers the completion, start-up, and close-out process

Typically, weekly site visits are made to review construction progress relative to the construction schedule and reports will made to the owner. Continuous onsite representation is not a part of basic services but can be arranged as well.

Design even continues through the construction process. Documents require interpretation and elaboration. Field conditions and other problems may force design modifications. Confronted with the reality of the project, the owner may request changes. The design team will integrate these conditions to maintain the design intent anticipated by the owner. The close-out punch list of omissions compares the construction with the plans to assure that all the details have been completed. This may take several weeks after the building is occupied to finish the details. This part of the work represents 20 percent of the architect's fee.

Getting the building that was designed within the budget is important. Attaining that goal requires considerable experience, time, and effort. This summary suggests that architectural design is a simple linear process. In reality, however, it is not quite so orderly and the design process can be compared to a learning curve in which each step reveals to the design team (including client, architect, consulting engineers, etc.) new opportunities, new problems, and new knowledge about the building. Evolving program requirements, budget realities, increased knowledge of site considerations, public agency reviews, and many other factors make it necessary to go back and modify previous steps. The design evolves as we become aware of additional design constraints and opportunities as we move through each design phase, building upon the last.

Furniture and Equipment Selection and Specification

In this phase the architect, library consultant, and staff work closely together to select, specify, and order the furniture and to design the complex staff work areas and public service stations. It will be useful to compare the workstations with the functional area sheet requirements prepared as part of the library building program to ensure that the stations work productively and efficiently.

This design work should commence during the design development phase and be completed nine months before the building is scheduled to be occupied so that the furniture, equipment, and millwork can be produced, delivered, and installed to coincide with the substantial completion and certificate of occupancy of the building.

Often an interior designer is retained to work with the architect and to prepare the detailed specifications. The process of installing the furniture and equipment should be assigned to the architect or interior designer as part of their contract. Budget priorities for furnishings should emphasize user comfort at chairs and workstations rather than expensive wooden book stacks.

Selecting an independent interior design firm provides the library with control over the selection of equipment but may result in furniture and equipment less well suited to the building design than retaining the architect to oversee interior design.

The cost for this may be 10 percent of the *net furniture bid* and may be paid to the architect or to an independent interior designer.

Moving

Moving to temporary quarters and into the new or renovated building requires considerable specialized expertise. An experienced library moving company will be helpful in this process. Weeding the collection of little-used materials and encouraging library users to borrow materials for long-term loans during construction will lighten the moving requirements. Equipment such as book trucks or boxes utilized for the move should contain a full three-foot shelf of books to simplify the location process to the new three-foot shelves. Try to avoid using cardboard boxes that will not coincide with a full shelf thus requiring complex box marking, sequencing, and laborious shelf checking.

Be sure to leave ample room for collection expansion on each shelf and try to predict differing collection growth rates for different portions of the collection so that in fast-growing subject areas there will be more empty shelf space than in slower-growing areas.

Computerized shelf lists in sequence may be helpful in predetermining space for each part of the collection.

Installing line-of-sight signs and shelf labels or book support label holders before shelving will help to assure that the materials are in sequence.

Several companies have developed stack movers that can manipulate several ranges of stacks loaded with books:

Library Liftman from DuPont Flooring Systems
1–800–4dupont
www.dupontflooringsystems.com

Nova Tech
1320 6th Ave. So.
Moorhead, MN 56560
218–236–2072

Post Occupancy Evaluation

The first step in post occupancy evaluation (POE) will be the development of a punch list of items not completed or improperly completed by the contractor. This should be done by the architect and library staff by careful comparing of the building with the contract document plans.

New or substantially improved libraries often generate considerable additional use. This may vary from 30 percent to 100 percent more use. Library use will also change as a result of the improved facility. Users may study for longer hours, children may come to the library more frequently, or teenagers may require additional group study opportunities. After the first year of occupancy the staff and library consultant should conduct a study to determine the changes necessary to respond to new library uses. The library should set aside 10 percent of the furnishings budget to respond to these changes. More information on POE may be found in Chapter 18.

6

Site Selection and
General Design Considerations

This chapter discusses site selection criteria, design considerations for convenient public use, and efficient staff operation including flexible planning. New buildings, additions, and adaptive reuse are discussed. Advantages of a single-story library are enumerated.

Locating the Library—Library Site Selection

Criteria—A site that encourages people to use the library is most important. This usually results from users passing the library in going to work and shopping.

Site availability—Is the site available for immediate use?
- Wetlands problems?
- Toxic materials?
- Historic buildings?

User convenience—Can people get to the site quickly and conveniently?
- Near retail shopping center?
- Visible and directly accessible on a well-traveled road?

Community access—Is the site in a useful location for the community?
- In geographic center?
- In population center?
- In future population center?
- Walking distance from a population concentration (one quarter mile)?

User and staff safety—Will the site be safe and secure at night?
- Well lighted areas?
- Active at night?
- Parking lot access to building does not cross traffic or road for child safety?
- Close to police station?
- Easily visible for police drive-by?
- Avoid major highway location for child safety?

Community synergy—Will community groups benefit easily from the new site?
- Near other evening community activities?
- Near schools (this may be a liability if students dominate the services, which is often the case when school libraries are inadequate)?
- Near businesses?

Size for future growth—Will the site accommodate expanded library facilities?
- Accommodates building?
- Accommodates parking and green space?
- Accommodates future expansion?

Cost factors—Will the site minimize cost?
- Purchase price?
- Site development cost—water, ledge rock removal, utilities?
- High community acceptance for public funding?
- Potential for private funding?
- State/federal grant potential?
- Minimizes staffing and operating costs?

School Locations

Although a school site may be inexpensive and has the great virtue of being convenient for school children and parents picking up children from school it also has several potential disadvantages:

- School children may dominate the building and discourage adults from using the library.
- School locations are often out of the normal traffic patterns for the community.
- Schools are often not clearly visible from the street so that people are not reminded of the library location.
- School materials are not suitable for adults who may be discouraged trying to find adult materials in this hybrid collection.
- Younger children may be intimidated by older, and possibly rowdy, school children.

Design Considerations

Designing a library often appears to be a struggle to achieve the impossible. A planning document may specify that the new facility have features and qualities that are not compatible with other features and qualities. The challenge that planners and the design team face is to arrive at a balance between seemingly contradictory goals. It often means striving to balance conflicting priorities so that the building exhibits the maximum of each. For example, the building should:

- Provide for the convenience of the library's users while maximizing staff efficiency.
- Provide a modern library with up-to-date technologies that reflect the cultural traditions of the community.
- Provide a comfortable and inviting ambience that encourages use but allows staff to maintain control and supervision.
- Provide a reference area that invites users to approach librarians but provides the option for private consultation.
- Provide an attractive, efficient design for today while leaving open the potential for future expansion.
- Provide a multi-purpose room that can be supervised when the library is open, and be accessible when the rest of the library is closed.
- Provide natural light to flood the library but control excessive heat gain from direct sunlight to minimize damage to materials and control energy costs.
- Provide plentiful artificial light without glare.
- Provide HVAC and electrical systems for future expansion, and for increased occupancy.
- Provide operable windows for between-season ventilation.
- Allow for future expansion for specific functions such as children's services, teen youth services, book stacks, and electronic workstations.

Handicapped Access

With an aging population and federal and state legislation delineating in detail how to make buildings, and libraries in particular, more accessible this consideration is essential in library design. Details vary slightly from state to state and are available from state libraries and other agencies, so this book will not attempt to repeat that material. In general these are some elements to consider:

- Handicapped people should be accommodated in the mainstream of the design rather than through special entrances or arrangements.
- Oversize handicapped parking spaces must be convenient to the entrance.
- Interior and exterior ramps should have gentle slopes 12 feet of horizontal travel for each foot of vertical rise.
- Aisle widths should be three feet minimum but we recommend four feet.
- Service counters no more than 36 inches high for handicapped.
- At least 5 percent of tables and carrels should accommodate wheelchairs with knee space 19 inches deep and 27 inches high from floor to underside of tables.
- Toilets should be designed for handicapped users.
- Reach height for magazines should be 48 inches maximum for front approach and 54 inches for side approach.

Spatial Relationships and Traffic Flow

Modern libraries provide an ever increasing array of services and materials. The design must make it easy for patrons to find and use these materials and services. It must be clear and logical to all, including first-time visitors.

LIBRARY SERVICE CHOICES AND TRAFFIC FLOW

The public entrance should flow naturally into the interior of the building. Visible at the entrance should be the most popular services the library offers. These services may include:

- Circulation—Returning, borrowing, and registration
- New material—Merchandising, including audio-visual services
- Public access terminals and other electronic reference resources
- Reference
- Magazine areas
- The major book stack
- Children's and young adult areas

The lobby/entrance should be compact and free of visual obstructions for safety and security reasons. Room for traffic flow and potential conflict in traffic patterns should be checked, since those entering and leaving the library or stopping to pick up tax forms or community brochures as well as others moving from one section of the library to another can be a problem.

The decor of the lobby should establish the library as a friendly but businesslike place. It should serve as a transition to the quieter areas within. Automatic opening of entrance doors will be useful for handicapped patrons as well as users with armloads of books, but as they tend to stay open longer, cold drafts on patrons and staff in close proximity to the doors will have to be eliminated by weather barriers.

Visitors should be able to visually orient themselves to the library's major areas while passing through the entrance area.

Those who come to the library will usually fall into one of the groups described below, and the building design must conveniently accommodate them all.

THE SHORT-TERM USER

Some users enter with the intention of making only a brief trip, often to return previously borrowed materials. Some wish to pick up reserve books or get a quick answer. Others wish to quickly browse new books or skim magazines and newspapers. Perhaps as many as one-third to one-half of the users fall into this category and stay 30 minutes or less.

THE LONG-TERM USER

The long-term user comes for extended periods of time to browse through collections, read magazines and newspapers, use materials in the library, search the Internet, or to study. Students will come to study after school or on weekends. These individuals need a quiet environment for their activities. They would especially appreciate small, acoustically separated rooms.

GROUP PARTICIPANTS
Some individuals will come to the library as a part of a formal or informal group to participate in a particular activity or program. Because groups can cause traffic problems and create congestion, noise, and confusion, access to meeting areas should be carefully planned to avoid routing through reading or stack areas.

DELIVERIES, LIBRARY STAFF, AND OTHERS
Library and delivery staff will normally use a special staff entrance. The delivery and staff entrance should be convenient and should not be visible from the public entrance or from public areas. It should have a buzzer to alert staff to deliveries, and a small storage room in which to lock delivered parcels.

SPATIAL RELATIONSHIPS FROM THE ENTRANCE

A key design challenge will be the integration of a wide variety of services, while maintaining acoustic separation and good visual control. Maps of the library can be useful, but only if placed in the direct line of sight. Maps or directories placed on a wall to one side of the entrance are seldom used.

MERCHANDISING—BROWSING
- New books, audio cassettes, videos, CDs, and special collection displays should be dramatically visible from the entrance and displayed with colorful front covers on attractively designed displays
- Spot highlighting would be useful here

CHILDREN'S, YOUNG ADULT, AND ADULT SERVICES: CIRCULATION SERVICES
Visitors should be able to see most popular areas from the entrance.

- The circulation desk, new materials, children's, young adult, and reference areas should all be visible
- It is important that this visual introduction be an inviting one featuring views of library materials and reader accommodations and lighted display units
- If adult fiction and non-fiction collections, children's services, young adult spaces, staff work areas, and study carrels are placed in one contiguous area, sound isolation is important for each; sound can be dampened by sound-absorbing materials or isolated by glass.

REFERENCE SERVICES ELECTRONIC REFERENCE EQUIPMENT
AND STAFF WORK AREAS
The reference and information area should be visible from the main entrance lobby and centrally-located.

- It must be convenient to the reference collection, the periodicals collection, and the browsing and audio-visual area. It should be near the bookstacks.
- Young adult and juvenile reference users should also have easy access to adult reference services.
- Terminals to access electronic sources should be readily available to the person entering the library.

- Terminals should also be distributed throughout the building for easy access by users in various functional areas. The placement of terminals must be given careful thought in designing the layout. Privacy for the public when using terminals is an important consideration. Is area suitable for wireless transmission?
- Public access and local area network terminals may not be interchangeable at first, but may become so in the future. Public service staff consult or trouble shoot these sources frequently, so equipment service points should be in close proximity to allow for easy staff access to equipment.
- Location of staff work areas is important to efficient operation. Work areas should be close to public services, yet acoustically separate.
- Traffic should not be routed through work areas. Staff security requires at least two exits in staff areas.

DRIVE-UP SERVICES

Drive-up access may be useful for the pickup or return of materials. Returns may be handled by using a curbside bin; however, these sometimes present a problem in inclement weather both for customers as well as for staff attempting to retrieve materials during rain or snow. Return bins should be located under cover if possible. Returns that come directly into the library building must be fire isolated by building a fireproof room and/or by using a special fire extinguishing device. A serious fire at the Danbury, Connecticut, library was caused by someone putting flaming materials into an interior book drop. The entire building was gutted by the resulting fire.

Staff attending drive-up facilities should be near the regular circulation desk so that they can work productively while waiting to be available for drive-up service. This requires that the building design locates the drive-up window near the regular circulation desk so that the same staff can provide both services.

Flexible Planning and Design

Libraries are organic buildings, ever growing and changing. The design should incorporate the following concepts to facilitate change:

- Vertical access elements such as elevators, stairs, heating, air conditioning ducts, and electrical risers should be kept on the perimeter of the structure to assure future functional flexibility.
- A master plan should be included in the initial stages of planning to accommodate change and growth both within and in addition to the building being constructed at this time. For example future expansion in collections, seating, and multi-purpose space should each be shown.
- Internal change scenarios should also be discussed, such as the change from material storage to computer workstations. Short-term, five-year changes are more useful than questionable longer-term plans. Change scenarios should include furniture and equipment sketches as well as footprint site expansion diagrams.

- Wiring for computers requires design for both power distribution and low voltage transmission such as telephone lines. These should run in separate conduits and the conduits should be easily accessible for increasing bandwidth. Improved bandwidth delivery systems may require rewiring during the life of the building, so electronic equipment centers and conduits should be designed for ease of rewiring.

- Computer workstations should be capable of easy movement throughout the facility. Such options as wireless, fiber optic cabling, carpet tile/flat wiring, power poles, Walker ducts, and floor grids for power should be discussed early in the planning stage. Wireless systems provide a useful option for new and old installations. Conduct a wireless evaluation to determine suitability and plan for future hubs.

- Special power and communication centers should be identified and receive special design attention early in the planning process to assure sufficient power for both overall and per circuit. Consider dedicated circuits, telephone transmission options, filtered, uniform and stable power delivery, ease of equipment exchange for repair, and ease of access to clearly labeled circuit breakers. These special areas will include:
  - Checkout locations
  - Reference services
  - Staff work areas
  - Multi-purpose and meeting rooms
  - Security systems
  - Electronic network center

The computer instruction area should be designed with large, double-opening doors so that it can be used as a flexible study area for individual electronic workstation use when classes are not in session.

The children's story and crafts area should be carefully designed for three very different functions:

- Story hour requires concentration on the story teller with sound separation from other library functions. A puppet stage and curtains for dramatizations with spot lighting may be helpful.
- Crafts requires a floor material that can be easily cleaned and a sink and counter.
- Study requires quiet and staff supervision and control.

About 10 percent of the equipment should be purchased after the first year of occupancy of the library addition in order to respond to the changing needs of library users. People will use the new facility differently than they used the old library and it will take a year before their preferences will be realized.

The flexibility fallacy refers to the assumptions that library functions are interchangeable and particular functions do not have specific design requirements. Beware assuming that a uniform design allows for functional change without major alterations. Putting stacks in a high ceiling area designed as a reading room requires lighting and HVAC adjustments that are difficult to achieve and which may look ugly. Electronic workstations in a former stack may not have adequate HVAC or lighting.

CULTURAL RESPONSE

The library design should be sensitive to opportunities for responding to the cultural esthetics of the populations to be served. Colors, patterns, furniture types, and decorative touches can be attractive responses. However, beware of rapidly changing demographics. An urban library selected German chair decorations and design for a branch library that rapidly became a Puerto Rican neighborhood. Avoid ethnic wall murals or major design elements that are difficult to change.

New Buildings, Additions, and Adaptive Reuse

Most architects and librarians would prefer to deal with a clean slate and design a brand new library.

New building has the following advantages over an existing structure:

- Massing and siting the building for new and future services is easier
- Sizing the building for future growth is easier
- Wiring for the future is simpler
- Cost effective staff adjacencies are not limited by an existing structure
- Handicapped accessibility is easier
- Unified library design can be achieved with less effort
- No need for temporary relocation

Disadvantages may include:

- New location for the community to learn about
- Loss of a historic structure familiar to the community

Addition and renovation of an existing site has these advantages:

- Known and familiar location and design
- Beautiful architectural detailing that may be difficult to reproduce
- Lower cost, but not always

Disadvantages:

- Bringing an older building up to modern building and life safety code compliance can be an expensive and time consuming process
- Temporary relocation may be necessary. Staying in a building while an addition is constructed is problematical because of renovation and construction activity— dust, electrical connection issues, and heating, air conditioning, and ventilating system shutdowns.

Adaptive reuse of other building types such as converting a shopping center or former school building to a library present interesting opportunities and problems.

Advantages:

- Retail stores are often in excellent locations for attracting library users
- They often have large parking lots and convenient access to the entrance
- The cost for abandoned buildings is often quite low

Disadvantages:

- Schools are often located far from retail or downtown locations
- High cost of renovations
- Floor load capacities for stores, offices, and schools are much lower that the 150 pounds per square foot live loads required for standard book stacks. Reinforcing floors is expensive and problematical

The Advantages of Locating Basic Library Services on One Level

Libraries smaller than 20,000 square feet should consider the advantages of locating basic library services on one level. These advantages become less as the building exceeds 20,000 square feet because larger buildings necessitate larger staffs to control these spaces, even on a single level.

Maximum and universal access to all materials—All materials will be equally accessible if they are all on one level. If materials are on a level above or below the entry level, they will be less used since more effort will be required to find them.

Public convenience—Services on one level will enhance public convenience since all services will be seen from the entrance and the public will be aware and have a clear choice of activities. The public is often unaware of services on other levels.

Staff productivity—Adding a single professional staff member will cost the library a million dollars over the 20-year life of the building. Locating public services on a single level will enhance staff productivity since staff can be involved in a variety of public services as they are needed, rather than having main floor staff be busy while second floor staff are idle. Experienced staff can assist newer staff better if they work in close proximity.

Lower cost—Elevators are costly to install and maintain, and require waiting when they are on other floors. Elevators also deny access to other floors when they are broken. Libraries are often open many hours a week requiring two shifts. Staffing another level on a two shift basis will greatly increase operating costs.

Improved security—Security of staff, public, and materials is better in a single-story library in which all activities are visible from a central service area.

Non entry level functions—Some functions can be located on other levels with some additional cost in staff and supervision. They may include:

- *Program, multi-purpose, and meeting rooms* are most usefully located on the same floor as other basic library functions such as the children's area. They are scheduled group activities that require access when other library services are closed, therefore an entry-level location is preferred. However, since they are scheduled they may be located on another level with staff supervision only during the actual program.

- *Mechanical building functions* such as heating, ventilating, and air conditioning can be located on another level to provide acoustical separation and separate maintenance.
- *Maintenance and custodial work areas*, offices, and storage can be located on another level but may not be as well supervised in that location.
- *Staff work areas* such as deliveries and processing can be located on another floor, but restricted communication and movement between levels may hinder productivity and public service staff will not be easily available to assist at public service stations.

Zones and Boundaries

Older libraries rigorously separated different library functions. Architects understood that libraries required different activities that needed to be expressed in the design. Therefore library book stacks were often dark, low-ceilinged spaces with lighting in the narrow aisles sometimes using the vertical stack support members to support the actual floors of the stack. Separate reading rooms on the other hand had high ceilings with tall windows carefully spaced to pour natural light onto the reading tables. These separate spaces were highly inflexible and often difficult to access since the reading room floor didn't always match the book stack floor level.

Flexible open plan libraries needed different ways to express different functions. Activities requiring zone and boundary definition may include:

- Age related differences such as young adult, middle school, and pre school
- Noise level functions such as staff service, listening, viewing, and group study
- High frequency of use new materials or low-use older materials
- Programs and meeting rooms
- Staff processing, ordering, and maintenance activities

Change in function within libraries requires several flexible methods to express functional zones and boundaries:

- Furniture types and sizes, such as widely spaced individual study tables for quiet study and sofas, lounge seats, and group study tables for noisier group or conversational activities.
- Colors can indicate bright noisy children's activity as opposed to natural subdued colors for study.
- Bright spot lighting indicates bustling display spaces while indirect low lighting indicates quieter spaces.
- Low partitions in the children's room set apart active from quieter areas.
- Glass partitions separate areas acoustically while allowing visual access. Glass should never be used on all four sides of an area because of the echo noise. Acoustical glass is expensive but may be used for group study rooms. Lighting that washes the face of the glass reduces reflections that often obscure areas set behind glass.

- Varying ceiling heights using suspended ceilings can indicate varying activities.
- Lower or higher book stacks and wider aisle spacing differentiate active display areas from the less-used book storage stacks.
- Vertical separation of areas by a few very low steps can differentiate functions, but ramps for handicapped access will have to be used.
- Standard book stacks are useful in sound absorbing and defining boundaries between functions.
- Graphics, especially back-lighted signs, are an excellent method of signaling important staff service points and defining their use.
- Passageways separate functions by not having any furniture and by high-hat lighting.
- Carpet color and pattern variations can differentiate function while facilitating recarpeting of more active areas.

Many zone requirements result from noise differences. Controlling noise in libraries may be achieved in several ways:

- Enclosing rooms is still the most effective method of isolating noisy or quiet activities. New construction methods make it easier to change partitions.
- Absorb sound with acoustical tile or anechoic foam wedges behind perforated metal screens. Books are excellent at absorbing sound while glass reflects sound and results in echoes. Carpets, cork floors, and upholstered furniture also absorb sound.
- Noise decreases greatly with distance.
- White sound generated continuously by small, distributed speakers can generate gentle ocean sounds to mask out traffic noise.

7

Review of Plans

Assuring that a library building project really works requires not only evaluating your clientele and services and preparing a carefully detailed building program, but making reality checks on the work of the architects and designers. A crucial step in the planning process occurs when the architect draws plans showing how the program will look as a building. These drawings should show furniture and equipment to scale and indicate proximities of major functions. A library should be easy to find, easy to enter, and easy to use. A library should be accessible and convenient. This begins with the site selection and extends through building design into the selection of furnishings and equipment.

The User Sequence

This sequence follows a user from arrival in the parking lot to departure. Look at the plan and trace the steps in the user's activities on the plan.

Sequence of use:

(1) Enter the building
(2) Return books
(3) Go to program or meeting rooms
(3) Browse in recent materials, look at a newspaper or magazine

(4)   Inquire at the information desk or conduct an Internet or database search
(5)   Look in the online public access catalog
(5)   Search for a particular book in the bookstack
(6)   Read or study in a quiet location
(7)   Take a drink or food break
(6)   Check out a book, leave the building

There are no obstacles to entering commercial buildings. We expect automatic operating doors in supermarkets, why not in libraries? The shopper carries parcels when leaving a store but the library user carries books, films, or other circulating materials both when entering and leaving. The path from parking space or sidewalk to entrance should be as direct as possible. The public must be able to see the entrance from the parking area rather than be faced with a twisting walk around a series of corners. Some other considerations follow.

Are parking spaces unnecessarily far from the entrance? Does the slope from the parking lot to the library meet ADA standards? Is the entrance clearly visible and inviting?

Plans may start as bubble diagrams suggesting proximities and relative sizes. The next step may be to relate boxes scaled to the sizes of functional areas. Finally, plans will show the footprint—the area that the building occupies on the site. Some architects will show bookstacks, tables, chairs, and staff work equipment at this step. In designing libraries it is essential that each piece of furniture for public and staff use as well as equipment be drawn on the plan in an early phase, since shapes of functional areas are often set at this time. Bookstacks, chairs, tables, and technical equipment are available in a narrow range of particular sizes. These sizes will determine if the shape of an area is workable for a library function. For example, a long narrow shape may contain the necessary square footage, yet be too narrow to accommodate the chairs and tables required by the program.

Capacities for books and seating in each functional area should be calculated by the architect and shown on the plan. The consultant and library staff should verify these capacities on the plans by counting the seats and stack sections.

An especially useful review process assigns the responsibility for plan review and approval to the library consultant and library director prior to plan review by the community building committee. This process clearly sets library function as the plan priority. If the building committee looks at a design before assuring its functional capability, the design may dominate the function.

Comparing plan and actual function is the process that occurs in plan reviews. This should be done from several points of view. Here are a few user considerations:

- When users enter the library, can they understand the layout?
- Are books visible and arranged in a clear and simple order?
- Are new materials displayed with the covers out near the entrance?
- Are reference librarians available for user assistance near the entrance?
- Are functions arranged with most-used functions near the entrance?
- Are noisy areas near the entrance so that users walk through noisy areas to reach quiet ones?

- Are audio-visual materials immediately available without time-consuming box matching or asking for staff assistance?
- Are readers offered a sufficiently wide variety of comfortable seats?
- Are chairs shaped with lower lumbar support and curved backs? Can they easily slide on carpets? Can wheelchairs fit under tables?
- Can children find their area easily?
- Within the children's area are there separate zones for pre-school and older children with different size and types of furnishings for each age group?
- Can teenagers find their area and listen to music or videos as well as study quietly and in small groups?
- Are there multi-purpose facilities for programs as well as meeting rooms available when the rest of the library is closed?

Staff productivity considerations:

- Are circulation areas designed in detail for efficient use of circulation systems now and flexibility for the future?
- Are dual-level service counters available to define user and staff functions?
- Is there a low checkout section for wheelchair access?
- Are technical service areas designed efficiently for rapid processing of library materials? Room for book trucks?
- Electronic workstations—For workstations with individual flexibility use adjustable terminal keyboards, seating, wiring flexibility.

Design Development

During this phase architects work on the details of the schematic plan including exterior elevations and heating, ventilating, and air conditioning machinery locations. Functions become fixed and sizes and relationship changes become complex and time consuming for the architect. Sizes and locations of library public service counters, bookstacks, and chairs and tables are fixed during this stage and equipment selections concerns begin to emerge.

Design development reviews should follow the same pattern as in schematic reviews by staff and consultant but now the size, location, and juxtaposition of each item is finally determined and detailed dimensions become more important.

- Do chairs swivel and tilt?
- Are multi-purpose tables large enough to be used by several people?
- Are there study carrels in quiet spaces far from noisy staff areas and entrance?
- Are oversize tables near the newspapers?
- Are computer workstations available for the public? With staff assistance nearby?
- Are children's services near the entrance?
- Are adult seats available in the children's area?
- Are story hour facilities available in the children's area and acoustically separated from children's study areas?
- Do children have a choice of single, group seating, and quiet areas?

The staff review examines a variety of library services from the staff point of view:

- Finding a book
- Answering a reference question
- Checking out materials
- Supervising public use of library services
- Ordering and processing new materials
- Security of valuable materials

Future Expansion

The next expansion of the library should be an integral part of the initial plan. A major building change will result in new and unanticipated changes in use. To respond to these changes 10 percent of the furniture budget should be available after the first year of operation to respond to use changes.

Furniture and equipment recommendations should be made before working drawings commence to assure that dimensions are accurate and equipment will fit comfortably into assigned spaces.

Lighting and graphics recommendations must be made before working drawings to assure that graphics are well lighted and appropriately placed.

- Is the graphic system coordinated with lighting for effective self-service?
- Are sign sizes proportional to distance from users and are signs sequentially positioned to make self-service work in this library?

Final Considerations

- How could this plan be improved?
- Is it easy to find things?
- Are there quiet places?
- Can children work together or find a quiet corner?
- Can staff see users?

III

The Planning
of Specific
Functional Areas

8

Parking, Entry, and Circulation

This chapter emphasizes the importance of the library as a community place and indicates a variety of considerations in designing the parking lot, driveways entrance, coffee food service, and checkout and return areas.

A Community Place

Libraries have always been centers for community activities. The library on the New England green was often the most beautiful building in town, the one citizens cherished for its classical exterior design. Libraries represent the sharing of community resources to create a building for everyone to enjoy. It should be designed, constructed, and furnished with the finest rather than with affordable, shabby materials and furnishings. Older libraries in small communities are often outstanding in the beauty and quality of their design. Library leaders should seek to demonstrate civic pride and spirit in the design of their libraries.

The Project for Public Spaces is an organization that wants to create public spaces in towns and cities. The critical combination of activities that result in these public spaces includes a market, a public transportation stop, and an eating place as well as a library.

Libraries can be important buildings in encouraging citizens to meet for exchanging information, learning about the world, and joyfully greeting one another. To do this they must have an open street presence related to other street functions. An indoor garden plaza with benches and coffee places might be one approach.

Currently there is a yearning for informal socialization. Older people, teens, and families need a place in town where they can meet others to share news and information. New immigrants, strangers new to town, and older residents with fewer family members would also come to the library to satisfy this basic human need. Garrison Keillor in his public radio programs conveys the essence of this idea in his skits on the Chatterbox Cafe in Lake Woebegon. Roxanne Coady in Madison, Connecticut, has created this in her R.J. Julia bookstore and the larger chain bookstores try to do this in their food service areas that are often crowded on weekends.

Libraries can easily become these kinds of places with an effort to create a community gathering place connected with their new books and magazines. How wonderful to discuss a topic in the midst of a collection of materials and a staff dedicated to the community and trained in helping people with their knowledge needs.

The Community Context

Libraries at their best create a welcoming space open to all that incorporates design features familiar to the community. In small town New England this may include some hint of a colonial past. In urban centers it may be a street presence that evokes activities involving families such as family centers with story chairs for parent and child to read together, or outdoor courtyards with music and dancing. The concept is for the library to come outside of its walls or to bring the outside into the building.

Approaching the Library

First impressions are important. The experience that library users have as they approach the building will influence their use of the library and their impression of service. People should see an open, user friendly, and esthetically pleasing place.

The view from outside the building should highlight the variety of activities that take place within, emphasizing the newest and most attractive aspects. Brightly lighted displays of the front covers of books, videos, CD/DVDs, as well as computer screens showing activity in the children's and library program areas might be examples.

Outside Signage at the Library Location

The library should be clearly identified to passing motorists and pedestrians by the provision of a lighted sign perpendicular to the road. If the sign is parallel to the road it will be nearly invisible to vehicular traffic. The sign should indicate hours the library is open, and should be resistant to vandalism. The purpose of this sign is not just to locate the library but to remind people of its existence so it should be sized to compete with other street signs.

Another sign with hours should be on the entrance door or immediately outside the door in the direct line of sight.

Parking

There should be parking spaces for easy access to the building with a covered drop-off point so that people can enter and leave without getting their books wet.

- The parking lot should be convenient to the entrance of the library so that users do not have to walk across streets.
- Trees in the parking area will be helpful to prevent car overheating. Trees should be selected to minimize leaf cleanup and minimize sap droppings on cars. Trees near the parking spaces should be protected from damage by cars. If possible, green landscaped "islands" should be incorporated into the lot to break up the expanse of cars and convey a park-like appearance.
- The parking lot should be lighted with vandal-proof fixtures on a timer.
- Future parking lot expansion should be designed into the plan.
- Clearly marked handicapped parking as required by code should be provided near the building. There should be a curb cut ramp to provide access for both wheelchair users and bicyclists. These curb cuts should be made from colored concrete to clearly delineate the slope of the curb from the flat concrete area. The drop-off area should be large enough to accommodate a van. The slope from the parking area to the entrance should meet the American Disabilities Act requirements to permit easy access for the elderly and handicapped.

The number of parking places is determined by several factors:

- Zoning regulations.
- Number of seats in the library and meeting rooms.
- Building size—one space for every 300–500 square feet of building.
- In some urban areas access to public transportation may lessen the need for parking.

Bicycle and Motorcycle Racks

There should be racks for bicycles. The racks should be sheltered from the rain and be lockable. A separate motorcycle area should be provided. This area should be in sight of the library entrance to prevent vandalism and discourage theft.

The Entrance—Outside

- A driveway two-cars wide with a drop-off point should include appropriate signage to prevent parking for a long time at the drop-off point.
- The entry should include a stroller storage area with covered protection from the rain.
- Glass at the main entry will allow users and passers-by to view the library before entering and give the library an open welcoming feel.
- The public entrance should be convenient to pedestrians and vehicular library patrons alike. It should be easily accessible for the physically challenged.
- There should be a separate entrance to the program, staff, and delivery areas that is accessible when the rest of the library is closed.
- Hose bibs for outside watering should be located in the building wall.

DRIVE-UP SERVICE AND AFTER-HOURS BOOK DROP

It may be possible to locate a drive-up window so that library circulation desk staff can assist users with driving in and picking up library materials. This activity often varies so care should be taken to locate the drive-up window so that regular circulation desk staff can occasionally service both in library and drive-up users. Library users need a place to return books when the library is closed.

- An easily accessible book return slot with a separate non-print return should be able to be reached from a momentarily parked car. People returning materials should be protected from rain.
- The book return must be accessible by the staff with book trucks to transport returns to the library.
- The book return should be lockable, and should include an automatic fire extinguisher and an automatic fire alarm. This area should have a fire barrier to the rest of the library to prevent smoke or fire damage. Air intake to the rest of the library should shut down in case of fire.
- A depressible book truck with a capacity of 200 books should be provided under the book drop, designed so that staff can easily empty the return without going outside the building.

The Entrance—Inside

When people enter the building they will pause to orient themselves. The lobby should be an open space to accomplish this orienting function. It will inevitably shape the attitude of the library user. Nineteenth-century public libraries often symbolized the "Temple of Learning" school of library design in which the building was set on a pedestal consisting of stone steps and classical columns flanked the entrance that was through huge heavy doors. This design is at its best in places like the great New York Public Library that had the virtue of calling attention to a grand spiritually uplifting place of major cultural importance.

At the same time handicapped access was non existent and the difficult access was exceedingly discouraging to many everyday users. Today, library designers want to encourage users to feel that the library still is a special and uplifting place, but also exciting and welcoming, and easier to enter.

THE LOBBY

The Lobby/Entrance should be compact and free of visual obstructions for safety and security reasons. According to Paco Underhill, retail store design should allow for a decompression zone of about 20 feet from the entrance to allow users to become oriented. Experience has shown that few shoppers will select in this zone. In libraries there may be the need for a similar open orienting space. This space may contain announcements and giveaway flyers for library or town events, tax forms, and a limited number of brochures neatly organized in open bins. Displays and artworks could also be located in the lobby area.

- The decor of the lobby should establish the library as a friendly place. It should serve as a transition to the quieter areas within. Visitors should be able to visually orient themselves to the library's major areas while passing through the entrance.
- Automatic opening doors allow users with armloads of books, baby strollers, and handicapped users to enter the building easily. In busy libraries a weather barrier blowing hot or cold air may be necessary if the doors stay open most of the time. In colder climates the doors should be offset to prevent cold winds from blowing in.
- Traffic flow must be smooth, since those entering and leaving the library or stopping to pick up tax forms or community brochures, as well as others moving from one section of the library to another pose a potential traffic conflict.
- A mat that removes dirt and drops it below and is easily removable for cleaning such as a Pedi-mat should be installed at the front door.

INSIDE SIGNAGE

The location of all areas of the library should be clearly marked on a sign at the library entrance. Library hours should be clearly listed on a sign at the door, so that users coming to the door when the library is closed will be informed when it is open. Be conscious of the line of sight of users when they approach the library. Signs hanging on walls to either side of the entrance are seldom noticed by users intent on entering the building. The sign must be actually on the door itself so that users see it when they enter without shifting their gaze to the side.

Coffee Bars and Food Service in Libraries

Some libraries have had food service for several decades, especially in New England. From a simple coffee cart to an elaborate restaurant, library users find this a helpful community service. A coffee shop near the entrance, such as in the Westport library, with a nearby display of the latest books, videos, and DVDs can create a friendly welcoming invitation to users. The key to success is the same as for all quality library service—good customer service with a friendly welcoming attitude on the part of every staff member.

This amenity may not be for every library, but many libraries have found these advantages to coffee shops:

- Set a welcoming tone and encourage an open conversational atmosphere.
- Provide places where people are encouraged to talk thus creating relief locations to the quieter parts of the library and preserving quiet elsewhere.
- Allow users to spend more time in the library since they have places to eat.

Disadvantages to be considered include:

- Responsibility for managing food service, including code requirements.
- Additional space required.
- Garbage disposal.
- Staff time.

Design considerations include plumbing and water heating, food preservation and storage, cleaning, maintenance, and garbage disposal. Seating and staffing should be flexible with additional event-related seating at busier times.

Circulation Area Design Considerations

The circulation desk may present a formidable and intimidating barrier to library users entering the building. It is often a busy, noisy, and messy area with masses of materials waiting to be reshelved and the inevitable clutter that is a natural consequence of hundreds of transactions taking place at a single location. For these reasons it is often useful to locate the circulation desk off to the left side of the entrance so it is convenient but does not present a barrier and a cluttered appearance to the library user eager to see the latest library offerings.

The design of the checkout area should not create a barrier to access, but should instead facilitate services, and be as unobtrusive as possible. It would be helpful for staff to have an option of facing the entrance. In case of users violating the theft detection system, the staff must be able to exit the desk toward the exit to remind users to check out materials.

Lighting

Staff activities require high-task lighting levels but glare on the computer screens should be avoided by location of light fixtures. Lighting should be easily adjustable as changes take place.

Durability

The surfaces of this counter receive extraordinarily hard use and will wear out rapidly if veneers are used. Consider using Corian, stone, or granite chips.

Flexibility

- Terminals should be near a telephone for easy diagnosis of problems and for renewals by phone. The circulation desk terminals should be easy to change and routine maintenance and replacement of broken machines should be easy to accomplish with plugs and connectors above the desk surface.
- Shell design of counters with mobile under-counter units is useful for flexibility since it facilitates easy change of drawers, shelves, files, and other under-desk components while retaining the basic transaction desk shell.
- Staff seating should be included.
- Bi-level design 39 inches/29 inches high with pass-through areas will define staff and public service locations. The top of the desk will be kept clear for public use. The area below the top surface, accessible only from the staff side, will be wider to allow for a variety of staff-only equipment, notices, and materials.

Circulation Functions

The circulation desk area should therefore be designed to facilitate the following distinct and different activities:

LEND AND RETURN

One of the most active services is to lend and return books and other materials. As a library improves its physical facilities, circulation of materials is likely to increase; therefore, the circulation area should be designed to accommodate at least 50 percent more activity than the current circulation of materials.

BOOK RETURN AREA

This is where library users drop off their returned library materials upon entering the building. Provisions should be made for quick and easy staff check-in of materials so users are not delayed waiting for a cumbersome check-in procedure. It may be helpful to provide a slotted return drop for users to place their books for later check-in. The drop may lead to a depressible book truck to minimize material damage. This truck must be emptied frequently and should be easy for staff to retrieve materials or to replace with another truck. Sensitizing equipment to resensitize theft detection strips should be near the book return. The lighting should be task lighting so that staff can quickly sort returns.

LENDING AREA

A 26 inch high area with knee space for users will be useful to persons in wheelchairs and children and will also permit staff to be seated. This is required by the Americans with Disabilities Act. Other circulation desk activities that require space include collecting of fines and fees, and answering circulation-oriented telephone questions. Space is also needed for storing supplies. Quick access to reserve storage is essential.

SELF-CHECKOUT MACHINES

These machines should be made available for users in good standing monitored by the staff. They should be like familiar ATM automatic bank machines built into a nearby wall. In some libraries they handle 90 percent of checkout transactions.

REGISTRATION

Registering new borrowers is a procedure that often requires a chair and writing surface to fill out registration forms. This is the library staff's first contact with a new patron and affords an opportunity for an orientation to library services. The new users' interests and preferences, an explanation of library services, and perhaps even a brief library tour can often be a part of this experience.

MATERIAL DISPLAY AT THE CIRCULATION DESK

Display units on the customer side of the desk will give library users the opportunity to browse through popular recently returned materials, brochures, or flyers while waiting for checkout. See Figure 8-1 for an example of a well-designed circulation counter. This can be accommodated in various ways, such as:

- Sloping display shelves built into the patron side of the desk
- Sloping display units placed near the checkout locations

Care must be taken to avoid blocking or obscuring exits with display units.

PARCEL SHELVES

Library users may need a place to rest their purses, parcels, and other hand baggage while checking out library materials. Security of personal belongings is a special consideration. See Figure 8-2 for an example of a well-designed parcel shelf.

STORAGE

Beneath and behind the counter should be a variety of mobile or fixed adjustable modular units. These can be used as flexible storage spaces for forms, books, machines, and supplies. This will help to keep the top of the counter clear of all clutter. In addition, the desk area should have:

- Wire management J channels to hold wiring off the floor
- Form dispensing slots and boxes
- Terminal keyboard, CRT, and printers
- File drawer and pendant side file
- Pencil drawer
- Cash register

A storage wall behind the circulation desk can be created by using built-in standards recessed into the wallboard installation. These provide a wide variety of shelf support brackets to accommodate storage of materials on the wall while allowing for book trucks to be placed underneath the shelves for easy access by the staff.

BOOK TRUCK STORAGE

Book trucks located behind the counter will make presorting convenient for the staff. Sorting at the desk can save time and effort.

BOOK TRUCK BROWSING

For easy browsing, book trucks loaded with newly returned materials may be placed near the areas where they will be reshelved. Each book checked out from the book trucks will save the library reshelving time.

THEFT DETECTION

Equipment must be located near the library exit and close to a staff location so staff can remind users of the need to check out theft-guarded materials. This can be done if the checkout location is near the exit door and staff can easily come out from behind the checkout counter.

STAFF WORK AREA

This area near the circulation desk will provide for an office, workstations, and a work counter with storage above and below. Operable windows with curtains or blinds will offer a choice of acoustical or visual privacy. Staff will be involved in processing reserves, overdue materials, interlibrary loans, or registrations. Staff should have visual access or an intercom or call button to the public desk so they can be called to assist at busy times. The area should be private and sound-isolated for efficient concentration. The multiple functions that take place in this area call for the utmost attention at the schematic phase of design. It is vital to emphasize a unified service area for public convenience and staff productivity.

READER'S ADVISORY

A staff location to assist users with selecting interesting books to read may be incorporated into the circulation area. Seating for staff and users will make this a pleasant experience. They should both be able to look at the same screen to select together. This area should be close to new material browsing but also close to the large book stack.

Summary of Circulation Area Design Considerations

- Consider the new projected daily volume of checkout, return, and registration in a more attractive new building or addition.
- Determine the number and type of checkout terminals.
- Consider ease of replacement and maintenance of terminals.
- Accomodate flexible location and configuration of computers above or below working surface.
- Provide bi-level or single level height adjustable counters with heights 29 inches–39 inches.
- Provide accessibility for children and handicapped users.
- Provide seats for the public for registration as well as for reader's advisory services.
- Consider a location to check in and sort recently returned materials and put them on book trucks presorted for efficient shelving. This may be at the service desk in small libraries.
- Provide nearby location for users to browse through recently returned, high demand materials.
- Consider an efficient location for staff monitoring of theft detection equipment.
- Provide reserve and interlibrary loan processing at electronic workstations as well as delivery and pickup of interlibrary loan materials.
- Provide space for processing of overdues, sorting of mail, collection, recording, and safekeeping of cash.
- Consider the location of self-checkout machines in relation to staff monitoring and servicing of equipment.

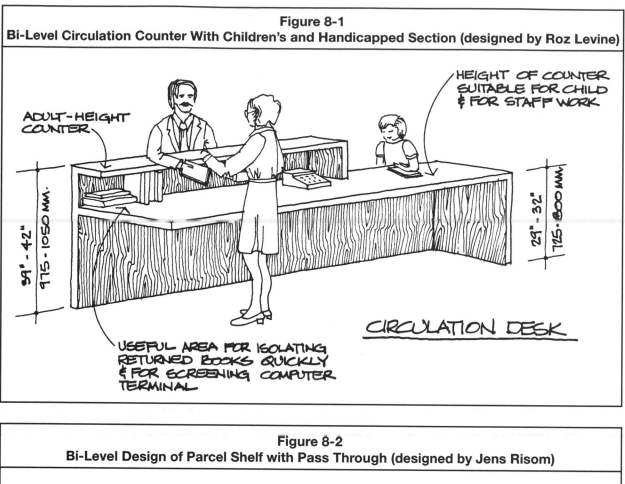

Figure 8-1
Bi-Level Circulation Counter With Children's and Handicapped Section (designed by Roz Levine)

ADULT-HEIGHT COUNTER

HEIGHT OF COUNTER SUITABLE FOR CHILD & FOR STAFF WORK

59" - 42"
975 - 1050 MM.

29" - 32"
725 - 800 MM

USEFUL AREA FOR ISOLATING RETURNED BOOKS QUICKLY & FOR SCREENING COMPUTER TERMINAL

CIRCULATION DESK

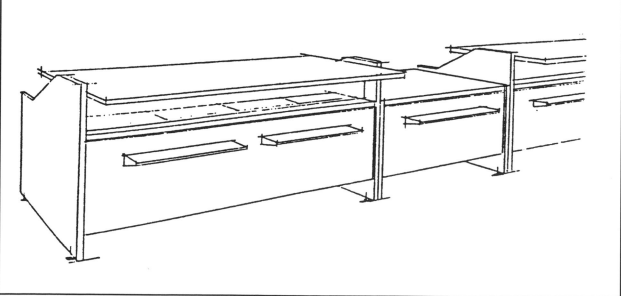

Figure 8-2
Bi-Level Design of Parcel Shelf with Pass Through (designed by Jens Risom)

9

Browsing and Magazine Display Areas

This chapter discusses general design considerations for the high use areas of the library close to the entrance, differences and similarities between libraries and bookstores, the Pareto Principle, and reader's advisory magazine and newspaper areas.

Merchandising and Finding—Libraries and Bookstores

About 20 years ago libraries began discovering the wonderful world of merchandising. We have gradually begun to look at the part of the building near the entrance as if it were a bookstore.

We have discovered what publishers have known for decades—that well designed front covers are the best means of getting users to take out books. However, this welcome change has brought with it a confusion in mission and design for our users.

The Pareto Principle and Library Use

In a wonderful article in the June/July 2001 issue of *American Libraries* (page 72) Walt Crawford discusses the Pareto Principle as it applies to libraries. This often quoted management concept indicates that in most fields a few of the contributors (20 percent) account for the bulk of the effect (80 percent). It is popularly known as the 80/20 rule in merchandising and in libraries it loosely translates into 20 percent of the materials accounting for 80 percent of the use of all materials. Crawford argues persuasively for libraries to pay more attention to the 80 percent of our collections that are less used because libraries not only need to give users what they want but more importantly we should focus on giving users what they need. As Crawford says,

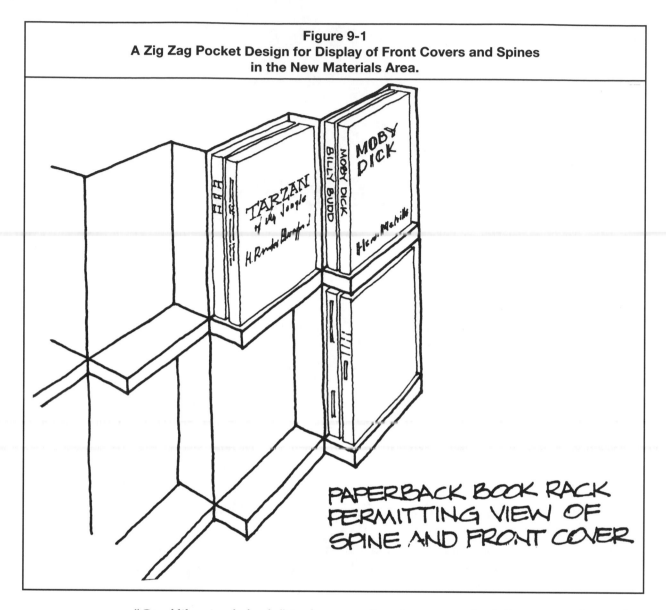

Figure 9-1
A Zig Zag Pocket Design for Display of Front Covers and Spines
in the New Materials Area.

PAPERBACK BOOK RACK
PERMITTING VIEW OF
SPINE AND FRONT COVER

"Good libraries do both." In the succeeding chapters methods for encouraging readers to use both the 20 percent most popular materials and the 80 percent that often languish in the stacks are discussed.

Display Devices

The most sought-after materials in libraries are the newer materials. They must be displayed with wider aisles and on easy to reach shelves because of the large numbers of users who seek them out. Library equipment manufacturers now include an amazing array of book displayers many interchangeable on the same system. These types of equipment may be summarized in the following categories:

- Tilted bottom shelves—Titles can be seen without bending down
- Modular spinners—High capacity but difficult to sequence
- Slatwall display units—Display of several different types of media

- Zig zag displayers—Show front cover as well as spine titles (see Figure 9-1)
- Wire vinyl shelves—Inexpensive but ugly
- Panel systems—Similar to pegboard or slatwall
- Tilt-and-store displayers—Older magazines stored under slanted display
- Book stop displayers—Combined book support and displayer for front cover
- Hanging bins—CD or DVD displayers on conventional uprights
- Stepped back shelves—Vertical stepped back display several shelves high
- Pyramids—Smaller boxes on top of larger ones
- Dumps—Movable slanted thigh-high boxes placed near checkout counter
- Bolt together boxes—Children's displayers configured flexibly
- Built-in lighting—Lighting attached to shelves
- Acrylic see-through displayers—Floor or wall mounted displayers

The introduction of popular new media such as DVDs, videocassettes, audiocassettes (including books on tape), CDs, and digital cassettes further complicate library browsing display. In some libraries, the result has been a chaotic melange of display devices jumbled together in a helter-skelter fashion.

Presented with this bewildering assortment, librarians, consultants, and architects have an increasingly difficult set of choices. How can we decide how much and what kind of shelving to use and where to put it in relation to conventional storage shelves?

Libraries and Bookstores

Understanding the differences and similarities of libraries and bookstores and how people use them may help us to formulate some design and furniture selection criteria:

- **A matter of scale**—relatively small libraries in communities serving 20,000 people may contain 100,000 items. The new so-called mega bookstores in their largest retail form will offer only 50,000 items. So libraries offer a wider choice.
- **Choice**—Libraries buy a smaller number of duplicates of new books, and they are often out in circulation, but they offer a wider choice of older titles than bookstores.
- **Centering the librarian**—The library professional makes twice as much as retail bookstore clerks and our services in advising library users on selecting and finding materials need to be twice as good. Librarians are still the heart and soul of quality service and our physical facilities should symbolize this difference by putting our library service centers at the front and center of our buildings not on the second floor or basement or in the back of the building.
- **Finding the right book**—Finding the right book for each patron and helping users to find their own perfect book for the moment is what libraries do.

Reader's Advisory Service

Identifying readers advisors by a sign at a service counter or by a badge can help with the user finding the right book. Locate a readers advisory desk near the major book stack. All library staff should be trained in the rudiments of useful customer service and they should all see how experienced staff help users to select books. Mentoring of staff and giving all staff an opportunity to observe a good readers advisor in action should be an essential part of every library employee's work experience. Visiting another library to observe this service or even visiting a good bookstore such as Roxanne Coady's RJ Julia store in Madison, Connecticut, can be a useful educational experience for staff.

Librarian Selected Displays

Librarians encourage users to pick books that will be useful in their lives. They may be selections particularly relevant to cultural segments of the community or to topical issues of importance to the community. Or they may be opportunities for entertainment or pleasure but they are selected because staff read the books or read reviews.

Sequencing

Ease of finding is more important in a library than in a bookstore so avoid rotating circular units like spinners that cannot be easily sequenced.

Line of Sight Graphics

These signs hang in the stack aisles showing users where to find particular subjects with their unique subject numbers. They are far more effective than end panel signs since they locate subjects right where they are in the stack ranges rather than at the end of each range. Labels attached to the shelves require users to turn their heads to see the labels.

OPAC Graphics

Online Public Access Catalogs (OPACs) should include a graphics display system revealing subject locations, sequencing, and leading users from a terminal location to the book on the shelf.

Provide Wider Aisles

Some libraries have bookstacks spaced 6 feet rather than the conventional 5 feet on centers, making it more comfortable to browse in the stacks.

Better Lighting

Use cool white deluxe lamps with better color rendition and louvers that direct light on the books not on the aisles. Lighting and graphics can be tools not only to display materials dramatically, but to create a clear understanding of subjects and sequencing.

Eliminate Bottom Shelves

Bottom shelves should not be used because the elderly and handicapped cannot easily access material placed on them.

DISPLAYS IN THE STACKS

Display shelving to accommodate front cover display of materials can be *interspersed* throughout the collection not just concentrated in the new book area. Shelf zig-zag inserts, two and three book displayers could be placed in every other three foot section of stacks at browsing eye height to quickly inform users about subject areas.

END PANEL DISPLAY UNITS

Using end panel display units throughout the book stack area has the twin virtues of displaying attractive front covers while graphically signaling the subjects in each range.

E PANELS

Electronic end panels incorporate flat screen computers and keyboards into the design of book stack end panels.

PLAN AHEAD

Plan ahead and anticipate new media collection growth so that shelving/display units purchased to accommodate the first year's worth of CDs can be modularly sequenced as the collection expands.

A better understanding of how library missions differ from those of bookstores can help librarians adopt the latest merchandising techniques while retaining traditional library values of variety and choice without price/sale objectives.

Browsing and Reader's Advisory Services

A person entering this part of the library should feel as if he or she is in a fine bookstore with a variety of materials. Covers should be attractively displayed. People entering the library will normally turn to the right and, therefore, if possible, the browsing area should be to the right of the entrance.

A reader's advisory desk will provide an opportunity for librarians to assist users in the selection of useful and appropriate materials. Users want a conversation with a staff member allowing time for the user to explain what they need; therefore, the user should be able to sit and talk with the reader's advisor. This service in small libraries may be part of the checkout desk or in larger libraries it may be located at the reference desk.

The browsing area is the busiest part of the library. Much of the borrowing is done in this area with users eagerly seeking the latest book, video, or CD/DVD. It should contain a library of ever-changing paperbacks, a selection of art and large format picture books, recently returned materials, and a new book, video, CD/DVD, and books-on-tape browsing section. Materials should be displayed on shelving no lower than ten inches and no higher than 54 inches to give an open, uncluttered appearance.

Research based on video analysis of how people behave in stores explains the necessity of having wide, 48 inch aisles in the browsing area. In this busy part of the library, the wider aisle width prevents people from bumping into one another or feeling uncomfortably crowded.

A density of five books per square foot in the browsing area rather than the ten for spine-out shelving in the larger bookstack should be the rule. There needs to be display shelving for front covers. Publishers spend a fortune to make these front covers attractive to users so we need to show them.

There should be a variable time limit for books to remain on the new book shelf. Books should be removed from the new shelf after two months if they have not been borrowed.

Browsing Design Considerations

- A sequential arrangement of materials will be helpful to patrons and staff trying to find a particular book.
- These materials should be arranged alphabetically by author for fiction and numerically by classification number for non-fiction so that users and staff can easily find a book.
- Circular spinners and towers are difficult to sequence and should be avoided.
- Sloping display shelves will impart an inviting atmosphere.
- Lighting should emphasize these colorful materials.
- Colors should be elegant, comfortable, and relaxing.
- Material displays should permit views of both front covers and spines.
- Genre shelving for special interest materials may be placed here.
- A choice of comfortable seating close to browsing areas offers the user an immediate opportunity to sit and read comfortably.
- Standing desks or reader stations close to the browsing area give users an opportunity to enjoy reading a few paragraphs to decide whether or not they really want to take a book home with them.

The Library Living Room

Some recently designed libraries such as the magazine room designed by Herb Newman Associates at Westport and the reading room at the Pequot Library in Southport create comfortable reading spaces with something of the feel of a living room. Comfortable upholstered chairs are offered with low side tables and large tables to read newspapers. Low-level ambient lighting supplemented by floor and table lamps and wall shelving illuminated by wall washers positioned three feet out from the walls combine to provide a relaxing atmosphere. This area may serve as a bridge between the active new browsing area and the magazine area.

Magazine and Newspaper Area

Magazines are used in two different ways:

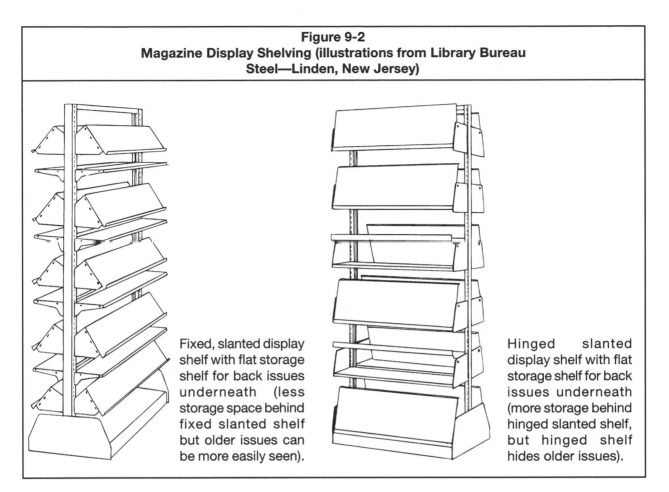

**Figure 9-2
Magazine Display Shelving (illustrations from Library Bureau
Steel—Linden, New Jersey)**

Fixed, slanted display shelf with flat storage shelf for back issues underneath (less storage space behind fixed slanted shelf but older issues can be more easily seen).

Hinged slanted display shelf with flat storage shelf for back issues underneath (more storage behind hinged slanted shelf, but hinged shelf hides older issues).

- Many library users come into the library to browse in current or recent issues.
- Other users wish to consult magazine indexes to look for articles on a particular subject.

Locating the magazine collection presents a special problem. Magazines can be located with other recent browsing materials or they may be located near the indexes in the reference section. Some libraries split their magazine collections locating the current year's issues with the browsing collection and older issues with the reference collection.

Non-print electronic access to periodicals presents a new option of providing access through electronic workstations and printers.

Locating magazines with other reference materials may be the most efficient service solution. Figure 9-2 illustrates two alternatives for displaying magazines. Displaying and accessing magazines should include these considerations:

- Sloping displays for current magazines with storage underneath for one year's back issues.
- Daily and weekly newspapers with one month's back issues stored using an Oblique filing system.
- Photocopy center with a sorting counter.
- Older magazines placed in a nearby storage area (high-density storage may be useful here).

Newspapers also create a special problem because of their flimsy large format and the tendency of users to tear out employment ads. Newspaper sticks for today's paper have the virtue of keeping all sections of the paper together but many users hate the cumbersome sticks.

Locating the previous day's papers can also be a problem. The Oblique hanging file system is useful in sequencing papers for the last month, but it does require staff monitoring. Keeping papers isolated at a service desk limits use and availability but secures the sections.

Electronic display of papers with printout capability may be a solution where electronic format is available.

A variety of seating choices should include:

- Comfortable lounge chairs with support for back and shoulders.
- Convenient side tables to accommodate books and bags.
- Oversize four foot × six foot tables especially for newspaper reading.
- Task chairs on casters with ergonomic support for the lower back.
- Floor or table task lamps are useful for older users reading small print.

10

Reference Services

This chapter discusses general design considerations for the reference area. Reading, study, consumer, business, local history, and genealogy areas are also discussed.

Reference Services

Libraries have increasingly become centers for information. Many of the people who enter library buildings do not borrow books. They read magazines and newspapers, ask questions, do research, use computers to search the Internet, watch videos, attend lectures and concerts, and talk with staff and one another. The complexities of modern life have led people to expand the ways they get information from the library.

A library is devoted to satisfying the individual information needs of citizens at every level of their life. Reference library users include students from elementary grades through graduate school and independent learners using the library for research. Patrons of all ages seek information on a wide variety of subjects relating to their personal, business, and family needs. They may select materials on topics such as career changes, job-related information, home repair skills, financial investment planning, gardening, arts and literature, health problems, crafts, and hobbies.

Reader's Advisory

In addition to using the Internet or a database to answer a user's question, good reference librarians are always alert to the possibility that users will require more extensive help to select one or more books that they will spend several hours reading. Some of the most important books in changing people's lives are stories or novels that capture their imagination and can lead to role models that affect how people behave.

Reader's advisory services may be located near the browsing area, as we discussed in the previous chapter, or they may be part of reference services. In some larger libraries they may be a separate function located close to the large book stack area. At this location staff will assist users with selecting interesting books to read so seating for staff and users will be needed. They should both be able to look at the same computer screen to select together. This area should be close to the large book stack.

Joan Durrance, a professor at the University of Michigan Library School, has devised what she calls a "Willingness to Return" survey that her students have administered to analyze several hundred reference transactions. The survey shows conclusively that library users are willing to return to a reference librarian when the reference transaction has lasted for several minutes rather then just a few seconds. It often takes time to carry on a conversation with a user to really understand what the user wants. A setting that encourages staff and users to spend some time sharing their information will be most conducive to satisfactory reference service and even more important when discussing a book reading recommendation.

On the other hand at busy libraries, where there are lines of users waiting to be served, efficient reference service requires that staff have computers handy and move quickly to respond to questions.

In most libraries these contradictory requirements will depend on the particular time of day. Libraries can be both very busy and relatively quiet. For these reasons the reference service desk should be designed for quiet conversation with chairs for both staff and users as well as with mobile stools and higher counters for quick mobility. Perhaps the working surface could be adjustable in height, or there may be both a sit-down and a stand-up section.

The Reference /Information Center

This is an area where technology is changing very fast. The multiple functions that take place in reference and information services call for careful consideration at the schematic phase of design. The likelihood of change in this area means that flexibility and ease of alterations are also major design considerations. The reference interview that takes place in this area requires staff to spend some time defining user questions and discussing solutions. Professor Durrance has shown that user willingness to return to staff depends on the time spent with the user, so user accommodations that include comfortable chairs are essential to the effectiveness of this service. The following considerations should govern decisions about the location and design of this area:

EASY ACCESS
- The reference/information center should be located so that staff are immediately visible to people entering the area from the street or parking lot or by stair or elevator (see Figure 10-1).

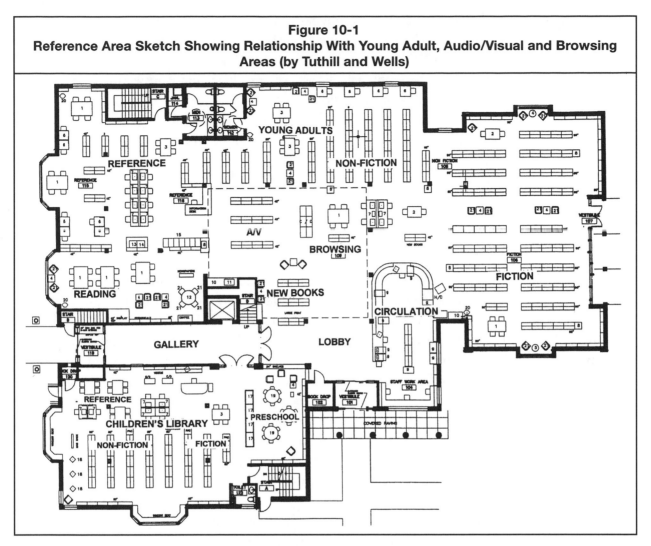

Figure 10-1
Reference Area Sketch Showing Relationship With Young Adult, Audio/Visual and Browsing Areas (by Tuthill and Wells)

- Library staff working in this area should have immediate access to a computer terminal visible also to the library user.
- Library staff must have easy access to the reference collection and other parts of the library where visitors need assistance.
- In smaller libraries locating the non-fiction collection close to reference staff enhances the opportunity for staff to help users select a book and enables reference librarians to use the non-fiction collection to answer reference questions.

LIGHTING AND CLIMATE CONTROL

- This area must have glare-free lighting that is intense enough to allow long periods of use with minimal eye fatigue.
- Since this area will be heavily used by staff and the public for long periods of time, both humidity and temperature must be carefully controlled.

FLEXIBILITY

- The reference area service desk design should be flexible.
- Staff will help patrons with a wide variety of materials and electronic reference resources.

- Computers should be easily reconfigured for public and staff convenience.
- Staff should be able to move freely from the desk to the bookshelves to answer questions.
- Hands-free portable telephones will greatly facilitate answering questions that require staff to go to the book stack.
- Mobile seating will be helpful in moving around this large area.
- Height adjustable counters may be reconfigured to accommodate changed activities.
- At slow times staff and users may sit together for conversation.
- At busy times lines may form waiting for assistance and both staff and users will benefit from a stand-up counter 36 inches high with stools.

DESK AREA

- A 29 inch high desk with seating for staff and public (kneeholes) is preferable. The desk should be easily convertible to a 36 inch high counter at busier times or have two separate sections, one low and one high (see Figure 10-2).
- Seating for staff and library users needs to be ADA compliant and ergonomically comfortable so that staff and users can move easily.
- Shelving for ready reference books, such as directories and handbooks, should have nearby resting places to open books in a variety of sizes.
- A minimal microfiche reader and microfiche storage must be nearby.
- Ergonomically designed electronic workstations for staff are essential.
- There should be mobile staff seating on comfortable ergonomic chairs.
- The desk area should accommodate telephones for answering questions, including a portable phone.
- Mobile workstation units with file drawers, and shelves, should be present.
- A small book truck for frequent checking of new reference materials is a good idea.
- Staff should be able to see down the stack aisles from this location.
- There should be a fax and copier nearby.

Reference Staff Work and Office Area

Staff in this area will be involved in Web design, newspaper indexing, community resource file maintenance, interlibrary loan, Internet searching, materials selection, program preparation, and staff research. This area must afford:

- Ergonomically designed electronic workstations for productive staff research.
- Work counter with shelves above and below for storage of materials.
- Lockable storage for handbags and personal materials.
- Controlled visual access to the information desk with operable window and curtains.
- Isolation from noise and distracting sounds.
- A room for staff communication and sharing of new materials, technology, and information techniques.

Figure 10-2
Reference Desk Design (by Jeff Hoover)

Reference Collections

Reference books on alternating full-height and counter-height shelving in the reference stacks in this area provide a space for users to rest books when doing a quick stand-up search. Sliding pull-out shelves located in every other section of the reference book stacks make it easier to consult books right in the stacks. An open space at counter height (36 inches) within each range will also be convenient for in-stack consultation of materials and note taking.

Reading and Study Areas

In older libraries one of the most glorious spaces was the main reading room with natural light streaming in from tall windows and rows of elaborately carved wooden tables and chairs. In addition, many old libraries had intimate reading spaces created by using low book stacks to form small alcoves with a few tables and lounge chairs. Both of these spaces should be considered for most libraries.

Some users will want to sit at a large table, others will be happier studying in alcoves. Comfortable lounge chairs will attract some users, but many will not want to sink down into an upholstered club chair that is hard to get out of. Individual study carrels spaced far apart and separated from the noisy activity of the library by being placed behind noise-absorbing book stacks will be useful for long-term study.

Designing this area will present a special acoustical problem since users will want quiet while staff will need to assist users with their searches. Staff and public will be using computers intensively for long periods of time, so glare-free controllable lighting, stable temperature, and comfortable seating are essential. Controllable natural light will be an asset in this area, but beware of heat gain from skylights and cold at night when the sun goes down. Long-term use may result in slowing of users' metabolism and consequent cooling of the body so that users initially comfortable or even overheated may become chilled after several hours without moving.

It is useful to remember that, except for children brought by their caregivers, most library users come to libraries individually and thus prefer individually defined user accommodations such as study carrels. These do not need to be high sided but should define the user space by sides that come to the edge of the writing surface. Even tables can use low dividers to define single reader space. Some libraries even use surface patterns on the tables to define user space.

The important point is that library users vary widely in their kinds of use and in their seating and study needs, so wise planners will give them a range of choices in seating accommodations, such as:

- A choice of tables or low carrels
- Group study rooms
- Electronic workstations with oversize collaborative workstations for staff to assist users with searches and for users to work together
- A computer training center with terminals acoustically separated from other areas but capable of being opened for public use when classes are not in session
- Alcove arrangement of furniture for more comfortable small-scale reading areas (see Figure 10-3).
- Single study carrels placed at the far end of stack aisles and spaced widely apart. Readers should be visible down the aisle.
- Comfortable chairs are enormously important in this long-term use area. Chairs should be mobile and users should be able to move about in the chair with considerable flexibility of accommodation. The UNO chair from Turnstone accomplishes this at a reasonable cost.

Electronic Resources

- E-Panels incorporating flat screen computers and keyboard at the end panel of each range will make it easier for users to search for resources right in the reference stack area.
- A local area network (LAN) will be needed to use a variety of computerized reference sources such as encyclopedias, hypertext, indexes, and full-text databases.
- Computers will provide access to materials in the library and on the Internet and they should be distributed conveniently throughout the library. Patrons should be able to download information onto their media or print it.

Figure 10-3
Alcove Arrangement

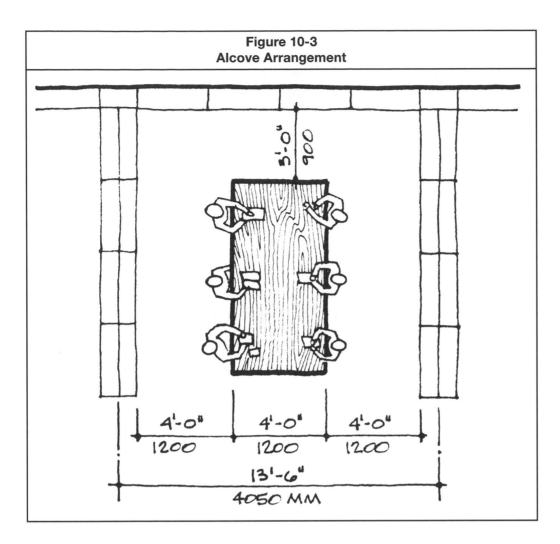

- Stand-up as well as sit-down electronic workstations will be needed, and should be handicapped accessible. Some companies are now making adjustable-height electronic workstations that can be easily changed from sit-down to standing height.
- Collaborative oversize workstations with two chairs that enable staff to work closely with patrons.
- Embedded terminal workstations make it possible for a workstation to become a reading table since the computer is embedded below the work surface

READING AND STUDY AREA DESIGN CONSIDERATIONS

The reading and study areas should be:
- Centrally located and convenient to the collections and stairs/elevator
- Located with clear sight lines so staff can monitor users
- Designed for easy modification
- In an acoustically dampened area to control noise
- Comfortable and inviting so users can sit

Other Specialized User Areas

Duplicating and Communications Center

Near the reference center will be a counter, with electrical receptacles above, large enough for a flexible array of machines such as copiers, computer printers, scanners, and fax machines that will be monitored by the staff.

A copy center with sorting counter, paper cutter, and stapler will be useful here. Pay telephones should be nearby. Data ports for quick transmission of data will be useful. Copyright signs explaining fair use are essential.

Special Service Centers

As libraries grow in size they may want to consider special service areas. These may just be signs hanging from the ceiling, small subdivisions formed by book stacks, low partitions, or separate rooms with large glass double doors for adjustable privacy and staff supervision. They may be clustered near the reference center for staff assistance.

Business Center

Near the duplicating and communications center should be a business center including business reference books and computer terminals with access to business databases. A ceiling-mounted business news ticker symbolizing the function of the area would be a useful amenity. Business services to the community will pay useful dividends to the library in achieving budgetary support. Maxine Bleiweiss at the Newington and Westport Libraries has shown how business outreach efforts bring useful support to the library at budget time.

Consumer Center

A consumer center in the reference area will contain several shelves of consumer materials that are in heavy demand. These need to be controlled for use only in this area.

Local History and Genealogy

Local history and genealogy are important materials in public libraries since they are often unique to a particular library. They need to be closely monitored by the staff and located near the reference desk. They require a climate controlled area. It is possible to purchase small packaged climate control units for these materials from:

Harris Environmental Systems
11 Connector Road
Andover, MA 01810
617–475–0104.

11

Material Storage

In this chapter collection management and storage are discussed.

Collection Cultivation

Charles Robinson, chief advocate for the popular library, remarked that a new library building reminded him of a "Museum For Books." As librarians we must be sensitive to the latest demands of library users if we are to encourage use.

However as publicly supported institutions we have the need to encourage the use of high-quality materials. Librarians read book reviews and are highly knowledgeable about the best books in all subjects. In addition to acquiring and building collections, librarians must promote the use of high-quality materials by seeking opportunities to encourage the use of these materials. Promoting the use of high-quality materials may be done in several ways:

- Classics shelved near the new book browsing area.
- Daily selection of a few older books with new topical community interest.
- Daily selection of books in the book stack for front cover display in the stacks.
- Curiosity or serendipity displays to pique the interest of readers in unusual topics.

A *New Yorker* article on "Sleepers" show how fine independent bookstores promote high-quality books of lesser popularity by scheduling programs, book discussions, and author signings. Libraries should emulate this activity and try to promote books by displays and programs.

Librarians have known for a long time that collection size has little to do with library use. In fact there is some evidence that reducing the size of collections may actually increase library use.

Just as in a beautiful garden, the weeding of library collections has several benefits:

- If the lesser-used books are removed it is easier to see the more desirable ones.
- If the poorer-looking books are removed the better-looking ones make the library seem more attractive.
- If there are fewer books it is easier to find the one you are looking for.
- Shabby, worn out, obsolete books make the library look ignored and dilapidated.

How should collections be cultivated? Library users are telling librarians each day which books they want to see on the shelves by checking some books out and leaving others alone. Modern computerized systems will list those books that have not circulated for easy weeding.

Rarely used books not found in the library can now be located so easily on the Internet that libraries no longer have to keep them. OCLC's interloan system can locate millions of titles. Amazon.com can get the book to you in less than a week.

Many classics are regularly used so they will rarely be discarded. Classics also make up a minor fraction of the collection, so they do not need to be discarded, and weeding rarely involves classics. What weeding does involve is the bestseller from 1990 that is no longer in demand.

The useful life of a book varies radically from title to title. A few titles are timeless. Some books have a heavy popularity of only a year. Others may circulate lightly but have a much longer life.

New-book shelves need to be lighted, designed, and shelved entirely differently than other library materials because they are so heavily used. Often 60 percent of the library's total circulation goes from the new-book shelf or from books that are seldom even shelved because they are so steadily reserved by users.

Encouraging stack use can be accomplished by several methods:

- Librarians can pre-select interesting books for browsers by reserving a space at eye height for the front cover display of a single book. A piece of tape marking the limit of book space for shelving staff on each eye-height shelf can reserve display space.
- Combining a book support with a cover displayer is an option.
- Wider aisles will encourage use.
- Occasional empty open shelves for resting books give users an opportunity to glance at several books before selecting one.
- Task lighting directed at the books not the aisles makes browsing the stacks easier.
- Line-of-sight subject signs tell users where subjects are located.

Collection Maintenance—Costs and Frequency of Use

Maintaining a large collection of books is expensive:

- Building costs to construct book stacks to accomodate each book to be shelved often equal the purchase price of the collection. If a library is heading into a building project and it is adding space for 10,000 additional books, that space will cost about $200,000. If the library discards 10,000 books they will save $200,000 in building cost.
- Utility costs to heat, light, and cool staff and clean and maintain the space of one book in the book stack may equal the cost of the book in ten years. If the planned book stack includes books that are used only once in five years, it would be cheaper to borrow from other libraries or buy the books on demand rather than house them.

Browsability and Serendipitous Discovery

It is wonderful to be looking for a particular book and then to discover another book that you weren't aware of. However, when book stacks exceed 100,000 volumes the size of the stack may actually inhibit browsing and make it more difficult to find a book.

Librarians have argued for decades about the merit of small, easily browsable collections compared to large more comprehensive collections. Few tracking studies have been done to see how users might respond to these different library models. However, tracking studies in department stores have consistently shown that shoppers respond badly to narrow aisles filled with goods, often leaving the store if the aisle is so narrow that they bump into one another.

With an aging population and an emphasis on handicapped access, libraries should abandon the bottom shelves seen in most stacks. The difficulty of browsing or even seeing the books on these lower shelves with low lighting levels make it highly unlikely that they are used as much as the more accessible higher shelves, so the bottom shelves should probably be eliminated.

The Internet has undoubtedly made it easier to locate a book thus making it less necessary to retain books that are not frequently used.

The Great Book Stack Area in Sequence

"It has been a fashion to make bookcases highly ornamental. Now books want for and in themselves no ornament at all. They are themselves the ornament." At the age of 80 and between Prime Ministerships, William Gladstone became fascinated with the problems of book storage, and made this statement during a visit to All Souls College, Oxford.

Book stacks should reveal and celebrate the beauty of books, not conceal them with end panels or canopies.

Reader's Advisory

The most important work librarians do is to recommend a useful book. Compared to answering a reference question that takes only a few minutes, librarians recommending a book are involving the reader in an experience that can take hours of time extended over weeks. This highly individual task has an important impact on the reader's feeling about customer service at the library.

Librarians should have the opportunity to sit with the reader or better still to walk into the book stack and handle books, discussing with the reader the relevance of a variety of reading choices. In our busy hyperactive lives librarians seldom have the time for this kind of leisurely exploration and many users do not need a lengthy interview, but providing the setting and opportunity for this to happen is an important design opportunity. Therefore the library reference and readers advisory service desk should be located close to the book stack and should include reader seating so that the opportunity for consultation is part of this setting.

The great book stack is one of the largest sections of the library. It represents materials selected by the library staff over a long period of time and carefully screened to supply the best current information on a wide variety of topics.

As it grows in size it becomes increasingly intimidating to first-time users. To make it a pleasant experience and to facilitate self-service browsing, the following design considerations may be helpful:

- Stack aisles should be visible for supervision and staff assistance.
- The numerical sequence of the ranges should be apparent to users approaching the stack end panels.
- A single continuous pattern in numerical sequence should be employed. Any break in the pattern, such as wall shelving at right angles to free-standing shelving, will be confusing to the reader.
- Materials shelved contiguously permit changes in the percentages of each subject as the collections change and grow.
- A standard section of book stacks is three feet long. Six sections connected together form a standard range 18 feet long.
- A double-faced section has an average maximum capacity of 240–300 volumes if five shelves on each side are used with space left for shelving returns. Reference or bound periodicals are wider so only 200–250 will fit in each double-faced section.
- Book stacks require a floor load bearing capacity of 150 pounds per square foot. Stacks must have web uprights to prevent collapse. High-density stacks require 300 pound per square foot live load capacity.
- To maximize capacity, oversized books can be removed from their regular sequence and shelved together in a separate stack area. In this case special location catalog entries for these materials and signs informing users of the special location will be helpful.
- Book stops prevent books from being pushed back off the shelves, but also result in wider books sticking out into the aisle, especially in the art area.

- Canopies are unnecessary for metal shelving and often create light shadows from overhead lighting and prevent the shelving of tall books.
- A 30-foot structural column module permits six-foot on center stack ranges to be converted to five-foot on center ranges to increase capacity.
- Tall art and oversized books will require 12 inch deep shelving. If tall books are kept in sequence only five shelves will fit in each section.

The design can easily become a sterile factory-like area unattractive for library users. To avoid this, some of the following design considerations may be helpful:

- Small bench seating perches within the stack will be useful resting places for users to browse briefly while choosing a title.
- A choice of electronic workstations, study carrels, table or lounge seating interspersed at the end of the stack will be helpful, convenient, and add interest.
- Digital end panels with thin computer screens and keyboard interspersed throughout the stack will make it easy for users to find their materials without the necessity of walking out of the stack.
- Front cover display fixtures for popular books on end panels and at eye-height spotted occasionally throughout the stack.

Browsing in the stack should be facilitated by these design considerations:

- Line-of-sight graphics over the aisles so that subjects are readily apparent.
- Sliding pullout shelves to rest books on for stand-up browsing.
- The standard handicapped accessible aisle width of 40 inches may be too narrow. Ranges should be spaced 72 inches on centers; this will leave an aisle 52 inches wide if ten-inch shelving is installed.
- For library users who are an aging population, bottom shelves are increasingly difficult to reach and should be abandoned in favor of a five-shelf pattern of easily accessible shelves in each section.
- Lighting the lower shelves is easier with lighter colored resilient flooring such as cork or vinyl instead of carpeting and light fixtures placed above the aisles and directed towards the books.

High Density Compact Stacks

Some larger public libraries use high density compact stacks to store seldom used materials. Essentially these stack ranges are mounted on strong steel rails and remain closed until a button is pushed or a wheel is spun to open a single aisle to retrieve a book. Only one aisle is available at a time and there are safety and maintenance considerations that make it advisable to have staff only operate the system (see Figure 11-1).

These stacks will hold three times as many books per square foot of floor space as standard stacks. They require a structural system rated at over 300 pounds per square foot live load to support the weight of these books twice the floor load required for standard stacks. Even when placed on grade the stacks require special assurance that the weight can be supported by the ground.

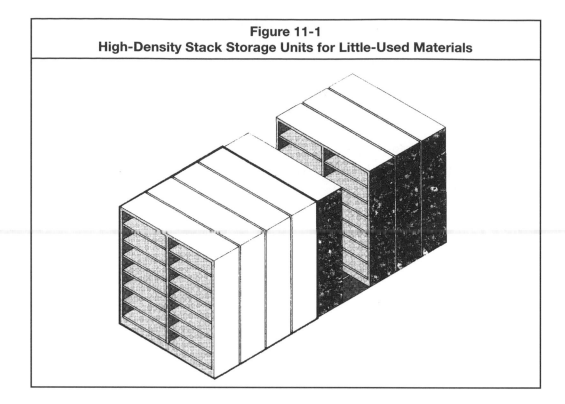

Split collections resulting from closed compact stacks for the least used materials make it necessary to look in two sequences to find a book. Browsing in the stacks to look over books on a particular subject is not possible if the stacks are closed. Compact stack aisles are often narrow and in spite of several safety features to assure that they will not close while a user is in the stack, people are often nervous about going into powered stack aisles.

The Portland Maine Public Library used electrically operated compact stacks open to the public to house their adult open stack books for over 20 years. They were finally converted to stationary stacks because the compact stacks were difficult to maintain.

Library Standard Cantilevered Bracket Shelving

This type of shelving can be specified in two ways:

- With end brackets securely attached to shelves.
- With shelves that fit loosely into end brackets after they are in place.

It is easier to adjust shelves if they are secured to end brackets because both shelf and bracket can be removed and adjusted in one piece rather than lifting out shelves and then adjusting end brackets individually before reinserting shelves into brackets (see Figure 11-2, illustration is Estey shelving from Dickson, Tennessee).

Figures 11-3 through 11-8 present illustrations and examples of many shelving and book stack options and considerations.

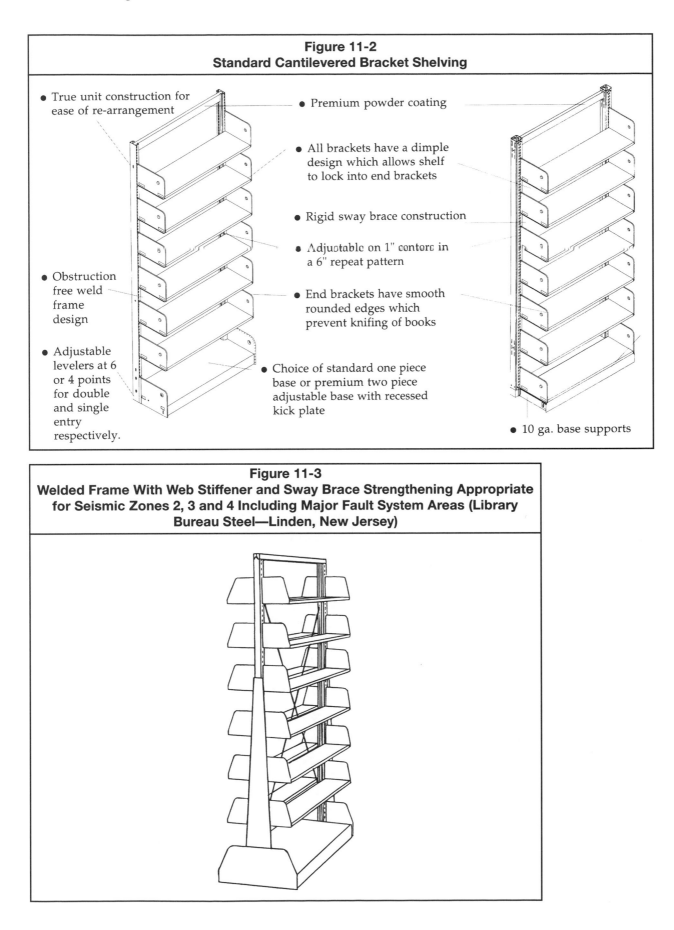

Figure 11-2
Standard Cantilevered Bracket Shelving

- True unit construction for ease of re-arrangement

- Premium powder coating

- All brackets have a dimple design which allows shelf to lock into end brackets

- Rigid sway brace construction

- Adjustable on 1" centers in a 6" repeat pattern

- Obstruction free weld frame design

- End brackets have smooth rounded edges which prevent knifing of books

- Adjustable levelers at 6 or 4 points for double and single entry respectively.

- Choice of standard one piece base or premium two piece adjustable base with recessed kick plate

- 10 ga. base supports

Figure 11-3
Welded Frame With Web Stiffener and Sway Brace Strengthening Appropriate for Seismic Zones 2, 3 and 4 Including Major Fault System Areas (Library Bureau Steel—Linden, New Jersey)

Figure 11-4
Multimedia Bin and Display Units Integrated With Cantilevered Standard Bracket Shelving
(shelving by MJ Industries, Georgetown, Massachusetts)

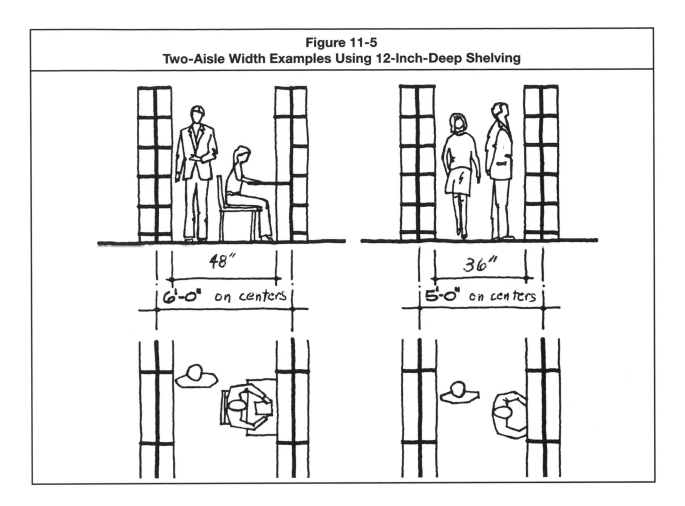

Figure 11-5
Two-Aisle Width Examples Using 12-Inch-Deep Shelving

48"
6'-0" on centers

36"
5'-0" on centers

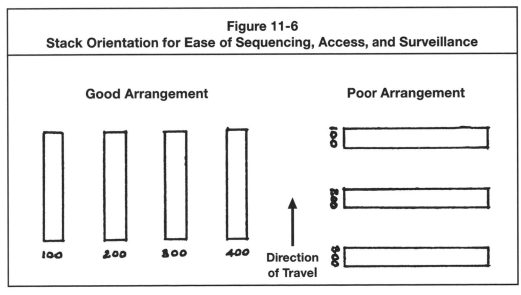

Figure 11-6
Stack Orientation for Ease of Sequencing, Access, and Surveillance

Good Arrangement

100   200   300   400   Direction
of Travel

Poor Arrangement

100
200
300

Figure 11-7
Line-of-Sight Stack Signage (by Brodart)

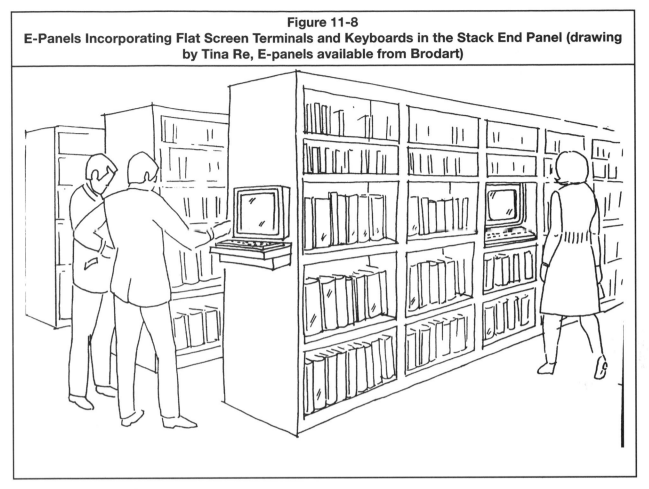

Figure 11-8
E-Panels Incorporating Flat Screen Terminals and Keyboards in the Stack End Panel (drawing by Tina Re, E-panels available from Brodart)

Audio-Visual/Non-Print Area

The Rights of the Right-Brained Library User

Most libraries underfund non-print media compared to its use by the public. In many cases this is the fastest-growing library service.

Studies in brain functioning show that people often emphasize one or the other side of brain function. Left-brained people have traditionally been intellectually dominant in our society because of their facility with verbal skills and libraries have traditionally catered to these left-brained people. The visually oriented right-brained user was often neglected by libraries. Now multimedia software is flooding the market with new forms of learning appealing to right-brained people. This is a strong argument to get tax funding to provide access to this new technology and attract new users to the library.

Audio-visual and non-print material should be on the entry level for public convenience and close to teen services since teens are avid users of these materials. Audio and videocassettes, compact discs, DVDs, computer disks, books on tape, and other audio-visual materials will be displayed and shelved here. These materials differ from books in that they cannot be taken from the shelves and browsed or sampled without the aid of a listening or viewing device. Therefore some consideration should be given to installing nearby listening or viewing stations to sample the materials.

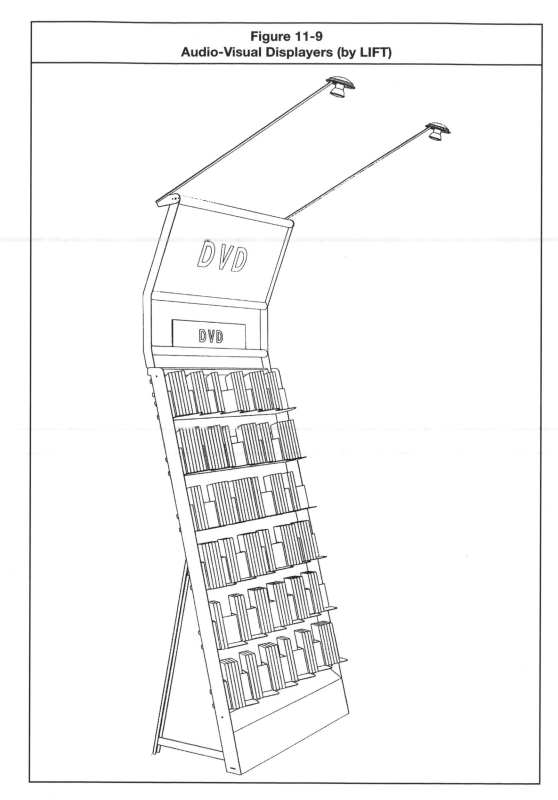

Figure 11-9
Audio-Visual Displayers (by LIFT)

This will be a bright, eclectic area showcasing the range of media available in the library. The following are considerations when designing such areas:

- Clear signage designating each collection and many subject dividers with alphabetic sub-dividers will be very helpful for browsing and reshelving.

- Formats will vary greatly in size and shape, so a system with a variety of flexible display and storage capabilities is necessary. CDs and DVDs, for example, will be displayed in racks while larger sets of audio cassettes with manuals or other written material will be stored on conventional shelving.
- The small size of these materials makes security an important design consideration. If possible, staff control and visual supervision should be maintained by locating this area close to a staff station such as the circulation desk.
- Sequential arrangement will be helpful for finding materials in this area.
- Front covers in bin type shelving will greatly facilitate browsing.
- LIFT, a company specializing in displays for retail stores, has a headphone listening tower that allows a choice of several CDs (see Figure 11-9). In addition they have a system that provides a brief preview of hundreds of CDs. This may be especially useful in teenage areas.

12

Special Spaces for Children and Teens

This chapter discusses design criteria for children's and teen services areas.

Children's Library Facility Planning

The children's services area will provide space for a full range of services and activities to promote and encourage learning, reading, and the enjoyment of books. The design and appearance of the children's room will make a lasting impression upon the child. There will be plants and pleasant outside views. The area should express warmth and friendliness and suggest to parent and child that this is the place to come in order to satisfy information and recreational needs.

Services and materials in this area must meet the needs of a range of library users, from the curious preschool toddler to the developing preteen with rapidly changing interests. It must also serve the needs of parents, child care professionals, teachers, psychologists, and others who will use the children's collection to support their work with children.

Design Options

Children's facilities are often designed to attract children with playful concepts. Typically a theme is chosen related to the history of the town. In Maine a small rowboat becomes a children's reading bench. In Pennsylvania couches are made to resemble a freight train. Creative treatment of ceilings, doors, windows, skylights, and furnishings should provide a strong immediate message that the children's room is a special place. However, libraries are special places in themselves. Books, videos, music, images, and words encourage children's imagination. These items themselves should be the theme and soul of the children's room. A large train can contain picture books using bins as cars in the train. A low platform overlooking the picture book train can hint at the captain's deck of an ocean liner, but trying too hard to make it into an actual ocean liner can look cute and corny and be boring in time. Murals, furnishings, and equipment should encourage children's imagination to make them what they will. The platform can be a deck, a balloon floating in the sky, or a space station depending on the child's imagination.

The character and history of the community should be expressed by distinctive images. Pictures and text from well-known children's books can be projected on a screen at the entrance. Classic and durable images should grace some of the walls of the children's areas and should flow naturally from the library's function to stimulate the imagination and offer children a variety of materials and ways to experience these materials.

Height

Children grow at varying rates and psychologically change with chameleon-like speed, so close attention should be paid to these characteristics in the design of the room. Adult designers should try walking around on their knees to get some sense of how children will experience these spaces. Sixty-inch-high book stacks can seem like dark caverns to 4 year olds. Conversely, any opportunity to give children some height in the room will be welcome. The innovative new designs in children's playscapes should give some clues to how children respond to height. A small, low platform with padded mats to soften the inevitable falls will be a valued place in the room, simulating the experience of reading in a tree house.

Displays

Changeable displays and seasonal decorations are an important aspect of the children's area. There will be tackable display walls in different parts of the room, as well as display cases.

Lighting

Indirect and diffuse ambient lighting will impart a quiet and cozy atmosphere by avoiding glare, but special adjustable spot lighting for materials and displays should provide strong visual punctuation for materials.

Openness and Stimulus Shelters

Spatial density and the degree of openness in the children's area present something of a design problem. The need to monitor children can conflict with their need for privacy. At the same time, research into the advantages and disadvantages of design options has produced somewhat contradictory and ambiguous results. Studies have shown that spatial density tends to increase aggression among preschool children. At the same time, open areas tend to result in running and cross-room talking. Research has also shown that activity areas with partitions tend to increase cooperative behavior. The answer may be low dividers between activity areas with higher dividers and increasing privacy for older children. Furnishings and dividers should always be low enough so that children can see and be seen by staff. Children may seek relief from over-active open areas in small stimulus shelters with just enough room to snuggle up with a book.

Developmental Areas

The children's room will have several distinct areas arranged to invite children and their care providers to move through the space and the service it supports in accordance with the child's conceptual development. Because of the wide range of ages and things done here, there will be a noticeably different ambience for these areas within the larger area. Transitional areas between each of these spaces will house services used commonly by both age groups such as the computer area between pre-school and middle school.

Vestibule Entrance

A display of children's art and community events invites users into the area. This space serves as a clearly organized orienting view of other children's service areas and provides direct access to the story room and performance space.

The Children's Service Desk

The service desk should be located close to the preschool entrance area and provide good supervision of the entire area. It will have sections for public assistance, including answering reference questions, and for sorting and repair of recently returned materials. There will be staff work locations at the desk, with computers, a printer, and telephones. A large display calendar will list children's events for the month. Several book carts of materials will be located near this service desk. See Figure 12-1 for an example.

Staff Work and Storage Areas

These areas should be in close proximity to the children's room. The staff work area will have computer staff workstations with CD and Internet access, a printer, a meeting table with folding chairs, and an art/craft design space with sink, design table, and a counter for laminating equipment. There will be an audio-visual preview carrel. Storage will hold posters, prints, mobiles, flannel boards, puppet tree, coats and personal belongings for the staff, and office supplies. The staff area might have the appearance of a small house within the library with operable double-hung windows and curtains to adjust the privacy of workers within the staff work area.

Office

The children's area office must provide good supervision of all children's activities. The staff should, however, be able to adjust privacy in the office by closing blinds on windows and the door. The office will include dividable space for the librarian. There

Figure 12-1
Children's Room Service Desk (designed by Jeff Hoover)

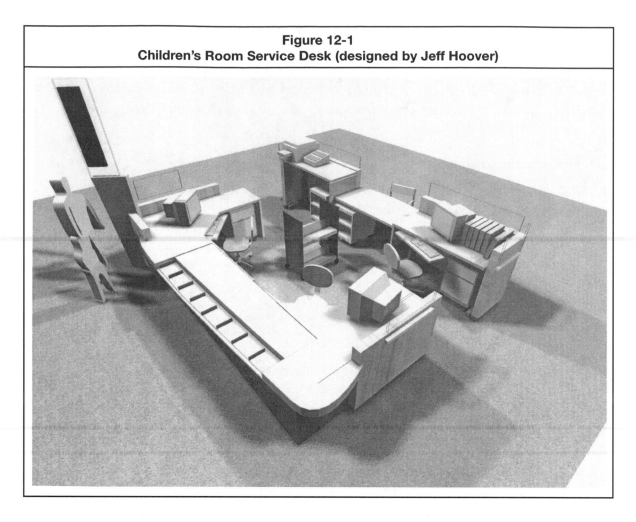

will be a workstation, which can be used with computer systems or typewriters. The workstation should allow for observation of active areas. Working materials will be kept in storage cabinets and on adjustable bookshelves.

Varied Children's Functions

Each of the areas listed below should serve as an imaginal landscape of the developmental period. The space should invoke a sense of liminality and containment for the projection and experience of the child's own imaginal field—a real field of dreams that encourages and supports a variety of imaginative feelings.

The sequence of areas should facilitate a successively more introverted relationship to the materials than the previous area, so that the preschool child will be engaged with parents and staff while the intermediate and young adult will work more independently.

INFANT, TODDLER, AND PRESCHOOL AREA

This is a noisy, whimsical area for children 2 to 5 years old. There will be very small "stimulus shelters" that children can crawl into in order to find quiet and security. These small cubby-hole areas will serve a protective function by providing shelter from overstimulation for children who need relief from the noise and activity of the open area. Wall-size murals, a large bulletin board for children, and a large, colorful clock will be visible from the entrance.

There are four collections of books in the preschool area:

- Bin shelving with alphabetical labels on each bin will hold picture books (see Figure 12-2).
- A "Toddler" section will have board books in colorful cubes.
- Easy books will be housed in low shelving.
- Big books will be housed in a mobile display/storage truck.

Seating will include:

- A rocking chair
- Oversize chairs for parents to read stories to their children
- Small tables and chairs (two sizes)
- A cradle or crib for infants
- Low ten-inch-high floor tables with cushions

At some distance from the preschool area will be a small-scale low platform or house with carpeted stairs for children to climb and scramble on and a triple-padded carpeted area at the foot of the stairs to minimize injury. The edge of the stair should have a contrasting color, and there should be a ramp for handicapped access. The location of this platform should be carefully chosen to avoid proximity to heavy traffic areas and to assure safety of children.

Parenting, Professional, and Reference Area

Parents, teachers, child care and home school providers in addition to children will use this active but quiet area. It will contain:

- Reference and parenting collection
- Database searching terminals
- Tables and chairs
- Large oversized chair-and-a-halfs so parents can read to their children here
- Tutorial rooms for individual consultation with children

Middle Schoolers Intermediate Browsing/Reading

A discussion with middle schoolers complaining that children's rooms were designed for little kids, and there was no place for them, suggests that a great effort should be made to differentiate this part of the room from the pre-school spaces. This part of the children's area will suggest a more contained behavior and more directed activity. It will include:

- Book stacks with wide aisles
- Display racks for new books, compact discs, and videocassettes
- Display shelving for magazines and paperbacks
- A variety of seating and table heights
- Electronic workstations with embedded terminals

STUDY AND HOMEWORK AREA

These areas will include:

- A quiet area with low individual carrels for study
- Computers for database and Internet searching
- Copier with sorting counter
- Group study areas for four people each

PERFORMANCE AND PROGRAM AREA

This is where story hours, puppet shows, creative dramatics, parenting programs, discussions, author talks, book groups, and video viewing take place. There will be a small, portable stage area and stackable chairs, and the room should have acoustical separation to keep noise from entering other areas of the building. Modest stage lighting capabilities, ceiling video projection screen and equipment, and several folding tables with storage for chairs and tables will be useful in this area.

MULTIMEDIA, AUDIO-VISUAL FACILITIES

These facilities will include:

- Display tower with several screens for silent display of multimedia
- Storage and display for games, puzzles, toys, and multimedia kits
- Listening and viewing stations
- Computers with printers on lock-and-roll storage carts
- Projection video with screen

ACTIVITY AREA FOR CRAFTS

This area will be constructed with tile flooring, including floor drain if possible. Sink, counter, storage for materials, and folding chairs and tables should also be included. A large format video screen for following demonstrations would be beneficial.

RESTROOM

A restroom for children with a changing table and nearby water fountain are essential.

Other Desirable Children's Features

Coat racks for children should be available near the performance area as well as distributed throughout the area for convenient access to seating.

Bicycle racks and stroller space near the entrance to the library should be protected from the rain and snow.

Flexibility and Mobile Furnishings

In the children's area there is often the need to reconfigure the area temporarily for special programs or weekly displays. Flexibility will be enhanced by:

- Mobile multimedia display units with flat screens, books, displayboard, and display shelving for quick setup of topics
- Low shelving on Darnell ball-bearing casters
- Sled-based chairs or chairs on casters that will glide easily (children may occasionally play bumper chairs, but the need for flexibility outweighs occasional discipline problems).
- Wireless wheelbarrow electronic workstations with two wheels and two legs afford the opportunity for rapid relocation while retaining some stability
- Electrical and low-voltage receptacles distributed throughout the area wall plugs at 36 inch height with child-proof guards
- Light fixture locations designed for task flexibility
- Acoustical adjustability by movable acoustical partitions and sound dampening materials

Design Result

The overall result of the children's area design should be an intriguing combination of creativity, function, and flexibility. Children should be engaged by areas that stimulate their imagination while suggesting a variety of behaviors. Alternating busy and quiet environments should offer children a choice. The area should be easy to change both for short-term display and long-term changes in function as children change. Parents and other caregivers should have an opportunity to sit with children to read to them and enjoy their reading skills. There should be an opportunity for individual consultation with children for teaching and discussion.

Sizes and Standards for Children's Facilities

The percentage of young children in a community will vary widely and will change constantly, therefore flexibility in the size subdivisions and furniture and equipment will be vital. Ideally children's areas should be redesigned every five years in light of changing library roles and missions.

STANDARDS AND GUIDELINES

MATERIAL REQUIREMENTS
- Picture book bins: 60 books per three-foot bin shelf (20 books per running foot). A double-faced two-shelf bin unit will house 240 books or ten books per square foot.
- Book stacks for children are often 60 inches high with 40 inch aisles accommodating 300–350 books per double-faced three-foot section and allowing 10–15 books per square foot of floor space.
- Media may be ideally accommodated in regular adjustable book stacks with special shelves for different kinds of media that hang on the same uprights.
- Spinners are usually to be avoided since they are difficult to sequence, making it hard to find a particular item; however, they do hold more items per square foot of space.

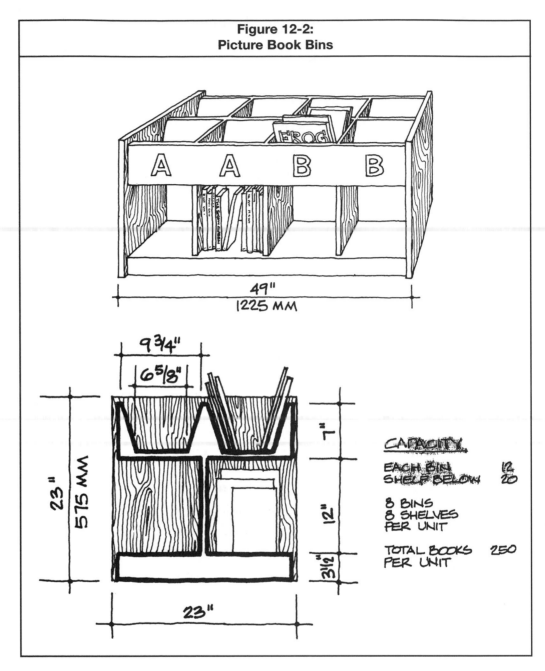

Figure 12-2:
Picture Book Bins

CAPACITY

EACH BIN   12
SHELF BELOW   20

8 BINS
8 SHELVES
PER UNIT

TOTAL BOOKS   250
PER UNIT

REFERENCE AND READING

Five seats per 1,000 children in the community is a useful starting point for determining seating needs. It may also be useful to do a behavior mapping study recording the number of children using seats at particular times and experimenting with table seating, carrel seating and lounge chairs to see how the mix of seating should be distributed.

Seats will require 25–30 square feet for each seat. Single carrels may require more space.

Electronic workstations with printers may require 40–60 square feet, especially for collaborative stations where children work together with staff or caregivers. Consider ergonomically designed office chairs for older children.

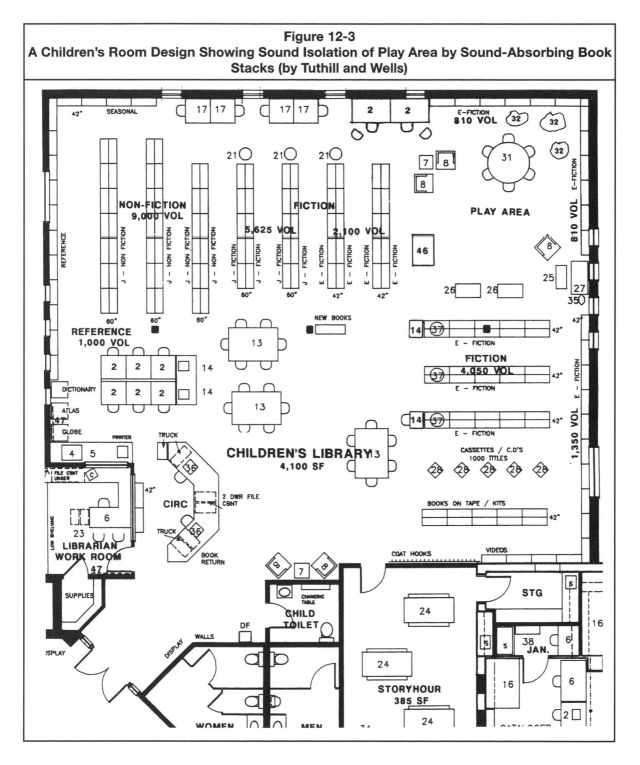

Figure 12-3
A Children's Room Design Showing Sound Isolation of Play Area by Sound-Absorbing Book Stacks (by Tuthill and Wells)

STAFF WORK AREAS

Design these spaces for 100–150 square feet per staff member.

HANDICAPPED ACCESS

In order to accommodate handicapped patrons, there should be lowered 26-inch knee clearances on desks and tables and no table skirts.

STORAGE

Children's facilities need several kinds of storage:

- Seasonal storage for materials most in demand at particular times of the year
- Audio-visual equipment storage
- Craft and story hour materials
- Temporary chair and table storage to open larger spaces in the area
- Staff supply storage for poster board, crayons, and poster storage
- Puppets, puppet stage, and story enhancers storage

Total area for children's services may vary from 20–40 percent of the total library assignable area. See Figure 12-3 for an example of a children's area design.

Teen Services

Library service needs of teenagers include space for social activities as well as space for age appropriate materials and studying. Young adults should feel that the library welcomes them, but the noise that often accompanies young adults should not disturb adults.

Locating teen services is often a puzzle. A location close to reference services provides the incentive to study but teen noise may disturb adult users. A separate location requires additional staffing. Placing teens close to or in the children's area would be very discouraging to most teenagers. Close proximity to the attractive display of new materials would be welcome to teens, but may also interfere with adult use. Teens and seniors are a questionable mix in many cases.

Young adults come to the library for several often contradictory purposes. They will alternate between the following very different sets of activities:

- Teens come to meet friends. This is a behavior pattern that libraries must design for if they are to be welcoming to this age group. An area designed for acoustical dampening of conversation, perhaps including a small coffee and snack service area might best accommodate this behavior and serve as a safety valve for noisy teens disturbing their peers in quiet study locations.
- Study habits of teenagers vary. Often they study in small groups so acoustically separated study areas for four to six people would be welcome.
- Music is very important for teenagers, especially music they can share. The LIFT CD listening station illustrated in Figure 12-4 allows them to sample CDs with headphones, but an acoustically separated area where they could listen together would be even better.

These conflicting uses require adjoining noisy and quiet areas. Careful acoustical design should allow noisy and quiet activities within this space, which in turn will be acoustically separated from other areas

Service Areas

THE NOISY RECREATIONAL USE AREA

This area should emphasize constantly changing popular video, audio, books, and magazines on a flexible linear display system so that particular titles can be easily located. It should also include an art display area, bulletin boards easy to move around, comfortable lounge seating with low tables, and mobile viewing and listening stations with easily repaired or replaced equipment. It may be located near a food service area.

THE QUIET STUDY AREA

This area should include.

- Oversize study tables with four chairs each
- Individual electronic workstations
- A place for coats and backpacks
- Group study rooms

This young adult area may have to be expanded and should be located and designed for considerable future flexibility.

New teen scene spaces at the Phoenix, Arizona, and Los Angeles public libraries include music opportunities, a cafe, dancing area, and group computer use facilities.

Anthony Bernier, now at the Oakland California library is an outstanding teen advocate and consultant. Bernier's concept for the Los Angeles Public Library's Teenscape Project that resulted from extensive conversations with teenagers included several zones with acoustical separation:

- The Cyberzone under a metal mesh awning lighted from below includes four circular wood cafe tables supporting 19 flat screen terminals with access to the Internet, 500 databases, and the library's book and magazine catalog.
- The Living Room has a 50-inch plasma-screen television, a Dolby surround sound system, and sofas and lounge seating, and magazine display shelving. It can also host small performances.
- The Lounge Zone with comfortable lounge furnishings provides for "out-of-the-way" activity.
- The Study Lounge Zone provides eight dedicated word-processing computers and shelves of ready-reference books.
- Three canvas-roofed group study rooms face a reference desk staffed with professional young adult librarians and paraprofessionals.
- The Teenscape collection includes 30,000 books, 150 magazine titles, graphic novels, videos, and CDs.

Design Considerations

- Ask teens what they want
- Alternating study and meeting areas
- Flexible size and furnishings

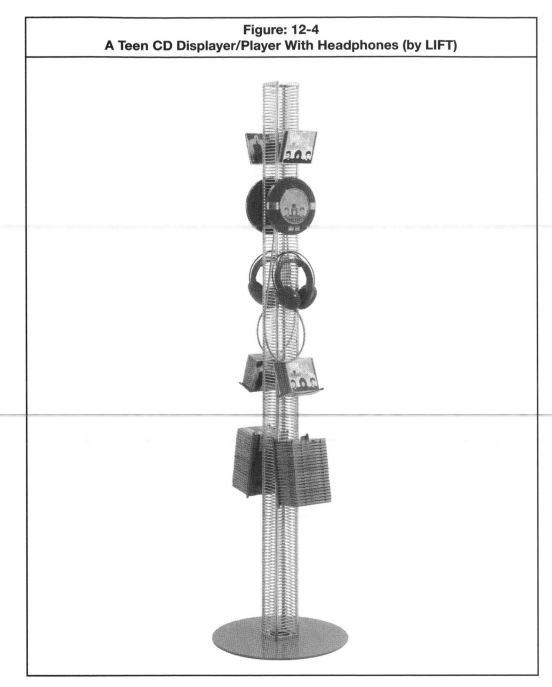

Figure: 12-4
A Teen CD Displayer/Player With Headphones (by LIFT)

- Music opportunities
- Food service
- Large projection screen for videos
- Community board for events
- Homework help
- Extended hours
- Large tables for interactive work
- Group study rooms or acoustical dampening
- Furnishings from Linea or other teen suppliers
- Special lighting effects

13

Meeting Rooms

Library Meeting and Program Rooms

This area should be on the main entry level so that it can be closed off from the rest of the library and have its own separate entrance and access to rest rooms for evening functions when the rest of the library is closed. This can be accomplished for an upper or lower floor location by screening off access to the library with movable roll-up screens. Some librarians argue that libraries are already open for a broad spectrum of hours and programs require staff presence at any hour so security for library materials may not be an issue depending on the community. A non-entry level location for the meeting spaces has the virtue of reserving entry-level space for basic library functions.

The larger program room may be used for a wide variety of activities including:

- Special children's and young adult programs and presentations
- Friends of the Library programs
- Lectures
- Book discussions
- Video and film programs
- Community organization meetings (when scheduling permits)
- Performing arts productions

Storage

Concealed, lockable storage will be needed for stacking chairs, coat racks, a lighted lectern with sound and light controls, and six-foot-long folding tables. Lockable storage for audio-visual equipment should be provided separately from other storage items.

Projection

A projection system with overhead projection, high-resolution video with in-room sound volume control should be provided. Computer connections with the video projection system, as well as receptacles for telephone line connection with computer terminals, should be provided. A wireless hub should be provided.

Conference Room

Conference rooms for 20 people with adjustable table system are essential. These rooms will also require after-hour access. They will need tackable walls and data delivery systems.

Small Meeting Rooms

Group study rooms for one to four people each may be located near the adult reference area.

Multi-Purpose Area

A multi-purpose area for seating people on comfortable stacking chairs with upholstered seats and backs should be part of any public library.

The multi-purpose room may be used for a wide variety of activities, including:

- Lectures by guest speakers
- Art shows
- Book discussions
- Video and film programs
- Musical concerts
- Children's programs

This area should be acoustically sub-dividable. Concealed, lockable storage will be needed, as well as coat racks, a lighted podium with sound and light controls, and folding tables. A projection system with overhead or rear projection should be supplied. Lockable storage for audio-visual equipment should be provided separately from other storage areas.

Multi-Purpose Facilities

VIDEO PROJECTION FACILITIES

The following facilities are essential in multi-purpose area:

- Overhead video with large-screen projection with 90 kilohertz scan rate high resolution.

- Three tube RGB input, one-inch conduit to two gang plate at control center with same phase alternating current hookup, and 15,000 frequency horizontal.

CABLE CONNECTION

Cable hookup to local cable network supplier from outside the building into the program room is necessary.

DATA TRANSMISSION

A data transmission line for digital display to overhead video projection needs to be installed. Connections are needed for laptop computers to receive and project Internet information from a wide area network (WAN). Connections for computers to access library LAN to project information from library databases are essential.

SOUND

A single amplifier controlling several sound sources and two separate speaker systems is needed.

Speakers at the podium and several ceiling-mounted speakers distributed throughout the area will be controllable from the podium or the rear of the room.

Volume control at the podium is necessary for control by presenters and separate volume control at the rear of the room allows sound at the rear to be monitored.

Floor microphone outlets provided at several locations allow convenient to audience access for group discussion purposes. Stage platform microphone outlets allow for additional microphones for group discussion on stage. Wireless microphone capability should also be installed. A separate film/video speaker system consisting of front-stage mounted speakers behind perforated projection screen is helpful.

Audio facilities for the hearing impaired should include headphone jacks and additional amplification capabilities related to handicapped accessible areas.

MULTIPLE COMPUTER USE

Installation of data transmission lines and electrical receptacles for electronic workstations to be set up and put away and stored in the storage room nearby is necessary. A wireless hub may be a useful alternative if bandwidth is sufficient.

LIGHTING SYSTEMS

Electrical panels in the auditorium should deliver sufficient power for additional stage lighting in the future. Hanging bars for overhead stage lighting system should be installed with related ceiling-mounted electrical receptacles, even if the fixtures are not installed initially.

Lighting in this room should include:

- Stage lighting with hanging bar and overhead lights illuminating the stage area that can be tilted and swiveled sufficiently for video camera work
- Audience area lighting
- Aisle lighting low-level directional lighting for finding aisles when other overhead lights are out

- Side wall washer lighting for art display; these may be elliptipar fixtures placed three feet from walls for good vertical distribution
- Emergency battery-supplemented exit lights

Lighting should include separate circuits for:

- Stage area spotlights
- Audience lights on a dimmer switch
- Perimeter wall lighting for art exhibits

Lighting controls should be duplicated at the podium and at the entrance behind a locked panel. They should include:

- Stage lighting with separate dimmer controlled hanging bar and overhead lights illuminating the stage area
- Audience area lighting with separate dimmer panel
- Aisle lighting with separate dimmer panel
- Side wall lighting with separate dimmer panel for art display

Toilet facilities should be available when the rest of the library is closed. Auditorium stage entrance doors should be wide enough to admit a six-foot-wide piano. Possible future expansion of this area should be an important design consideration.

Design Considerations

Many of the following considerations will only apply to larger libraries with more elaborate programming requirements. See Figure 13-1 for an example layout.

- Kitchen and serving facilities
- Access to wide loading doors or dock for bringing in equipment
- Pay telephone
- Storage for tables and chairs
- Acoustics should accommodate musical performances, speeches, discussion groups, and projection of films or video (considerable flexibility and adjustability of acoustics may be necessary for these different requirements)
- Acoustically sub-dividable into smaller areas
- Wired for data delivery, CATV outlets, and wireless hub
- Wall spot lighting on a separate circuit will be needed for art displays
- If the space is to be used for dance performances a wide stage will be needed with crossover space behind the stage
- Changing rooms and restrooms for performers
- Sufficient power for theater lighting

Figure 13-1
Meeting Room Layout Showing After-Hours Access to Meeting Room, Bathrooms, Kitchen, and Chair Storage While the Rest of the Library Is Closed (by Tuthill and Wells)

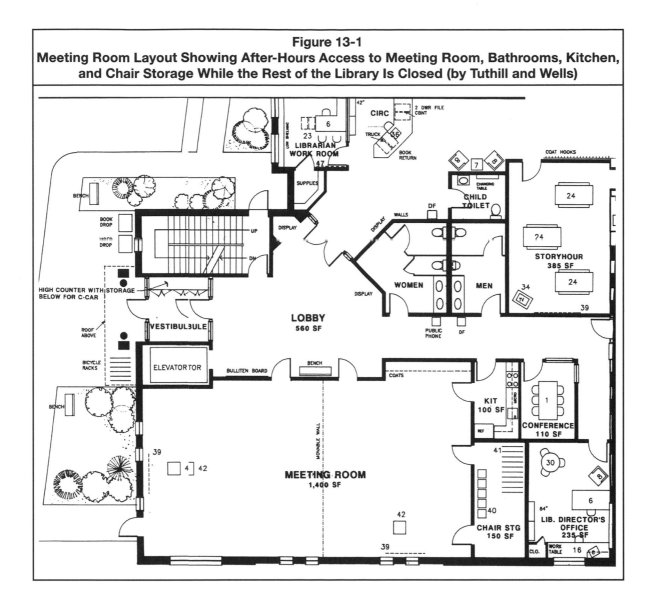

14

Administration and Staff Work Areas

Design considerations for staff work, administrative, and technical service areas.

These areas house behind-the-scenes functions that are necessary to support successful and efficient public services. There will be several staff work areas:

- The circulation work area will be adjacent to the circulation desk near the library entrance.
- The children's work area will be adjacent to the children's room for convenient staff access.
- The technical services and administrative work areas may be on a non-public floor.

The following recommendations apply to all of these work areas:

- Safety and security of staff, materials, and equipment should be a primary consideration in locating work areas. Work areas should not be dead-ended enclosed space where staff may be confined or isolated with patrons.
- The arrangement of work spaces, the location of equipment, and most importantly in the design stage, acoustical dampening, lighting, and color scheme, should promote productivity and attention to detail over relatively long periods of time.
- Natural lighting from windows should be augmented by task-oriented lighting from lamps and fixtures. These should have flexible switching patterns.

Workstations

Space for individual expression, such as areas for green plants and wall space for posters and decorations, is helpful where work is unrelieved by the variety and the immediate satisfaction of public contact. Cork bulletin boards or a tackable surface should be placed at workstations so that staff can easily refer to schedules, procedural memos, and other temporary notes. All work areas will have coat space and individual half- or box-lockers for employees' personal possessions. Other factors in workstation design include:

Climate Control

This is essential for staff who spend long hours at workstations. Insofar as possible, staff should be able to control their own climate.

Lighting

Natural lighting from windows is important for the morale of the staff. Natural light should be augmented by task-oriented lighting from lamps and fixtures. These should have flexible switching patterns. Under-shelf lighting should be avoided. While glare can be a major problem, dim lighting can cause the operator to strain to read a CRT screen or paper documents on the desk. Adequate lighting during the day may be completely inadequate in the evening. Because proper lighting is relative, adjustability in task lighting at the workstation is important. Workers are more productive when they can adjust the intensity, location, and the angle of light in their work area.

Comfort

The seating, work surfaces, and other furnishings must be comfortable and provide good support, especially to the sacro-lumbar area, for staff who must sit at the workstations for long periods of time.

Adjustability

All aspects of the workstation should be adjustable and adequate for staff with special problems, e.g. back problems, eye glasses, or different heights. This flexibility is critical because staff differ in size, bodily configuration, and work preferences.

Seating

The staff member should be able to adjust the height of the seat and the backrest. Furthermore, the backrest and seat pan should be laterally adjustable so that the user can move the backrest fore and aft and change the seat deflection from flat to a somewhat backward angle. All adjustment levers must be readily accessible and easy to use—staff should not have to turn chairs upside down to make adjustments. Hydraulic mechanisms are necessary where two or more people use the same workstation. Arm rests should be adjustable and removable. The chair itself should move and swivel to allow the worker to perform a wide range of activities. Chairs should be designed for simple maintenance, including replacement of upholstery and mechanical controls.

Desks and Work Surfaces

Ideally library workers should have desks and work surfaces that can be adjusted from 22 inches to 45 inches from the floor. Normal desk height is 26 inches to 30 inches. The flexibility to raise the work surface to counter height permits workers with a back injury to use a keyboard or library materials while standing. Knee hole space should be available so chairs can be out of the way when not needed.

At minimum, the work area must include an adjustable keyboard pan that enables a sitting worker to maintain their upper and lower arms at a 90-degree angle (upper arm vertical, forearm horizontal) and their wrists at 10- to 20-degrees from horizontal. A tilting keyboard pan would also help improve the wrist angle. Lack of adjustability may be a major cause of repetitive motion syndrome in those working at keyboards.

The ideal work area is 60 inches wide but should be at least 30 inches wide to permit opening books or use of documents or other media. Leg clearance should be at least 24 inches wide and 16 inches deep. Space for book trucks at each workstation is imperative.

Computer Equipment

The librarian's role in the information age demands increased reliance on computers and related technology. Librarians create, maintain, and search local and remote databases; they use word-processing equipment to write reports, letters, and other documents; they use spreadsheets and other productivity software to plan budgets and manage the organization.

Local Area Networks (LANS) and connectivity are important aspects of a library's use of technology. Design features must reflect the need to power and connect equipment in each workstation as well as between the different departments. J-channels, ramps, grommeted openings for bundled cables, and power poles will be important design features. The workstation will need room for a variety of hardware, including some bulky equipment like printers and paper supplies, and storage devices such as hard disks and CD-ROM systems. Shelving for manuals and supporting documents is also important.

Screens

Placement of the CRT or VDT screen is also a primary concern. The screen should be approximately 18 inches from the worker's eyes and as low as possible. The screen should never be above normal eye level. In the best situation, the user will be able to raise, lower, tilt, and swivel the screen to suit their individual physical requirements.

Visual fatigue can be minimized by correct lighting. Artificial or natural light that is too bright can cause glare or a "wash-out" effect. VDTs should not be placed next to windows. When this is necessary the screen should be at a right angle to the plane of the window. Polarized glare screens may be helpful while blinds can also control reflected glare.

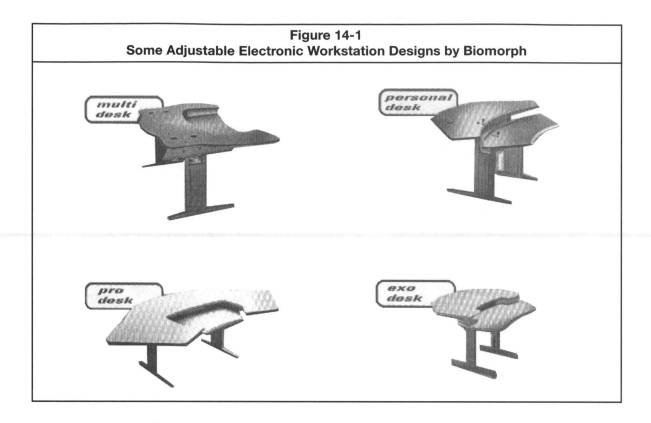

Figure 14-1
Some Adjustable Electronic Workstation Designs by Biomorph

Cost

Purchasing workstations of this quality may be an expensive investment on the part of the library. However, staff productivity and public comfort should become high priorities in library planning. Libraries who specify expensive marble checkout desks and wasteful atrium spaces should not be reluctant to also spend money on user comfort. All equipment does not need to be in place on the day the new library opens. It can be phased in and purchased over a period of years.

In some cases repeated motion syndrome injuries to staff resulting from poor ergonomic design and the resulting loss of time may more than compensate for the cost of an ergonomic chair and workstation.

Costs for these well-designed workstations are also decreasing rapidly. The Charles Perry designed Uno chair is less than $200 and the new Biomorph workstation costs less than a good quality wooden study carrel (see Figure 14-1). The New York Public Library has been the trendsetter by specifying expensive Aeron chairs for all of the workstations at its Science and Business Library.

Technical Services

Location of this area is important to efficient operation. It should be close to an elevator and delivery entrance for deliveries and mail. However, traffic from other departments or to frequently used areas should not be routed through these work areas. See Figure 14-2 for an example layout.

Receiving and shipping should be near the elevator and delivery entrance but in a

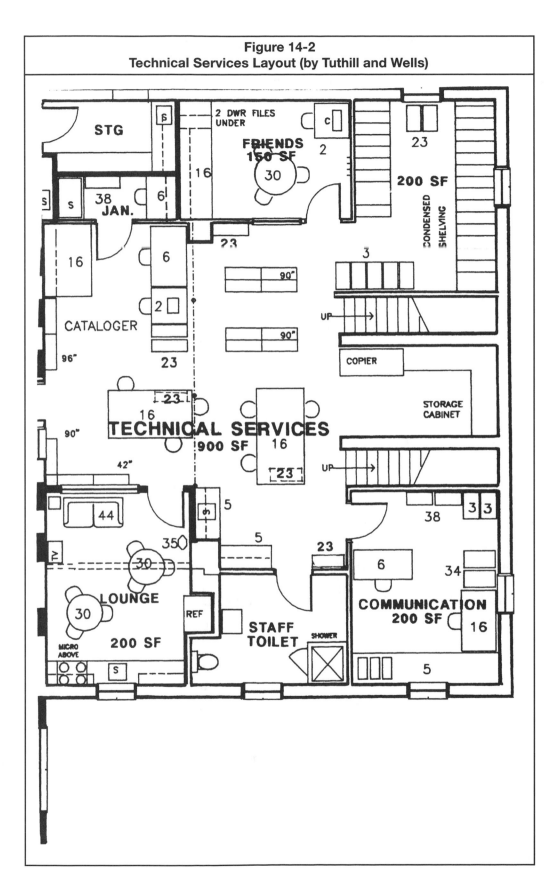

Figure 14-2
Technical Services Layout (by Tuthill and Wells)

separate room. Counters for receiving and shipping, and a system for storing and distributing materials will be provided.

Acquisition and processing functions for library materials in both print and non-print format, including receiving and processing periodicals, are all accomplished here. This area should be a large, flexible, open area subdivided by movable office landscaping.

A 36-inch-high work counter will serve as a receiving and processing location. Twenty-nine-inch high workstations on the perimeter of the area will have cabinets above and knee holes below.

Ample electrical outlets will be provided at mid-wall height. There will also be file cabinets and wall shelving. The area will also have a storage room separate from other library storage areas.

Book truck space for maneuvering heavily loaded trucks should be included beside each workstation. There may be dozens of book trucks in this area in various stages of processing. Plans should include book truck locations. The permanent staff will be supplemented by part-time staff who should have lockable, movable files that can be moved to any workstation location.

Technology Support

Electronic Repairs

Technology support services include a bench for repair of computers with six electrical outlets and a telecommunications line. The bench will have shelves above for tools and drawers below for spare parts. There will also be several 24-inch-deep shelves nearby for equipment waiting to be sent out for repair. This area should be able to be locked off from the rest of the technical services area and should be near the server room and the delivery entrance.

Audio-Visual Test Equipment and Repairs

These may be accomplished in a nearby space using some of the same facilities.

Network/Server Room

Servers, CD towers, and other electronic and communications equipment should be located in this general area with special considerations given to:

- Acoustical dampening
- Wiring access to outside and inside the building
- Air conditioning appropriate for equipment

Administrative Offices

Electronic workstation design concerns discussed earlier in this chapter should be carefully followed when designing work stations in all administrative offices. See Figure 14-3 for example layouts. Administrative offices will include:

Figure 14-3
Some Sample Office Layouts

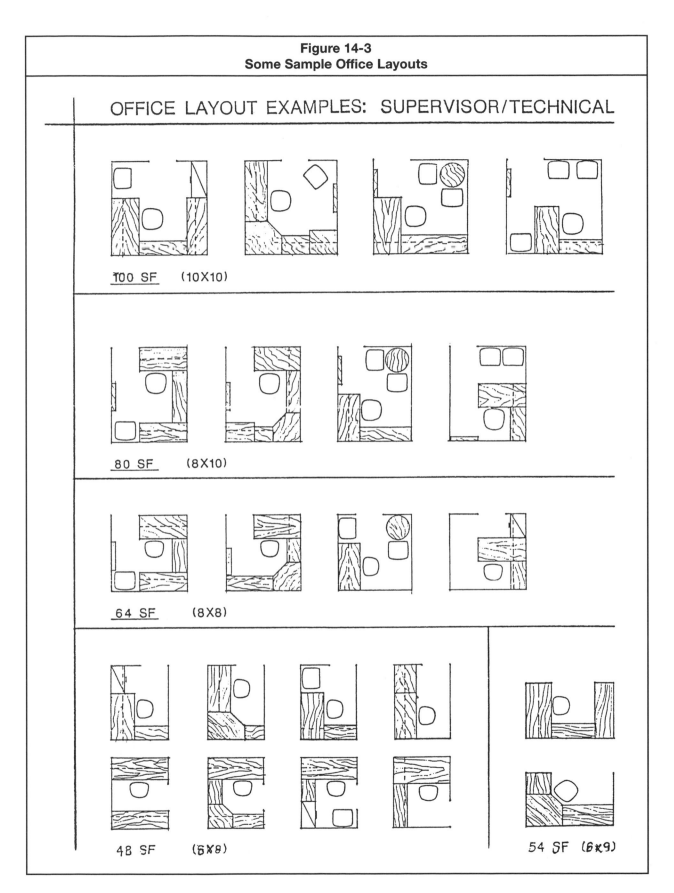

OFFICE LAYOUT EXAMPLES: SUPERVISOR/TECHNICAL

100 SF   (10X10)

80 SF   (8X10)

64 SF   (8X8)

48 SF   (6X8)

54 SF (6X9)

- Director's office
- Assistant Director's office
- Administrative Assistant's workstation
- Bookkeeper's workstation

Other administrative functions may also be needed in larger libraries such as personnel manager, public relations, and development officer.

A central shared staff office area will include:

- Copier, fax, side files, scanner
- Lockable storage cabinets for office supplies

The Library Director/Assistant Director's offices will include:

- A large outside window as well as an operable inside window with curtains
- Electronic workstation with ergonomic chair
- Large desk with upholstered chair, two visitors' chairs, coat rack credenza, side files, and shelving
- Large work counter for projects with shelving above
- Conference table for meetings
- Multiple exits so that administrators can exit without being seen by visitors.

Administrative workstations will include:

- Visitors' chairs and coat rack
- Large work counter for projects with project shelving above
- Electronic workstation with printer, sorting table, and ergonomic chair
- Various filing cabinets

Friends and Volunteer Activities

A flexible area for Friends and volunteer activities should include:

- Reception and lounge area with chairs and lockers for coats and personal belongings
- Friends store with counter, chair, display shelving, and cash register
- Tutorial rooms for literacy tutoring
- Office area to include:
  - Visitors' chairs
  - Large work counter
  - Electronic workstation with printer and ergonomic chair
- Book storage stacks for sale books

15

Climate Control, Staff Lounge, and Restrooms

This chapter deals with the important infrastructure support elements of the library.

Climate Control: Heating, Ventilating, and Air Conditioning

This is a very complex subject with mechanical engineers working on intricate systems to provide the necessary controls. This chapter includes general guidelines for librarians and consultants to discuss with the experts. A library consists of different areas with a variety of control requirements. These areas have the following considerations:

- Storage of library materials requires shelter from direct sunlight and consistent temperature ranging from 55–75 degrees Fahrenheit with average humidity. However, archival storage of old materials that are unique to the library requires more consistent temperature and humidity.
- The entrance to the library should be protected from weather extremes by having a sheltered canopy and offset doors with a transition zone that tempers outside weather extremes by the introduction of hot or cold air. In the case of automatic doors care should be taken to protect door controls from freeze up and to temper extremes that occur when both sets of doors remain open for long periods.
- Long-term use areas for quiet study should be located to assure consistent temperature of 72–75 degrees Fahrenheit. Users in these areas will find that a gradual lowering of body temperature often takes place after an hour of inactivity

and a formerly comfortable temperature becomes too cool. Direct sunlight or large windows make this consistency difficult to achieve. Perimeter study carrels should be located near small view windows and should be sheltered from direct sunlight with dark glass and building overhangs. Ideally they would have separate control zones for heating and air conditioning.

Staff and users' control of temperature and ventilation is desirable from the user perspective but engineers dread this because users make frequent adjustments expecting instant response while the system struggles to respond rapidly and then breaks down. Rapid system response will often result in hot or cold air blowing uncomfortably on the user. In a public space with multiple users there will be differences in perceptions of hot or cold.

Location of sensors can be very important in large spaces with few controls. If direct sunlight hits the sensor it will shut down the heat or activate the air conditioning while other parts of the room suffer from excessive heat or cold.

Variable air volume controls with mixer boxes provide useful localized control. Windows that open and local supplementary heating and cooling devices are often useful, especially in areas where library staff spend long hours in the same location. However, caution must be exercised to control opening of windows especially in public areas.

Quiet air distribution can be accomplished by lined ducts and machinery rated for quiet operation, as well as remote location of noisy mechanical equipment. However, duct lining can come unglued and block air distribution so lining should be mechanically secured.

Cost savings can be achieved by building insulation and by the use of outside air for cooling in the early morning summer hours, and hotter outside air for heating during the spring and fall.

Staff Lounge

This area should be as comfortable as possible so that staff may relax and enjoy their meals with relief and privacy from their service duties. It should have natural light. This area must be acoustically isolated from public service areas.

Equipment might include:

- Double sink and dishwasher
- Four burner stove and oven
- Full size refrigerator
- Microwave
- Tables and chairs (quantities may differ in relation to the availability of in-library or nearby restaurants)
- Quiet room with sofa
- Telephone
- Restrooms
- Hot and cold water dispenser

Public Restroom Facilities

Design considerations for bathrooms include:

- All restrooms will be equipped for handicapped accessibility according to current codes
- Ratio of four stalls for women, two for men
- Program area restrooms require more stalls than library restrooms because audiences will use the rooms before, after programs and at intermissions while library rest room use is individual use distributed over a longer time period
- Children's restrooms near children's staff service area for close supervision
- Water fountains on all levels
- Baby changing facilities in men's and women's restrooms
- Floor drains and cantilevered lavatories in all restrooms for ease of cleanup
- In larger libraries doorless restrooms such as are frequently seen in airports may be helpful in reducing vandalism because they offer less privacy
- Single-stall, lockable bathroom doors allowing users to exclude others from the bathroom sometimes result in destruction of facilities because users have more assurance of not being discovered during acts of vandalism

Parking

The parking lot should be convenient to the entrance of the library so that users do not have to walk across streets. It should be lighted with vandal-proof fixtures on a timer. Light fixtures can be either high mounted general illumination for maximum safety in an urban environment or low walking guides in a residential location

Trees near the parking spaces should be protected from damage by cars. If possible, green landscaped "islands" should be incorporated into the lot to break up the expanse of cars and convey a park-like appearance. Trees should be picked with care and should not exude sap or droppings on parked cars. Tree selection should also minimize leaf pickup problems by choosing trees dropping small leaves that disintegrate easily.

Clearly marked handicapped parking, as required by code, must be provided near the building. There should be a curb cut ramp to provide access for both wheelchair users and bicyclists. These curb cuts should be made from colored concrete to clearly delineate the slope of the curb from the flat concrete area. The drop-off area should be large enough to accommodate a van. The slope from the parking area to the entrance should meet the Americans With Disabilities Act (ADA) requirements to permit easy access for the elderly and disabled.

Parking Spaces

The number of parking spaces available for library purposes differs widely. Local building codes often determine the number of spaces. This can vary from one space per 150 square feet of building area to 1 space for every 500 square feet. One space for every two seats in the library and meeting rooms is another measuring gauge.

Provisions should be made for meeting room seats in addition to library seating, perhaps one parking space for every two seats might be a reasonable amount. At least 5 percent of spaces or more as required by code and ADA Guidelines should be designed as oversize handicapped spaces.

Bicycle and Motorcycle Racks

Racks for bicycles should be sheltered from the rain and be lockable. A separate motorcycle parking area should be provided so that motorcycles will not take up the larger spaces required for cars. This area should be in sight of the library entrance to prevent vandalism and discourage theft.

Hose bibs for outside watering should be located in the building wall.

Maintenance Area

This area should include:

- Office desk, chair, and vertical file
- Plan file with large surface for viewing plans
- Lockers for custodians
- Lockers for tools
- Workbench
- Storage for supplies and work materials

It should be located in close proximity to loading dock and elevators.

Loading Dock

The loading dock and adjacent storage should be convenient to the elevators with large doors and passages to assure accommodation of oversize items. Although the loading dock may be outside the building, lockable storage to hold materials for distribution throughout the building must be nearby.

Access to the building from the loading dock should be as direct as possible to avoid turning corners with heavy objects. Large double doors that can easily be propped open will be helpful to get big objects into the building as quickly as possible.

A raised loading dock is helpful if truck and dock match in height. But smaller van deliveries must also be possible near the dock. A weather cover over the dock may prevent damage to library materials during inclement weather. But low overhangs can be damaged by large trucks. Backing a large truck into a dock can be tricky, so visual safeguards for the truck and building should be carefully thought out.

Combination staff and delivery entrances sometimes cause traffic congestion and can lead to theft of deliveries by staff or salespeople using the staff entrance. To avoid this situation, delivery entrances should never serve a dual purpose as customer entrance and delivery entrance.

16

Computer Areas

This chapter discusses how computer use may affect a library design. Different types of computer use and electronic workstation design are also discussed.

The Effect of Access to Electronic Information on Library Design

What Are Library Services? What Do Librarians Do?

Library services make individual connections between people seeking knowledge and people who know how to help them find that knowledge. Knowledge is information that is related to a social purpose. Examples include information about:

- being in business to make a profit
- improving health
- finding a job
- understanding current events
- moving to a new area
- choosing a college
- learning about different people
- enjoyment and recreation

Electronic means are only one of a variety of resources that librarians use to accomplish these objectives. The librarians' skill is in communicating effectively with users to determine their needs and successfully using the resources to satisfy these needs. Libraries are organized to make these connections as convenient as possible, both for staff services and for self-service. By far the largest number of library transactions are self-service.

How Are Library Facilities Organized to Accomplish These Goals? Building Objectives

Library buildings are organized to make it easy for people to:

- Discuss their needs with a knowledgeable staff member
- Find the latest information on popular topics by displaying popular materials in a sequential fashion so that they are easy to find
- Look up a subject, author, or title and find a particular item in a large clearly organized collection of materials
- Use a computer:
  - ◆ to get an article or a piece of information in a local area
  - ◆ to access a network of items of particular interest to the community
  - ◆ to obtain an article or a piece of information from a wide area
  - ◆ to access a network such as the Internet
- Attend a program of particular interest to the community
- Attend a small meeting of people with a shared interest

How Electronic Information May Affect Building Planning for the Short Term—Five Years

Periodical research, formerly done with print indexes and large back files of magazines, will increasingly be done electronically, reducing magazine storage requirements.

Electronic workstations that require more space than a seat and chair, and are more expensive to acquire and maintain, will be increasingly needed by libraries and used both by staff and by patrons independently.

Libraries have often been used extensively by telephone. It is not uncommon for libraries to do 40 percent of their reference service over the telephone. Now users will get information through their home computers as a substitute for using libraries, if their ability to navigate these networks is sufficient. Many users will continue to use these networks through their local libraries because the skill of the librarians using the networks is frequently greater than the skill of the occasional user.

How Electronic Information May Affect Building Planning for the Long Term

REMOTE ACCESS TO MATERIALS BY FORMER LIBRARY USERS

Users will access lengthy documents electronically with the advent of high resolution technology. The role of the librarian in assisting people making knowledge connections and navigating networks may occur remotely with fewer people enjoying the face-to-face encounters that now characterize many library transactions. People who have the choice between face-to-face and electronic contact may realize the benefits and disadvantages of each and continue to choose the appropriate venue for their particular needs.

THE LONG-TERM FUTURE OF LIBRARY BUILDINGS

Places where connections can be made face-to-face will continue to exist. Choices of material formats will change over time. The idea of community will differ from place to place as it does now. Many communities will recognize the value of face-to-face communications in information-seeking knowledge connections as symbolized in the library building and choose to build structures that enhance these connections and offer a wide choice of services.

How Many Electronic Workstations?

The first question asked by most clients at the outset of library facility planning is how many electronic workstations are needed. This is a difficult, essential, and constantly changing question. Many libraries are considering designing all study carrels as potential future electronic workstations. Good planning requires that this question be answered in the context of the community the library serves and the variety of uses that community makes of computer functions.

- *Library Use*—If in-library use is as high as seven to ten uses per capita, libraries may need more computers. Libraries with high entry counts may also require more terminals than a library with less use per capita.
- *Library Staff Leadership, Technical Staff Training and Development*—Libraries that have well trained technical staffs may use more terminals.
- *Population Served*—Well-educated and technically oriented populations may require more terminals.
- *Local Educational Emphasis*—Schools that have a strong computer emphasis will affect public library use of computers.
- *Library Budget*—Libraries with high budgets per capita may also have high budgets for the purchase of licenses for databases.
- *Building and Collection Size*—Libraries containing major collection resources may require additional terminals because of increased in-depth use resulting from extensive collections.

Wireless

Wireless installations in libraries can provide very useful flexibility in locating and moving computer access locations. Currently wireless transmission can be ten megabytes in band width but in the near future may go up to fifty megabytes. Ten megabytes band width can support Internet access for text and pictures but fifty is better for sound and video transmission.

Users' laptops as well as library laptops may be used.

A site survey is required to determine reception requirements in each area. Constraints to reception may include:

- Metal wire mesh used under plaster walls
- Aluminum sheet rock studs

A hub is needed for every ten terminals. A Cisco wireless work group bridge may facilitate transmission. Codes are assigned to each access point. The protocols for wireless are 802.11B and the newer 802.11A which supports fifty megabyte transmission. In new buildings wireless may reduce wiring requirements by 75 percent by using wires only to each area hub.

Web site addresses for wireless technology vendors:

- www.3com.com,
- www.cisco.com,
- www.linksys.com
- www.lucent.com/products/subcategory/o..ctid+2007-stid+10209 LOCL+1.00html
- www.proxim.com
- Newsletter—Networkworld fusion www.nwfusion.com

Variety of Uses

Almost universal in libraries is the Online Public Access Catalog or OPAC. This device is used by library patrons to find out if a book is available in this or other libraries. This type of use is often very brief, suggesting a stand-up environment except for first-time users who will need to be seated to learn how to use this new device. As users become more familiar with technology fewer sit-down terminals will be necessary. OPACs are needed in quantity at the entrance to the library, and in lesser quantity in the stacks. They are very useful in the stacks when the books sought by the users are not in place and they need to look for alternatives.

OPACs are increasingly becoming database providers. A variety of bibliographic, abstract, and full-text databases are downloaded onto the same hard drive as the library's catalogs, so all OPAC terminals also become reference tools. This use often requires longer consultation, so there needs to be a choice of sit-down and stand-up environments. Preferably terminals are adjustable for sitting or standing.

Local Area Networks have more complex uses and offer a wider choice of databases and more extensive full-text offerings requiring a sit-down environment with the capability of printing out or downloading data onto the users' media.

Wide Area Networks such as the Internet offer a bewildering array of complex choices requiring long-term, sit-down environments together with print and download capabilities and the necessity for a large collaborative carrel to ease instruction by staff or other users.

Library users may want to use their own software on library equipment. They will bring in disks and use library software. They will download data for use on their home computers.

Group instruction is a requirements in school, academic, and sometimes in public libraries requiring ganged workstations and an acoustically separated area.

Appropriate Environments

Brief lookups require a stand-up environment except for first-time users who will need to be seated to learn how to use this new device. This area requires 20 square feet of space for a stand-up workstation.

Collaborative carrels are very useful since staff instruction is a necessity. In addition more knowledgeable users instruct their fellow users. This is especially true in the children's room where kids frequently help one another. Carrels need to be large enough to accommodate two chairs and two users at a single terminal. Plan on these areas taking up 60–80 square feet of space.

Longer consultation requires a sit-down environment with noise absorption. Long-term use, sit-down environments together with print and download capabilities take 40–50 square feet of space.

Group instruction requires ganged workstations and an acoustically separated area.

Computer Readiness Phases

Stage 1—Install empty conduits for data transmission and low and high voltage lines. Consider wireless infrared requirements, raised floors (especially Milliken Powerflor system [Charlotte, NC 704–523–9441]), flat wiring, power poles, Walker Duct, Shielded, Type 5, twisted pair, and fiber optic cabling. Consider uninterrupted power supply systems (UPS) for the building. These will often include batteries and surge protectors to assure constant filtered power.

Stage 2—Install electrical and low voltage transmission with Type 5 wiring. Minimum of six electrical receptacles for each terminal at 32 inch height.

Stage 3—Install workstation furniture with "J" channels for wire management, grommets large enough for plugs or wiring troughs.

Stage 4—Install computers.

Technology Support

Electronic Repairs—Technology support services should include a bench for repair of computers with several electrical outlets and a dataport telecommunications line. The bench will have shelves above for tools and drawers below for spare parts. There will also be several 24 inch deep shelves nearby for equipment waiting to be sent out for repair. This area should be able to be locked off from the rest of the technical services area and should be near the server room and the delivery entrance.

Audio-Visual Test Equipment and Repairs—These may be accomplished in a nearby space using some of the same facilities.

Network/Server Room—Servers, CD towers, and other electronic and

---

Figure 16-1
Electronic Workstation Design Considerations

- 6–10 electrical receptacles per terminal at 32" height.
- Wireless systems.
- Raised floors (especially Dupont or Milliken Power floor system).
- Flat wiring with carpet tile.
- Power poles.
- Walker Duct.
- Shielded, Type 5, twisted pair wiring.
- Fiber optic cabling.
- Uninterrupted power supply systems (UPS) for the building.
- Surge protectors to assure constant filtered power.

---

communications equipment should be located in this general area with special considerations given to:

- Acoustical dampening
- Wiring access to outside and inside the building
- Patch panel and cabinet for LAN and Internet access
- Firewall/proxy server
- Rack system for hubs and routers
- Wide conduits for fiber optic and category 5 wiring
- Uninterruptible power supply (UPS)
- Telephone

Electronic Workstation Design Considerations

(This section is based on work done by Dr. James Kusack of Southern Connecticut State University)

Comfort

The seating, work surfaces, and other furnishings must provide ergonomically designed relationships for users who sit at the workstations for long periods of time. See Figures 16-1 and 16-2 for design considerations and workstation/body relationships. See Figure 16-3 for an example of workstation design.

Adjustability

All aspects of the workstation should be adjustable and adequate for staff with special problems, e.g. back problems, eye glasses, different heights. This flexibility is critical because staff differ in size, bodily configuration, and work preferences.

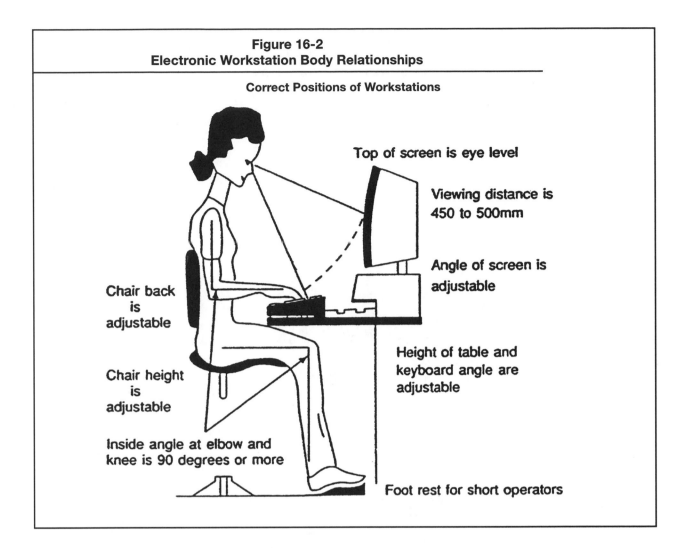

Figure 16-2
Electronic Workstation Body Relationships

Correct Positions of Workstations

Top of screen is eye level

Viewing distance is
450 to 500mm

Angle of screen is
adjustable

Chair back
is
adjustable

Height of table and
keyboard angle are
adjustable

Chair height
is
adjustable

Inside angle at elbow and
knee is 90 degrees or more

Foot rest for short operators

Seating

The user should be able to adjust the height of the seat and the backrest. Furthermore, the backrest and seat pan should be laterally adjustable so that the user can move the backrest fore and aft and change the seat deflection from flat to a somewhat backward angle. All adjustment levers must be readily accessible and easy to use—users should not have to get on their knees or turn chairs upside down to make adjustments. Hydraulic mechanisms are necessary where two or more people use the same workstation. Arm rests should be adjustable and removable. The chair itself should move and swivel to allow to facilitate a wide range of activities. Chairs should be designed for simple in-house maintenance including replacement of upholstery and mechanical controls.

Desks and Work Surfaces

Ideally, desks and work surfaces should be adjustable from 22 inches to 45 inches from the floor. Normal desk height is 26 inches to 30 inches. The flexibility to raise the work surface to counter height permits workers with a back injury to use a keyboard

Figure 16-3
Electronic Workstation Designed for Bretford by Formway Design
Studio of Wellington, New Zealand

or library materials while standing. Knee hole space should be available so chairs can be out of the way when not needed. At minimum, the workstation must include an adjustable keyboard pan that enables a sitting user to maintain upper and lower arms at a 90-degree angle (upper arm vertical, forearm horizontal) and wrists at 10- to 20-degrees from horizontal. A tilting keyboard pan would also help improve the wrist angle. Lack of adjustability may be a major cause of repeated motion syndrome in those working at keyboards.

The ideal work area is 60-inches wide but should be at least 30-inches wide to permit opening books or use of documents or other media. Leg clearance should be at least 24-inches wide and 16-inches deep.

Computer Equipment

The library's role in the information age demands increased reliance on computers and related technology. Librarians create, maintain, and search local and remote databases; they use word-processing equipment to write reports, letters, and other documents; they use software to plan budgets and manage the organization.

Local Area Networks and connectivity are important aspects of a library's use of this technology. Design features must reflect the need to power and connect equipment in each workstation as well as between the different departments. J-channels, ramps, grommeted openings for bundled cables, and power poles will be important design features.

The workstation will need room for a variety of hardware, including some bulky equipment like printers and paper supplies, and storage devices such as hard disks and CD-ROM systems. Shelving for manuals and supporting documents is also important.

Screens

Placement of the CRT or VDT screen should be approximately 18 inches from the worker's eyes and as low as possible, ideally flat in the desk surface itself. The screen should never be above normal eye level. In the best situation, the user will be able to raise, lower, tilt, and swivel the screen to suit their individual physical requirements.

Visual fatigue can be minimized by correct lighting. Artificial or natural light that is too bright can cause a "wash-out" effect. VDTs should not be placed next to windows but when this is necessary, the screen should be at a right angle to the plane of the window. Polarized screens may be helpful while blinds can also control reflected glare.

Embedded Terminal Technology

Computer terminals placed below the work surface within enclosed workstations (see Figure 16-4) have many advantages and some disadvantages:

Advantages:
- Enclosed wiring is neat and prevents tampering
- CRT screens do not have to be cleaned as frequently
- Multiple uses—The workstation can be used as a standard study carrel
- More space is available for papers and books
- Some experts believe this is the most ergonomic design

Disadvantages:
- Difficult to load floppy disks or CDs
- Overhead lighting often causes reflections
- Some users do not like this methodology and some experts criticize its ergonomics

Web Sites for Electronic Workstation Vendors and Designers
- www.biomorphdesk.com—Height adjustable workstations
- www.bretford.com—Wrap around and height adjustable workstations.
- www.sitincomfort.com
- www.sishft.com
- www.laptop-laidback.com—Laptop workstations
- www.haginc.com—Ergonomic workstation seating

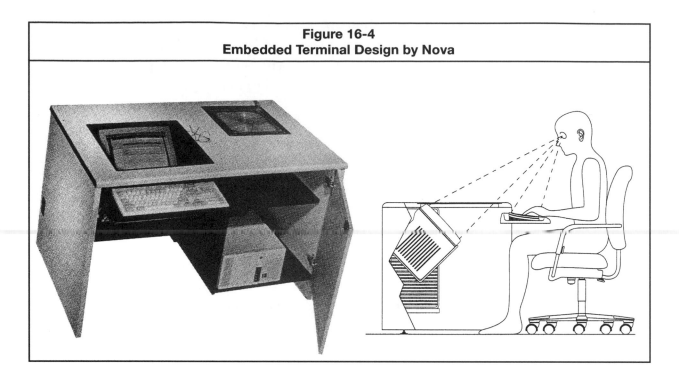

Figure 16-4
Embedded Terminal Design by Nova

17

Graphics, Lighting, and Chairs

In this chapter we suggest some design characteristics for graphics and lighting that will make the library easier to find and use. Chair comfort and ergonomic basics are also discussed.

Library Graphics

Exterior Graphics

A public library is a multi-service community resource for individuals. Unlike town halls, police stations and fire stations, citizens are coming to libraries for their own particular individual needs and not for emergencies or mandated governmental purposes like paying taxes. Libraries are also competing for an individual's time with recreational entertainment as well as educational places. For these reasons a library's external signage assumes great importance. In our busy modern lives external library signs serve as a constant reminder of the library's availability to help people with their everyday informational and educational needs as well as helping people find the library.

Public libraries receive public funding as a benefit to citizens for many purposes. Their effectiveness in serving people depends to a great extent on their ability to get people to come in the front door.

We live in a world of media hype. Our streets are flooded with signs that seek to get people to spend money. Libraries are valuable free community resources that need to compete for attention in this media frenzy or find themselves ignored.

Wayfinding in Libraries

A library is to a great extent a self-service operation, but the wide variety of services and materials offered by libraries require explanation and guidance. Graphic signs help users find their way to a particular book with minimal staff assistance. Lighting, furnishings, and colors work together with graphics to assist users in differentiating among services. For graphics to work effectively they must be planned early in the design sequence to coordinate with furnishings, colors, and especially lighting. The following guidelines should be helpful in planning graphics:

- The front door of the library should be directly in the line of sight of people entering the building and should include a clear reminder of the hours that the library is open. Exceptions to these hours, such as special holiday schedules, should also be posted here.
- In selecting size consider background and distance. One-inch high letters for every 50 feet of visibility would call for two-inch high letters on a sign designed to be seen 100 feet away.
- Consider how the sign compares with the background. A dark background sign with light white letters is easier to read and avoids the glare reflected from a light background.
- Use a simple, direct, familiar type style that is easily obtainable and easy to read, such as Helvetica.
- Graphics can be esthetically pleasing as well as functional, and should be designed to coordinate with the architecture and furnishings at an early stage in design development.
- Location, colors, furnishings, lighting, and graphics can be helpful in affecting behavior and locating materials. They should all be coordinated at an early planning stage, not after construction is completed.
- Avoid negative signs, especially large permanent ones that are difficult to enforce such as "No food in the library."
- Fliers, posters, maps, and directories may be more useful than signs in some cases.
- Standard height center point is 54 inches.
- Use capitals and lower case rather than all upper case type.
- Never stack letters one on top of the other.
  Don't stack letters this way:

  B
  O
  O
  K
  S

- Arrow panels used to indicate directions should be produced separately from letter panels so that letter panels can be changed without changing arrows.
- Exterior signs should be lighted, include hours open, and should be perpendicular to traffic. Signs intended to be noticed by people in cars may have to be larger

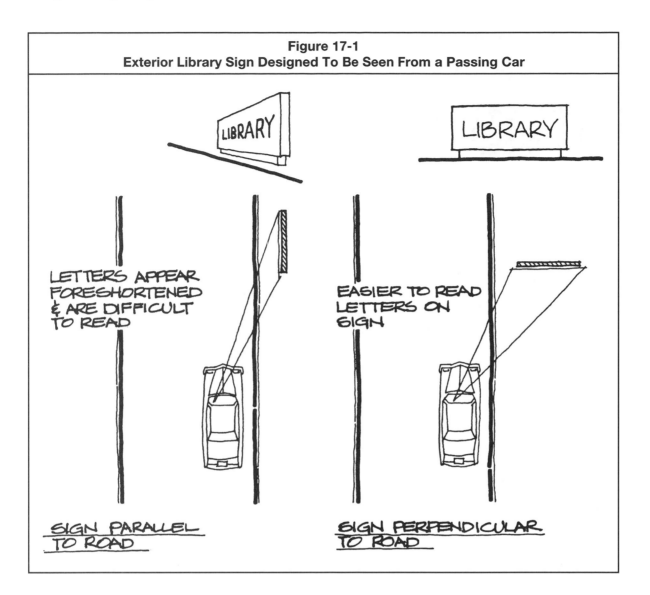

Figure 17-1
Exterior Library Sign Designed To Be Seen From a Passing Car

LETTERS APPEAR FORESHORTENED & ARE DIFFICULT TO READ

EASIER TO READ LETTERS ON SIGN

SIGN PARALLEL TO ROAD

SIGN PERPENDICULAR TO ROAD

than normal. Outdoor signs are useful reminders of a library's availability, not just its location.

- User categories should be identified and destinations charted in preparation for specifications. Plan by:
  - ◆ user category
  - ◆ user destination
  - ◆ traffic flow
  - ◆ decision points where patrons pause or turn
- Projected signage using laser beams can be very effective in locating a library building during the evening.
- Signs located on the front of busy counters such as the circulation or reference desks become quickly invisible when library users are standing in front of the desk. Instead use signs raised above the desks.

See Figures 17-1 through 17-3 for illustrations depicting different signage issues.

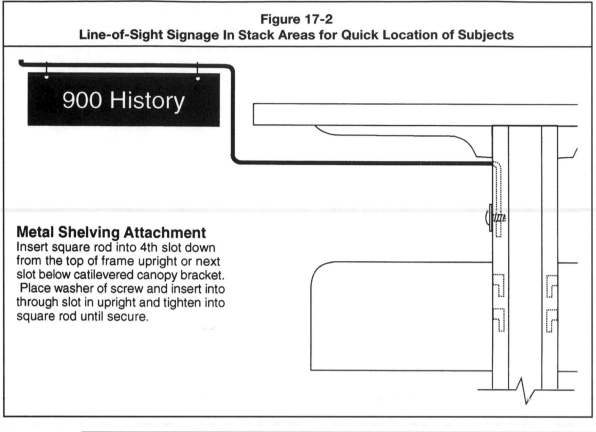

Figure 17-2
Line-of-Sight Signage In Stack Areas for Quick Location of Subjects

900 History

Metal Shelving Attachment
Insert square rod into 4th slot down
from the top of frame upright or next
slot below catilevered canopy bracket.
Place washer of screw and insert into
through slot in upright and tighten into
square rod until secure.

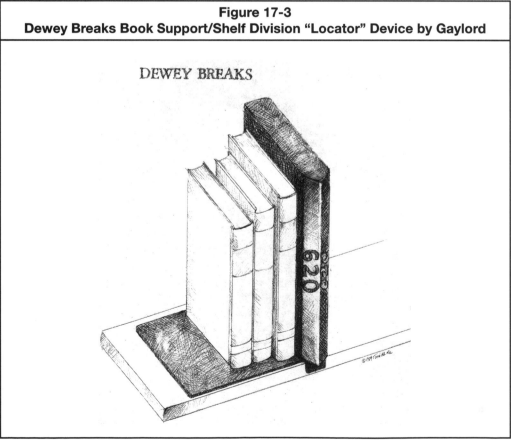

Figure 17-3
Dewey Breaks Book Support/Shelf Division "Locator" Device by Gaylord

DEWEY BREAKS

620

Figure 17-4
Elliptipar Wall Wash Lighting Fixture Designed by Sy Shemitz

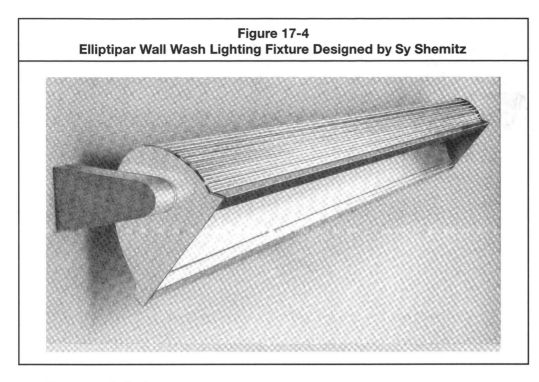

Library Lighting

Louis Kahn, one of the greatest of modern architects, wrote in his program for the Phillips Exeter school library in New Hampshire that libraries are about books, people, and light. How the library is lighted can make the difference between a bland gray industrial look and an exciting glorious space in which the materials become the decoration and people have a marvelous choice of sunlit reading and study spaces and cozy comfortable individual study carrels. See Figures 17-4 and 17-5 for examples of lighting design. Here are some ideas about lighting that may be useful in achieving a beautiful and functional library:

- Indirect natural sunlight is wonderful for library users and should be introduced into all library areas except perhaps the program rooms. It can be brought into the center of the library by clerestory design that lifts part of the roof to make windows inset from the side of the building.
- Be careful of direct sunlight, it is unpredictable and difficult to control. Instead consider clerestory windows set back from the side walls to bring natural indirect light into the middle of the library. Ultraviolet light from the sun damages paper and bindings. Use overhangs and awnings to control direct sunlight. New products are available that filter sunlight and reduce the heat gain that formerly made perimeter window seats unusable in hot summer days.
- Select lenses for light fixtures that will diffuse light and prevent glare.
- Lamp choices include:
  - Fluorescent lamps that provide high light output for low cost, burn for over 10,000 hours, and provide a useful selection of colors.
  - High Intensity Discharge (HID) lamps that provide more even high light

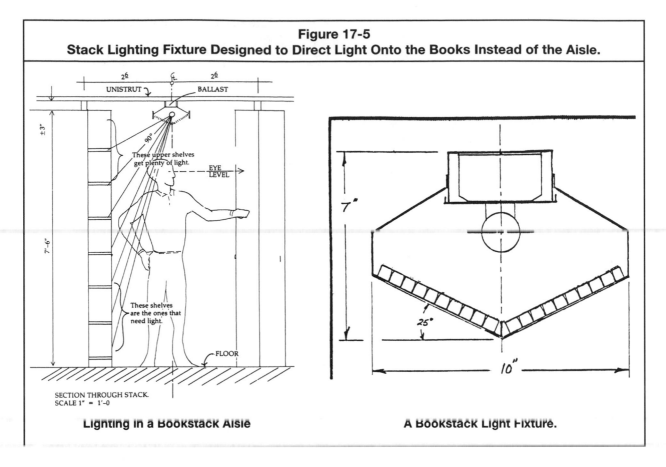

Figure 17-5
Stack Lighting Fixture Designed to Direct Light Onto the Books Instead of the Aisle.

Lighting in a Bookstack Aisle   A Bookstack Light Fixture.

output than fluorescent and an equal lamp life but a lesser range of color choices.

- ◆ Incandescent lamps that burn for less than 1,000 hours and provide lower light output than the other two types. These can be spot or flood lamps.
- Locate fixtures to minimize ceiling brightness and ceiling reflectance caused by light striking the viewing surface at a 45-degree angle.
- Limit light intensity variation in small rooms or in contiguous areas.
- Use low intensity light in non-reading areas, such as traffic aisles.
- Maintenance, ease of replacement, and fixture cleaning as well as energy efficiency (electronic ballasts), life of lamps, and initial and replacement cost should be considered in selecting and locating fixtures.
- Costs for electricity and maintenance will increase, so select fixtures, lenses, and lamps that are easy to clean and replace and burn cool for longer life.
- Control glare and reflection by diffusers, louvers, and light locations.
- Computer use areas should meet preferred standards for VDT lighting in IES standard practice for office lighting.
- Let users control task lighting. Use table and floor lamps.
- Parawedge louvers minimize ceiling brightness and ceiling reflections, but provide very directional lighting and do not eliminate direct glare.
- The bat-wing reflector spreads light over a wide area and provides good, inexpensive, evenly distributed stack lighting when fixtures are mounted directly

above and parallel to stack ranges, provided fixture height is correct in relation to the reflective ceiling.

- White ceilings and white walls will increase light, especially in small rooms.
- Visibility in a room is affected by:
  - ◆ size of room
  - ◆ color and contrast within the room
  - ◆ brightness of lamps
- Select incandescent lamps for concentration (very narrow spots) or spreading of light (flood lamps), and for color rendition.
- The color of light from warm white fluorescent lamps (not deluxe) provides better rendition of skin tones than cool white lamps. Cool white deluxe lamps are even closer to the color of sunlight. Color rendering Index (CRI) of 75 is preferred.
- Light-colored reflecting floor materials increase light on bottom shelf compared to carpeting. Cork floors are reflective and absorb sound.
- Indirect light intensity depends on the color and distance of the ceiling from the light source as well as the brightness of the lamps.
- Consider heat gain from lighting in air conditioning and heating control.
- Ceiling light fixture locations must be coordinated with location of graphics to assure that light does not obscure signs. This can only be achieved by planning graphics and lighting at the same time during the project. Too often graphics planning comes too late to coordinate with lighting.

Layered Lighting

Layered lighting combines ambient and task lighting:

- **Ambient Lighting**—A low level of ambient lighting will provide for general illumination. This ambient lighting will be low-glare, and accomplished by perimeter luminaires as well as hanging lamps that indirectly reflect light from a white ceiling.
- **Task Lighting**—Non-glare task lighting will be directly related to the functions such as illumination of displays, reading surfaces, and lounge seating. This can be accomplished by floor or table lamps or recessed ceiling fixtures. Task lighting should be as adjustable as possible including long, flexible electrical wires attached to ceiling fixtures that may be easily relocated when functions change. Task lighting should be capable of being controlled by the user, with lamps on swivel arms.

WALL WASH DISPLAY LIGHTING

Perimeter, ceiling-mounted wall wash book display lighting fixtures should be installed at least three feet out from the walls and include elliptical reflectors in order to cast light all the way down the wall.

LIGHTING STANDARDS

The Illuminating Engineering Society Handbook suggests the following levels of maintained lighting intensity (taking light loss factors into consideration). Foot candles measure the light falling on a surface equivalent to the number of candles placed one foot from the lighted surface:

- Public service desks—50 foot-candles average measured horizontally at the counter top.
- Staff areas—50 foot candles average measured horizontally at the desktop.
- Small conference room—30–40 foot candles measured horizontally at the desktop with dimmers for AV.
- Large multi-purpose room—40 foot candles average with all lights on separately controlled lighting from the front of the room. Lighting dimmable to 2-foot candles for note taking during AV presentations.
- Reading areas—30–40 foot candles measured horizontally at the desktop.

These figures do not always translate into visual acuity. Factors such as glare from bright lamps, light absorbing materials on the floor and walls, and contrast can dramatically affect people's perception.

INDIRECT AND SPOT LIGHTING

In some areas of the library where a variety of tasks are performed in close proximity it will be useful to consider a system that will deliver uniform indirect light over the entire area. This can be accomplished by installing indirect lighting fixtures under a white reflective ceiling so that the light will shine up and be diffused by the ceiling over a wide area. This indirect light strikes the viewing surfaces from many angles thus diffusing glare and providing a comfortable reading level for most tasks.

If the light source is hidden from view there will be no glare from the light source to disturb long-term users. This follows Frank Lloyd Wright's dictum "Hide the luminaires." Computer screens will also be protected from annoying reflections. An excellent example of this type of indirect lighting is the computer room in the Science Industry and Business branch of the New York Public Library at 42d Street and Madison Avenue in New York.

The disadvantage of this indirect system is that the ceiling becomes the brightest object in the room, and the rest of the room may be darker and less interesting as a result. It also requires high levels of light output from High Intensity Discharge lamps with unpleasant colors that change over time and supplement it with dramatic spot lighting of materials.

Wall wash lighting with elliptical reflectors intended to light the entire height of the wall must be mounted at least three feet out from the side walls in order to cast light all the way down the wall.

MEETING ROOM LIGHTING

In meeting rooms light dimmers will be especially useful to vary the intensity of light depending on the program content. The controls for these should be mounted near the stage or speaker area in the front of the room and there should be separate light controls for:

- Stage or podium
- Audience
- Aisles
- Perimeter walls

Theatrical lighting is expensive and requires elaborate ceiling racks and special wiring. The fixtures produce considerable heat and thus require special cooling.

Workstation, Table, and Seating Choices

People need a wide range of choices in seating because people come in different sizes and forms and use libraries in different ways. A sedentary 200-pound person coming to the library for several days of genealogical research has different needs than a restless 100-pound teenager coming to listen to the latest CD.

Stand-up workstations will be useful for quick location of materials in the library or for a brief reference question. They should be available at the entrance and in the stack area. Biomorph, Highsmith, and other manufacturers have introduced hi-lo workstations that can be used in either a sitting or standing configuration.

Individual study carrels can be located so as to be visible down the stack aisles so that a person selecting a book to read has ready access to a place to read it. If carrels are located far from supervision they should be single carrels spaced far apart to discourage talking.

Four-person tables should be four feet by six feet, not the standard three foot by five foot library table. The small tables discourage use by more than two people while the larger tables are more likely to be used by four. Alcove arrangements with low shelves on three sides of the table are highly desired by many library users for privacy and to separate user groups.

Tutorial rooms are essential in the children's and teenage areas for collaborative study and teaching.

Oversize collaborative electronic workstations with two chairs and one monitor will be useful near the reference desk for assisting users unfamiliar with searching and for doing complex searches.

Library Seating Design Considerations

A library chair is the most important piece of equipment in the library. It should be the first priority for equipment expenditures and there should be no compromise with comfort and durability. Library users will sit for hours of intensive study and their comfort will determine their level of satisfaction with the library study experience. If libraries want to distinguish themselves from bookstores, chair comfort is an important factor in that distinction, The following information may be of value to those making decisions about chairs and seating in the library:

COMFORT

Chair comfort is not simply a function of hard or soft surfaces. In fact, hard surfaces shaped carefully to human bone structure may be more comfortable than rectangular slabs of foam. Chairs that afford users the opportunity to both move within the chair and to move the chair itself will be preferred over handsomely sculptured stiff shapes such as the Barcelona chair.

People spend a great deal of time in library chairs. Therefore, chairs should be extremely comfortable and conform to the human body. Ergonomically designed chairs not only conform to the curve of the back, but also provide side-to-side support for the lower back. It is important to get in and out of a chair with ease. Pregnant women and older people may experience difficulty getting out of low lounge chairs. People vary in size, so a variety of chair designs may be useful. Woven fabric tends to be more breathable than vinyl, and more comfortable to sit in.

ADJUSTABILITY

Seat height is adjustable usually with a gas cylinder lever on the side of the chair. The cylinder should be easy to replace when it malfunctions. Lower back lumbar support should be firm and adjustable up and down. The seat back should move with the body and be adjustable back and forth for different tasks. An electronic workstation should be equipped with a chair that supports the back in an upright position, while a lounge chair in the magazine reading area should recline and support the back as the reader's body moves. Chairs should accommodate to movement of the body. The chair should flex and support the body as it moves within the chair.

DURABILITY AND COST

Library chairs tend to last many years in regular use, twelve hours a day seven days a week. It is difficult to get an inexpensive chair that will hold up and still be handsome over that span of time. Hundreds of people will use the chairs each day, therefore it is important to select fabric, materials, and structure that will last a long time. Wood frames should be carefully examined for their construction before a decision is made as to their durability.

The Eustis chairs with their epoxy injected gluing system are an example of wooden chair durability.

LOUNGE CHAIRS

A stressless reclining chair and footstool constructed of tubular steel that is leather upholstered with a curved foam back is an extremely comfortable chair that can be easily adjusted to fit any size person, and it is relatively easy getting in and out. A spare set of cushions can be purchased and installed if the upholstery is damaged. See Figure 17-6 for example of lounge chair construction.

TASK CHAIRS

Mobile task chairs for electronic workstations are available in a wide variety of price ranges. The Charles Perry designed UNO chair from Turnstone (see Figure 17-7)

Figure 17-6
Lounge Chair With Lumbar Support

Figure 17-7
Adjustable Mobile Task Chair UNO Designed by Charles Perry Turnstone

is adjustable in height, and flexes and moves with the user. The Herman Miller Aeron chair is an ergonomic design classic and is the standard chair used in the Science, Business Branch of the New York Public Library. It has a ventilated seat and back to prevent heat buildup. The Steelcase Criterion chair has a back that moves in and out for lumbar support while working at a computer. The newer Leap chair by Steelcase has a height adjustable lumbar support for the lower back.

Carpet Compatible Design

To move chairs easily on carpeting, they should be on casters or with a runner on the bottom so that they can glide easily. Heavy wooden four-legged chairs are harder to move and difficult to pull back from a table when standing up. They may also damage the carpet in a short time. They often tip over when they are tilted back. Two-position wooden chairs with increased stability and two-position bases are available.

Maintenance

Select easily replaceable gas cylinders for height adjustment. Upholstery should be easy to replace by simply unscrewing the seat or back and installing a new seat or back. Button/sling backs or velcro on some lounge seating permit even faster replacement. Darnell casters on chairs facilitate easy movement.

Floors

Carpeting is obviously the preferred library flooring material for its acoustical absorbency. It should be:

- Low pile (less than 1/4 inch high)
- Looped through the backing for durability under heavy book trucks
- Minimum face weight of 25 ounces per square yard
- Install different color/pattern carpeting in heavy-use areas and plan to replace these areas more often than light-use areas
- Carpet tile may be useful for flat wiring access in small areas
- Mixed tweed colors will look better than solid colors when dirty

Entrance mats should allow dirt to drop below the walking surface and should be easily removable for frequent cleaning. Cork floors are durable and sound absorbent and have a high reflectance to increase light on the bottom shelves of book stacks.

18

Quick Improvements

This chapter outlines how libraries can be improved quickly without a costly and lengthy renovation or addition process.

Quick and Inexpensive Improvements

Physical improvements to a library do not always necessitate a costly and time-consuming process. Quick improvements to a library can often be accomplished by employing some basic principles of library design and executing:

- Improved staff productivity by careful planning of electronic areas in relation to changing staff functions—electronic reference
- Lighting improvements and energy savings
- Increased use by better display throughout the library

Easy Access To the Most Popular Materials

- Creating clear pathways so users can travel throughout the library and see from one end to the other will encourage users to walk throughout the building. Lighted signs in the pathways can then direct users to the variety of services.

Grouping popular materials to the right of the library entrance is important because retail store studies have shown that people entering stores have a natural tendency to turn to the right.

Since there is a relatively small number of popular materials, it is useful to spread them out on sloping display shelves so that many people can enjoy them at the same time. These units may be purchased from several manufacturers, such as MJ or Lift. They allow books, CDs, videos paperbacks, and picture books to be grouped together in a wide array of display shelving choices on the same upright frames. Bins, sloping display shelves, and zig-zags can all fit together.

Signage such as line-of-sight fixtures from Brodart can be hung in the stack aisles to give users a continuous orientation to the sequence of subject numbers. They will make it easier to find subjects and to inform users of the meaning of the numbers.

Book holders to display the front covers of books can be placed in the book stacks on eye-height shelves to provide users with an opportunity to see quickly the best books in each section.

Tilt-and-store magazine shelving can group current and back issues to make it easier for users to find magazines.

E-panels incorporating flat screen computers with keyboards at the end of each stack range can make it easier for users to find handy computers near book locations. Low boxes covered with a handsome cloth and placed at pause places such as elevators, stair landings, near telephones, and computers can give users the opportunity to look at a few carefully selected books throughout the library.

Comfortable Seating

The UNO mobile upholstered chair adjustable in height may be purchased for a reasonable price from Steelcase Turnstone division. These chairs are on wheels, upholstered in a durable fabric, and easily adjustable in height. They also move and flex with the body so as to remain comfortable for long periods of time. Choices in seating types can be matched to appropriate library services:

- Technical chairs with electronic workstations
- Oversize tables near the newspapers
- Leisure lounge seating near the magazines
- Varying seat and table heights in the children's room
- Study rooms for group study projects and tutorials
- Stand-up counters in the new book section and in the reference area give users an opportunity to rest heavy materials and use them standing up

Improved Lighting

A dramatic improvement in appearance and lighting comfort can be achieved by substituting cool white deluxe lamps for the cool white or warm white fluorescent lamps currently in use by most libraries. The new color is more like daylight.

Floor or table lamps in seating areas can also markedly improve visual acuity by providing light where it is needed and by allowing users to adjust the light location and intensity by moving the lamp.

Wall wash lights placed at least three feet out from the walls and equipped with high intensity discharge lamps and elliptical reflectors cast light all the way down the wall and improve the appearance of wall shelving.

Pendant swivelier fixtures screwed into existing ceiling receptacles can quickly and inexpensively give libraries the flexibility to direct light where it is most needed. In addition, very narrow or narrow spots can replace flood lamps and impart a spotlighted dramatic appearance to display fixtures.

Improved Control

Staff control of public behavior can be enhanced by better sight lines for visual surveillance by moving furniture and replacing high sided carrels with low sided carrels.

Outdoor Mobile Book Trucks

Providing outdoor book trucks for lunch hour quick sidewalk service on good days will vastly improve user satisfaction.

Improved Staff Productivity

Improved staff productivity can be achieved by:

- Ergonomic comfort designs for staff workstations
- Bi-level service desks to define public and staff work surfaces
- Check-in location near several book trucks to allow for presorting of materials to be shelved
- Improved heating and cooling controls located where staff can adjust them
- Standing work counters to give back relief by allowing workers to stand for part of the work day
- Adjustable, locally controlled lighting to allow for variations in the need for light intensity
- Attractive lunch and coffee break facilities located close to work places with a choice of healthy alternative foods

IV

Library Design
Source Box

Source 1

Post Occupancy Evaluation Criteria

Post Occupancy Evaluation (POE) was pioneered by a few architects in the 1980s and 90s. Preiser, Rabinowitzi, and White published a book called *Post Occupancy Evaluation* and Morans and Spreckelmeyer's *Evaluating Built Environments* shows how to use surveys.

A library POE was conducted by Jane Goodwin, Coordinator of Evaluation and Information Development for the Fairfax County, Virginia, Public Library. This evaluation consisted of surveys of building users and staff as well as trained observer studies. They collected a sample of over 500 surveys from each of three libraries. The information was very specific. Users spent a surprising amount of time in the library, over 80 percent spent more than ten minutes. Adult users and staff did not always agree on such questions as temperature control and storage space. Comfort levels for temperature and lighting were carefully measured to test staff perceptions in these areas. Comfort was indeed a problem, sometimes caused by such design features as skylights. The user questionnaires for seating preferences indicated that all three seating types (table, lounge, and carrel seating) were liked by users with a relatively small difference in preference. How do people actually behave when they are browsing for books? In the Fairfax County study more than a third of users were browsers not looking for specific materials.

Dr. James Kusack, a professor at Southern Connecticut State University Library

School worked on several POE studies in Connecticut libraries at about the same time. Some of these studies used behavior mapping techniques that showed in one memorable case the problem with locating a branch public library next to a school with school age children dominating the small library and discouraging adult users from 3–6 p.m.

A recent post occupancy evaluation of the San Francisco Public Library was highly critical of the building and recommended many useful improvements.

A useful method for conducting the post occupancy evaluation of the library might include behavior mapping and user focus groups as well as trained observer studies that are similar to the tracking studies used by Paco Underhill discussed earlier in this book.

The POE should include:

- An analysis of library use as compared to the previous year.
- A tracking study of user behavior.
- A focus group of library users.
- A focus group of library staff.
- A review of the building by the staff.
- Behavior mapping of seating types and comparative intensity of use.
- A review of the building by an independent library consultant (not the consultant who wrote the original program) using the library program and plan review process.
- A review of the building by a different architect.

After this evaluation the remaining 10 percent of the furniture budget can be spent in a way that is appropriate to the changing use of the facility.

The plan review process is the key to producing library facility improvement emphasizing public self-service convenience and improved staff productivity.

Source 2

Model Template for Library Specifications

Sample of a Spreadsheet Showing Areas, Materials, and Seats

This spreadsheet for a heavily used library serving a population with a projected size of 30,000 summarizes the sample functional area sheets that follow.

Centralton Public Library	Areas	Materials	Seats
Functional area			
Circulation service area	400		
Circulation work area	250		
Circulation supervisor's office	150		
Adult services			
browsing and magazines	1800	1450	40
reference/information	4000	10000	60
reference work and office	400		
computer instruction	900	40	20
book stacks	11000	90000	20
audio visual	2000	20000	
Adult services total	20100	121490	140
Young Adult services	1000	6200	16
Children's room			
parents and pre-school	1600	10000	12
children's study and materials	5200	40850	40
children's service desk	300		
children's staff work and office	500		
children's librarian's office	200		
story and craft area	600		*50
Children's total	8400	50850	52
Conference room	400		*20
Program room	1800		*150
Director's office	250		
Administrative offices	500		
Technical processing	1000		
Network center/computer room	200		
Staff room	400		
Total library function	34850	178540	208
Non-assignable area	10455		
Total area of library	45305		

In the seating column the asterisk * indicates that the seating is for program purposes not for library purposes therefore these asterisked seats are not included in the seating total.

Samples of Functional Area Sheets

These sheets are the result of consultation with the library staff to list equipment needed for each functional area.

Name of area   **Circulation Area**   **Dimensions**   400 Sq. Ft.

Activities Staff greet public, operate terminals to check out or renew up to 1,500 items daily, check in approximately the same number of items.

Register users for library cards, collect fines and fees, answer circulation-related questions, answer telephones, make change for patrons, assist with equipment malfunctions and contact other staff members to help users.

Occupancy   Public   15–25   Staff   1–4

Major design features and ambience of area

Area must be inviting to the first time library user.

Graphics should define functions for the public such as checkout, registration, and return of materials.

Desk should be visible from entrances and at a comfortable height for both staff and library users.

Acoustical dampening, glare-free lighting, thermostatic control, adequate ventilation, and protection from cold drafts in winter and heat from summer sunlight are important design considerations at this location.

Floor should be anti-static with extra padding under the carpet.

Traffic flow of staff and users into and out of this area will require careful planning.

Disabled, elderly, children, and parents with children in strollers must be accommodated here.

Lighting must be carefully coordinated to prevent glare on the CRT screen.

Furnishings & equipment

A U-shaped counter 15'–20' long, 30'–39' high and 24–30" wide constructed as a "shell" desk with modular units independent of the structure to be flexibly configured for files, shelves, drawers, as required for library processes. Five computerized workstations will be at this desk. Computer screens may be placed below a glass counter top with the keyboard on the counter top for an uncluttered appearance and ample workspace.

The counter should open at each end to allow staff to exit easily to assist users.

The desk area should open into the circulation work area.

Staff must be able to sit comfortably on easily adjustable stools with backs.

Staff work activities by many people in a small, noisy area require space to maneuver book trucks and walk around.

Acoustical dampening, task lighting, and thermostatic control are essential.

Book return area will have two terminals with printers, space for eight book trucks for returned materials.

Check-out area will have two terminals with printers.

Registration area with terminal staff facing entrance area/lobby, visible from all public areas.

Space for registration forms, space to log statistics, and lost and found storage for ten items.

J channel for wire management and grommeted wiring slots for terminals.

This area may in the future be adapted for self-service check-out

Large bulletin board behind desk for library announcements.

Seating   5 staff seats, 1 public at registration desk

Materials   1,000 returns

Proximity Entrance, Information Service Desk, Circulation Work Area. Locate away from quiet area.

Name of area   **Circulation Work Area**   **Dimensions** 250 Sq. Ft.

Activities Circulation processing activities including reserves, overdue notices, and bills.
Staff use fax machine, computers, photocopiers, and typewriters.

Occupancy
     Staff 2

Major design features and ambience of area
Large window to the circulation desk with one-way glass and curtains.
12' long 29" high counter around the walls with cabinets below and shelves above.
Staff requested "places to put things down."

Furnishings & equipment
12' long, 29" high, 30" deep work counter with knee spaces and cabinets under and shelves above.
Fax machine with stand.
Two ergonomic staff chairs with carpet casters.
Two wall-mounted telephones.
Six book trucks.
Two wastebaskets.
Photocopier and sorting counter.
Counter with computerized workstation.
Four three-foot long wall-mounted shelves for 200 reserves.
Clock.
Space for staff to store personal belongings.

Seating
     2 staff chairs

Materials
     150 Books   50 Non-print materials

Proximity to
Circulation Desk

Name of area Circulation Supervisor's Office **Dimensions** 150 Sq. Ft.

Activities Circulation office activities.

Occupancy
Staff 2

Major design features and ambience of area
Private staff consultations.
Quiet working area.
A large window.

Furnishings & equipment
Work counter with cabinets under and shelves above.
Desk with ergonomic staff chair with carpet casters, electronic workstation, telephone.
Space to store personal belongings.

Seating
1 ergonomic staff chair, 1 visitor chair

Materials
150 Books

Proximity to
Circulation Desk

Name of area Browsing, Magazine, Reading Area   **Dimensions:** 1,800 Sq. Ft.

Activities Display and promotion of high-demand, high-interest new books and audio-visual library materials. People will look, browse, and select items to borrow or read in the library. Most readers will stand but some will sit in nearby lounge seats to enjoy their materials.

Occupancy

Public 30–45   Staff 1

Major design features and ambience of area
This is prime retail space. Materials should be spot-lighted.
Uniform, flexible, highly attractive shelving with clean lines.
Hardcover books, paperbacks, cassettes, compact discs, videos, and other new materials beautifully displayed, many with front covers showing.
Tackable wall covering for display.

Furnishings & equipment
Copier and public fax machine with sorting table near entrance.
Integrated flexible shelving with shelves ranging from 10" to 48" above the floor so they are easily accessible by elderly and handicapped users, with a variety of shelf configurations to display and store:

500 paperbacks
750 hardcover new books
200 non-print media, videos, compact discs, books-on-tape

300 linear feet of shelving to house the materials listed above.
12 lounge chairs with tables and table lamps.
7 tables for 4.

Seating 40 public
7 tables with 28 chairs   12 lounge chairs

Materials
Books 1,250   Non-print media, videos, compact discs, books-on-tape 200

Proximity to
Entrance, Circulation Desk.   Distant from quiet study area

Name of area   **Reference/Information Area**   **Dimensions** 4,000 Sq. Ft.

Activities Answer research questions for people of all ages, in-house and by telephone.
Provide reference and directional help. Provide reader's advisory services. Monitor and instruct in use of
terminals and electronic resources

Occupancy
   Public 10–60   Staff 4

Major design features and ambience of area
Clearly delineated staff and patron areas. Information Service Desk should be visible from the entrance.
Entire area should be inviting with no architectural barriers and handicapped accessible.
Computers, printers, and user conversations contribute to noise which should be acoustically dampened.
Many electrical floor outlets and low voltage data transmission lines will be needed.

Furnishings & equipment
Modular "shell" information desk 28" high with mobile file units, drawers, and shelves.
1 printer, 4 electronic workstations with ergonomic seating at information desk.
2 collaborative workstations for mediated searching with the public.
CD-ROM capability for all workstations.
Mobile, portable, and fixed wired telephone with data transmission lines.
1 three-foot section double-faced 42" high shelving to hold 120 ready reference books.
6 ranges of six three-foot sections double-faced 60" high shelving to hold 10,000 ready reference books.
Photocopier and sorting counter.
2 small book trucks.
4' x 8' display bulletin board for public postings.
6 four-drawer vertical files.
Atlas stand.
Dictionary stand.
30 electronic workstations.
8 single seat, low sided carrels.
5 tables for 4 (4'x6') tables.
2 microfilm/fiche reader printers.
6 microfiles.

Seating   60 public seats, 4 staff

           2 collaborative electronic workstations
           30 single electronic workstations
           20 table seats
           8 single carrels

Materials
   Books 10,000   2 microfilm/fiche reader printers, 6 micro files

Proximity to
Reference Office and Collections, Microform Area, Adult Non-Fiction.
Visible from entrances and in line of sight with the Circulation Desk.

Name of area   **Reference Work and Office**   **Dimensions** 400 Sq. Ft.

Activities Staff research reference questions, prepare programs, edit newsletter, select reference materials, search databases, answer mail reference questions. Interlibrary loan staffer borrows materials, packs and unpacks materials, and returns materials.

Occupancy
          Staff 4

Major design features and ambience of area
Private, quiet area for reference staff. Excellent lighting—high intensity, low glare.
Acoustically but not visually separated from the reference desk.
Many computers in this small space will require cooling from air conditioning and a separate thermostat.

Furnishings & equipment
4 desks with electronic workstations, modems, ergonomic staff chairs, wastebaskets, and telephones.
9-foot-long counter with 2 knee holes for staff, storage shelves above and file units below.
Printer, fax machine, and copier.
4 book trucks.
Clock.
Wall shelving for professional library books—20 lineal feet.
Space for staff to store personal belongings.

Seating
          4 staff

Materials
          Books 100

Proximity to
Away from the public, next to Reference /Information Area.

Name of area   **Computer Instruction**   **Dimensions** 900 Sq. Ft.

Activities Public use of computer-based resources including CD-ROMs, software programs, and online services devoted to research. Staff will deliver bibliographic instruction here.

Occupancy

Public 20   Staff 1–2

Major design features and ambience of area
Excellent non-glare lighting positioned to avoid reflections on CRTs. Filtered and voltage regulated.
Floor or built-in electrical outlets for user-owned as well as library-owned electronics.
Telecommunications and modem connections.
Countertop space for documents and materials.
Acoustically separated but visible from reference desk.
Large double half glass doors that will open 180 degrees to make this area seem like part of the reference area when it is not being used for instruction.

Furnishings & equipment
20 electronic workstations with ergonomic, mobile, and adjustable chairs.
4 printers.
Lockable shelving for 40 books.
Locked closet for equipment and tools.
Coat racks.
Projection screen for group demonstrations or large CRT monitor.
1 staff electronic workstation.

Seating   20 public   2 staff

Materials
40 books

Proximity to
Near the Reference Work and Office.

Name of area   **Non-Fiction/Fiction Bookstacks**   **Dimensions** 11,000 Sq. Ft.

Activities
Browsing, reading, and research.

Occupancy
         Public 30   Staff 1

Major design features and ambience of area
Line-of-sight signage system attached to metal stack uprights and easily adjustable.
Well-defined sequential layout.
Easy to browse—nothing too high or too low.
Good lighting.
Comfortable work space.
Quiet.
Plenty of space between units.

Furnishings & equipment
Two 4' x 6' tables with 4 chairs each.
10 carrels with chairs.
2 electronic workstations for public access catalog standing use only.
Wastebaskets, clocks.
2 electrical receptacles dedicated to Public Access Catalogs, 6 others.
2 book trucks.
10,000 linear feet of shelving to house 90,000 books.

Seating   20
          8 table seats at 2 tables   10 carrels   2 electronic workstations

Materials
          Books 90,000

Proximity to
Near Reference/Information Area.

Name of area   **Audio-Visual Area**   **Dimensions** 2,000 Sq. Ft.

Activities Select popular videos, compact discs, audio cassettes, books on tape, video discs, and computer program disks.

Occupancy
> Public 10

Major design features and ambience of area
Brightly lighted bookstore display units.
This area will be intensively used, therefore aisles should be wider.
As this is a high-growth area, it should have a flexible design for future expansion.

Furnishings & equipment
Flexible shelf display system that will accommodate a varied array of videos, compact discs, audio cassettes, books-on-tape, and future materials with varying sizes.
1,000 linear feet of shelving with display, no lower than 18" off the floor.

Materials
> 20,000 non-print materials in varying formats.

Proximity to
Near Circulation Area to discourage theft of small, easily concealed items.

Name of area   **Young Adult Area**   **Dimensions** 1000 Sq. Ft.

Activities Teenagers find materials of interest, browse, relax, gather, talk, listen to music, view videos.
Use computers to get information of interest, do homework, book reports, and other research assignments.

Occupancy
     Public 5–20   Staff 1

Major design features and ambience of area
Comfortable, attractive informal for browsing, reading, study.
Visible from circulation area.
Acoustically isolated from adult reading and study.
Sound dampening materials on walls, floor, and ceiling—area carpet.
Tackable wall surfaces for a bulletin board.
Electrical and low voltage wiring in place for wide area network connections.
Wireless hub.
2 group study rooms.

Furnishings & equipment
Flexible display shelving for 500 front cover display of materials.
Paperback racks for 500 paperbacks.
Displayers for 1,000 CDs and cassettes, 100 videocassettes, and 100 audio book cassettes.
Shelving for 4,000 books.
10 magazine titles on tilt and store shelving.
Tackable wall surfaces for posters and student art.
4 electronic workstations with listening headphones.
2 4' × 6' tables with 4 mobile comfortable chairs with ergonomic support for each table.
4 lounge chairs with support for back and shoulders—easily reupholstered.
2 mobile carts for materials.
2 standup CD listening stations.
1 overhead video projector with screen.

Seating   16
          2 tables with 8 chairs
          4 electronic workstations
          4 lounge chairs

Materials   6,200
          500 front cover display of materials, 500 paperbacks
          1,000 CDs, cassettes, 100 audio books, 100 videos
          4,000 books

Proximity to
Accessible from the entrance without going through Children's or Adult areas.
Adjacent to Browsing, Audio-Visual Areas.
Visible from Circulation Desk.

Name of Area   **Parents And Preschool**   **Dimensions** 1,600 Sq. Ft.

Activities Parents and children select materials, browse, and read.

Occupancy
              Staff 1   Public 10–15

Major design features and ambience of area
Parents will read with children.
Sound absorbing materials will be helpful.
Lighting should emphasize the colorful book covers.
Visually and acoustically separated from children's study area.

Furnishings & equipment
12 oversized adult lounge chairs for parent and child to read together.
8 floor cushions.
16 picture book bins for alphabet, picture book classics, and toddler books.
Low mobile shelving for 8,000 picture books and easy readers.
Framed off play center with large interactive toys.
Small parent resource section.
Space for parking strollers.
Coat racks.

Seating
              12 lounge chairs for parent and child to sit together, 8 floor cushions

Materials
              8,000 picture books, 1,600 easy readers, 400 toddler books

Proximity to
Entrance to Children's Room.

Name of Area   **Children's Study and Materials**   **Dimensions** 5200 Sq. Ft.

Activities Children and parents will browse, and look for particular books.

Occupancy

        Staff 2,   Public 50

Major design features and ambience of area

Task lighted book stacks in one uniform pattern for easy finding of materials.
Task lighting for each reader and workstation.
Good visibility from staff service area.
Children's librarian wants a "prominent, gorgeous Study Center."
Visually and acoustically separated from preschool area.

Furnishings & equipment

24–66" high shelving ranges 6 sections long – 18' long double-faced book stacks to hold 40,000 books
2 revolving magazine display racks shelving 40 titles.
Paperback display shelving for 200 books.
Multimedia kit racks for 50 kits.
Video shelving for 600 videos.
Computer center with 8 individual workstations with LAN wiring, Internet access.
4 4' × 6' rectangular study tables with 4 chairs to each table.
8 electronic study carrels for quiet work.
6 comfortable lounge chairs sized for children.
6 OPAC terminals, 3 clustered near entrance, 3 dispersed around room.

Seating   40

        4 tables with 4 chairs each
        8 station computer center
        10 study carrels
        6 lounge chairs

Materials   40,850

        40,000 books
        600 videos
        200 paper backs
        50 multimedia kits

Proximity to

Children's Service Desk but far from Preschool Area.

Name of area   **Children's Service Desk**   **Dimensions** 300 Sq. Ft.

Activities Check-in, check-out, helping children, registrations, reference, reader's advisory, technical assistance, telephone, interlibrary loan, program sign-up.

Occupancy

        Public 15   Staff 4

Major design features and ambience of area
Acoustically dampened.
Task lighted.
Places to exhibit children's posters and art works.

Furnishings & equipment
Staff service counter 12–15 feet long (no sharp edges) with child-size height at one end for library.
Registration area with 1 adult sized chair, 1 child sized chair.
2 60"-high single-faced sections of shelving.
4 electronic workstations with OPAC terminals and printers.
4 ergonomically designed upholstered swivel chairs on carpet casters.
6 book trucks.
Photocopier and sorting shelf.
2 phones.
Large display calendar will list children's events for the month.

Seating

        4 staff seats
        2 public chairs

Proximity to
Entrance. Staff should have visibility to the entire Children's Room.

Name of area   **Children's Staff Work and Office**   **Dimensions** 500 Sq. Ft.

Activities
Administrative, answer telephone, cataloging, processing children's materials.

Occupancy
Staff 4

Major design features and ambience of area
Support staff work activities with adequate shelving for books in transit.
Window to Children's Circulation Desk and visibility to Preschool and Study Areas.

Furnishings & equipment
4 desks with computerized workstations, ergonomic chairs, telephones, and wastebaskets.
2 visitor chairs.
Table for processing.
2 sections of single-faced shelving for books in process.
Typewriter and typing table.
Lost and found area.
2 4-drawer file cabinets.
4 book trucks.
6 telephones.

Seating
4 staff chairs, 2 visitor chairs

Materials
Books 100

Proximity to
Children's Circulation Desk.

Name of area   **Children's Librarian's Office**   **Dimensions** 200 Sq. Ft.

Activities
Plan programs, professional reading, meet with parents, children, staff, and salespeople.

Occupancy
  Staff 2

Major design features and ambience of area
Visibility to Children's Staff Workroom.
"A place to think."

Furnishings & equipment
Desk with electronic workstation, ergonomic chair, telephone, and wastebasket.
Professional reading shelving for books and journals.
2 4-drawer file cabinets.
2 visitor chairs.
Table (3' × 5').

Seating
  1 staff chair, 2 visitor chairs

Materials
  Books 100

Proximity to
Children's Staff Work Area.

Name of area   **Story and Crafts**   **Dimensions** 600 Sq. Ft.

Activities
Preschool story hour and after-school and summer programs for children. Children's films and/or videos, and craft activities.

Occupancy
                Public 50   Staff 2

Major design features and ambience of area
Safe, warm, and friendly place for young children that also can serve for elementary school children's programs.
Warm, light, neutral wall colors with tackable wall surfaces.
Visible through glass but acoustically separated from other Children's Areas.
Lockable entrance.
Washable, easily maintained floor covering.
High intensity lighting (70 foot candles) with low glare.
Capable of being darkened for films/video.
Large storage closet for tables, chairs, and floor cushions.
Cable TV hookup.
Sink and counter area.
Emergency exit.
Separate HVAC with quiet air conditioning.

Furnishings & equipment
6 folding adjustable-height modular tables.
50 stackable chairs, 50 floor cushions for story hour, 1 large chair for story telling.
9' long, 36" high, 30"-deep counter with sink and storage cabinets above and below.
Ceiling video projector, pull-down screen.
8 child safe double electrical receptacles at 38" height distributed around room.
2 cork bulletin boards

Seating
                Staff 1   Public 50

Proximity to
Children's Preschool Area. Distant from Children's Study and Materials.

Name of area   **Conference Room**   **Dimensions** 400 Sq. Ft.

Activities
Discussion, tutoring, small group study, quiet study.

Occupancy
          Public 20

Major design features and ambience of area
Acoustically dampened.
Incandescent lighting controlled by rheostat, 70 foot-candles at 30" high work surface.
Electrical receptacles at 32".

Furnishings & equipment
Blackboard/bulletin board combination with lighting.
Flexible table arrangement such as the Rudd System.
20 chairs with upholstered seats and backs.
4 4' × 6' folding tables adjustable in height with dollies for easy storage.
Small wheeled cart for audio-visual equipment.
White walls for projection purposes.

Seating
          20

Proximity to
    Library Program Room.

Name of area   **Library Program Room**   **Dimensions** 1,800 Sq. Ft.

Activities A variety of library programs for adults, children, and teens. Community programs and study groups. Meetings, lectures, video showings, displays, art exhibits, and book sales.

Occupancy

           Public 150   Staff 1–2

Major design features and ambience of area
Acoustical qualities appropriate for video, music, speakers, and audience participation,
Loudspeaker system permitting control of sound from the podium as well as from the rear of the room.
Lighting on dimmers controlled from the podium and the rear of the room.
Window/doors open to the outside desirable, light-proof drapes/shades will be necessary to darken room during daytime use.
Accessible when the rest of the library is closed.
Bathrooms accessible independently of the library.
Child-proofed electrical receptacles throughout the room.
Computer connections with video projection and jacks available throughout the room.
Cable access for video projection.

Furnishings & equipment
150 chairs with upholstered seats and backs.
Ability to hang "things" on wall—displays.
12 tables.
Storage for 12 tables and 150 chairs.
Telephone.
Outside exit (so entire library can be locked up).
Kitchen facilities including refrigerator, sink, microwave, and storage.
1 unisex restroom.
Partition capable of dividing room in half.

Seating

           150 chairs with upholstered seats and backs.

Proximity to
Public restrooms, elevator.

| Name of area | **Director's Office** | **Dimensions** 250 Sq. Ft. |

Activities
Administrative, small group meetings, individual meetings.

Occupancy

Staff 1–5

Major design features and ambience of area
Soundproof.
Natural light.
Windows—fresh air.

Furnishings & equipment
Large desk—at least 5' x 3'.
Executive office chair.
Computer desk with printer.
2 visitor chairs.
Conference table with 4 chairs.
Telephone/Fax.
Shelving for 200 books.
Minimum of 18 linear feet of wall shelving in addition to that for 200 books.
8 file drawers.

Seating

7 chairs

Materials

Books   200

Proximity to
Administrative Offices.

Name of area   **Administrative Offices**   **Dimensions** 500 Sq. Ft.

Activities Library administration/clerical staff.

Occupancy
> 4 staff

Major design features and ambience of area
Sound proof.
Natural light.

Furnishings & equipment
4 desks, minimum 3' × 4', with computerized workstations, ergonomic chairs, telephones, and wastebaskets.
Laser printer.
Clerical supplies.
Fax.
Copier.
4 5-drawer file cabinets.
Open shelves for visibility and ease of location.
1 locked cabinet, minimum 70" high and 3' wide.

Seating
> 4 ergonomic chairs

Proximity
Next to Director's Office.

Name of area   **Technical Processing**   **Dimensions** 1,000 Sq. Ft.

Activities
Order and receive books, magazines, and non-print materials.

Occupancy
   Staff 4

Major design features and ambience of area
Near delivery point for delivery and distribution of materials.
Windows that open, very well lighted, individual heating and cooling thermostat zone.
Spacious, elbow room, adequate space to move book trucks is essential.

Furnishings & equipment
4 desks with drawer files, ergonomic chairs, electronic workstations, telephones, and wastebaskets.
Acoustical dividers between desks (staff complain "can't hear when answering phone").
10 book trucks (need 4-foot-wide walk spaces).
L-shaped counter 5' by 3' 28" high, 30" deep for book covering and repair with nearby sink.
Printer.
Typewriter and copy machine.
Shelving no higher than 5-1/2 feet (higher than that is wasted space for staff with arm loads of books).
Storage shelves in closet for processing and mending supplies which can accommodate both book- and bulkier cases for non-print materials.
Clock.
Bulletin board.
Receiving area with a 6–8 foot table or counter with 3–5 sections of single-spaced shelving plus space for storing, loading, and unloading boxes of books.
Space for staff's personal belongings.

Seating
   4 staff chairs

Materials
   Books 200   Non-books 50

Proximity
Near Service Entrance

Name of area   **Network Center/Computer Room**   **Dimensions** 200 Sq. Ft.

Activities
Work area for computer repairs, telecommunications center for equipment storage, parts, and supplies, automated systems consortia equipment storage,

Occupancy
Staff 2

Major design features and ambience of area
Near delivery point for delivery and distribution of equipment and wiring.
Well lighted, individual heating and cooling thermostat zone.
Spacious, elbow room, adequate space for present and future equipment.
Work area separate from storage and system equipment.
Wide doors for access to equipment and wiring.

Furnishings & equipment
Patch panel equipment and cabinet for LAN and Internet access.
Server, monitor, and printer for library automation system.
Telephone line switch closet with work space for rewiring.
Windows NT server, monitor, and printer for Internet.
Firewall/proxy server.
Uninterruptible power supply (UPS) cabinet.
Rack system for hubs and routers.
Work bench with lockable drawers for tools, with dataports and electrical receptacles above work surface.
Ergonomic chairs, electronic workstation, telephones, and wastebaskets.
2 equipment trucks (need 4-foot-wide walk spaces).
Deep storage shelves and closet for equipment and supplies.
Wall clock.
Bulletin board.
Receiving area with a counter with 2 sections of single-spaced shelving above plus space for storing, loading, and unloading equipment.
Space for personal belongings.

Seating
2 staff chairs

Materials
Books 20   Non-books 10

Proximity
Near Service Entrance and Technical Service Area.

Name of area   **Staff Room**   **Dimensions** 400 Sq. Ft.

Activities
Staff eat lunch, take coffee breaks, relax.

Occupancy
        Staff 10

Major design features and ambience of area
Comfortable, relaxing room with natural light.
Efficient kitchen with ample storage.
Incandescent task lighting with an area that can be darkened for resting.

Furnishings & equipment
Lounge seating for 6.
Table with seating for 8.
Sofa/couch, place for cot to lie down when ill.
Lockers for 20 (box lockers).
Refrigerator.
Microwave.
Sink.
Cabinets.
Restroom adjoining.
No carpeting under table seats.
1 shelf for reading materials.
Telephone.
Small bulletin board area (3' x 4').
Coat rack for 20 coats.

Seating   14 staff
               12 chairs, 1 sofa/couch, 2 lounge chairs

Proximity to
Restrooms. Possible future shower/exercise room area.

Source 3

Steel Book Stack Specifications

Part 1—General

A. Proposal is to include all costs of items including delivery, unloading, installation, and assembly in completed library building, and necessary cleaning, polishing, or adjustments, removal of all shipping and packing materials; final installation complete and ready for use.

B. No sales tax is to be included.

C. The owner reserves the right to increase or decrease the quantity of the final order by 25 percent of the total proposal cost at the same unit price of the basic proposal.

D. All products to be guaranteed against defects in materials workmanship or installation for a period of one year after installation. No bent, scratched, rubbed, or otherwise damaged or deformed items will be accepted.

E. Temporary storage in the library will generally NOT be available in the event items are delivered prior to required installation date; therefore, include any necessary storage charges in bid proposal.

F. Anticipate installation on or about _____. Telephone before delivery.

Part 2—Products

A. General: All components to be first quality and meet manufacturer's standard recommended details of gauges of metals and finishes. Sheet steel is to be cold rolled, Class I steel. Gauges are U.S. Standard.

B. Type of Bookstack: Steel book stacks shall be cantilever with each unit having a welded frame assembly. Commercial or case type shelving or sway bracing will not be acceptable.

Shelving Units: Provide complete free-standing steel book stack units as follows. All framing sections 36 inches wide, with welded frames and steel web upright braces to conform to state of California seismic standards to eliminate sway bracing and top bracing.

Upright columns of welded frame shall be formed of not less than #16 gauge steel into channel shape with no less than one-half inch stiffening flanges measuring two inches in the web and 1–1/4 inch at front and rear. Uprights are to be slotted with a series of 3/16 inch × 5/8 inch slots spaced one inch on centers. Every sixth slot shall be shaped differently to ease visual leveling of shelves.

Bottom spreader of welded frame shall be formed of #16 gauge steel channel shape measuring at least one inch by 1–3/4 inches in cross section and be equipped with two adjustable plastic covered levelers to provide protection to floor surface and to prevent the sections from "walking." The outer end will receive pre-drilled weld nuts to receive floor levelers. Bottom spreader to be welded to uprights with open portion facing upward.

Top spreader of welded frame will consist of #16 gauge tubular steel shape measuring at least one inch by 2–1/2 inches in cross section. Top spreader to be welded to uprights at concealed locations.

Closed base shelf: Base shelves shall be one piece construction formed of no less than #18 gauge steel designed to fit around the welded frame uprights and snap into the base brackets without the need for fasteners. Front edge of base shelf shall be three inches and sides shall have stiffening flanges.

Base Bracket: Base brackets shall be one piece and shall fit snugly around the welded frame uprights. Brackets shall be formed of #16 gauge steel and shall have a flange that will rest on the floor. Bracket shall provide a positive leveling capability. Top and front edge of bracket shell be flanged outward one-quarter inch and profile of base bracket shall be sloped 15 degrees to match the shelf end brackets. Base bracket shall have an impression with a hole in it for attaching adjoining base bracket fasteners contained within the impression.

Adjustable Shelf: All shelves shall be capable of supporting book loads of 50 pounds per square foot without deflection in excess of 3/16 inches. Nominal shelf sizes shall be eight, nine, ten, or 12 inches formed of #18 gauge steel. Actual dimension of shelf shall be one inch less than nominal dimension. Front and rear edges of shelf shall be box formed three-quarter inch high. Sides of shelf to be flanged downward to allow locking into end bracket grips. Each shelf shall measure 35–3/8 inches clear between end brackets.

Shelf End Bracket: Shelf end brackets shall be formed of #16 gauge steel with a 15-degree sloped front edge. Top, bottom, and front edge are to be flanged outward one-quarter inch. Rear edge shall have two crimped hooks at top and a positioning tab at bottom for engaging into frame slots. Two grips are to be provided for engaging side flanges of shelves. Brackets shall extend at least 6 inches and have an impression to prevent brackets from overlapping.

Optional T-Bar Construction: T-Bar Leg Base where specified shall be constructed of a horizontal member measuring one inch by 2–1/2 inches, #16 gauge steel tubing with welded four nine-inch #11 gauge vertical channel members and a #11 gauge pan clip welded at bottom to serve as bearing surface for the welded frame. Extreme ends of tubular members shall have weld nuts pre-drilled to receive floor levelers. Open ends of tubular shape will be closed with black vinyl cap. T-Bar units shall be starter and adder combinations.

C. Guarantee: Manufacturer shall guarantee the durability and stability of his components for the intended library use.

D. Alternates: If alternates are available within the descriptions that follow, quote on the basis of least expensive with an alternate for the more expensive. Equipment to be equal to MJ Industries, Estey, Montel, Scania, BCI, or Aetnastack.

E. Finishes: Finish for all metal to be factory finished baked-on or powder coated medium gloss enamel in selected standard colors.

Item 1—90-inch-high, double-faced, 12-inch-deep base and six additional 12-inch-deep adjustable shelves at each face.

Item 2—90-inch-high, single-faced, 12-inch-deep base and six additional 12-inch-deep adjustable shelves.

Item 3—90-inch-high, single-faced, 12-inch-deep base and four additional adjustable tilt and store periodical shelves. Each shelf will have one fixed and one hinged display shelf.

Item 4—30-inch-high, single-faced, 12-inch-deep base and one additional shelf. This unit will have a plywood/plastic laminate canopy perforated at the rear. It is located in front of baseboard radiation that requires free air passage below shelving, which makes wall anchorage impractical. The hot air should also be able to freely pass up the window to the rear of the book stacks, so that these book stacks should be anchored to the floor with a perforated plywood/plastic laminate canopy above the radiator.

Item 5—End panels—Provide cost estimates for three alternate choices:
Alternate 1—Plastic laminate with bull nose edges as in item 4.
Alternate 2—Slat wall with bull nose edges.
Alternate 3—Steel end panels.
Alternate 4—Birch or teak plywood with bull nose edges.

End panels will be required only for range ends facing the building interior. Do not supply end panels for range ends facing walls.

Provide one pull-out sliding reference shelf for every other section.

Provide one combined book support and displayer for every section (Gaylord).

Provide one non-losable large oversize steel book support with cork base for each shelf except those with combined book support and displayer.

Install all units plumb and level.

Plastic laminate canopy: 3/4-inch minimum thickness particle board both sides covered with plastic laminate sheets with putty color and pattern throughout Nevamar plastic or equal. No visible seams. 3/4-inch solid wood rounded bullnose on front with three coats of polyurethane clear dull finish varnish. Securely attached to the top of the steel book stacks.

Schedule of Book Stack Equipment

Item A
Seven (7) double-faced ranges 12"/24"/90"—15 feet long comprised of five (5) 3' double-faced units.

Item B
One (1) double-faced range 12"/24"/90"—12 feet long comprised of four (4) 3' double-faced units.

Item C
One (1) double-faced range 12"/24"/90"—9 feet long comprised of three (3) 3' double-faced units.

Item D
Three (3) single-faced ranges 12"/24"/90"—6 feet long comprised of two (2) 3' single-faced units.

Item E
One (1) single-faced range 12"/24"/90"—18 feet long comprised of six (6) 3' single-faced units.

Item F
One (1) single-faced range 12"/24"/90"—12 feet long comprised of four (4) 3' single-faced units.

Item G
One (1) single-faced range 12"/12"/90"—24 feet long comprised of eight (8) 3' single-faced units of tilt-and-store periodical shelving with integral lighting on each shelf similar to Scania Hy Lyter.

Item H
One (1) single-faced range 12"/12"/30"—21 feet long comprised of
seven (7) 3' single-faced units with plastic laminate canopy. This range is located in front of baseboard radiation that requires free air passage below shelving, which makes wall anchorage impractical. The hot air should also be able to freely pass up the

window to the rear of the book stacks, so that these book stacks should be anchored to the floor.

This range will include a plastic laminate canopy with a perforated rear section to let hot air rise from the radiator to the rear of the window.

Source 4

Library Equipment Suppliers

General Equipment

Abodia
slide storage system
Elden Enterprises Box 3201
Charleston, WV 25332-3201
304–344–2335

Adden
furniture—wooden
165 Jackson St.
Lowell, MA 01852—2199
978–453–6484

American Seating Meeting
room chairs
401 American Seating Center
Grand Rapids, MI 49504
800–748–0268

Art Directions
pendant lighting
6120 Delmar Blvd.
St. Louis, MO 63112–1204
314–863–1895

Russ Bassett
files
8189 Byron Rd.
Whittier, CA 90606
800–624–4728

BCI Danish Library Design
multimedia display units
2216 Bisonnet
Houston, TX 77005
713–522–9715
www.bciusa.com

Beemak
plastic displayers
7424 Santa Monica Blvd.
Los Angeles, CA 90046
213–876–1770

Biomorph
Electronic workstations
11 Broadway, Space 10
New York, NY 10004
212–809–4323
www.biomorphdesk.com

BKM Office
furniture dealer
340 Woodmont Road
Milford, CT 06460-3702
800–786–4350

Bretford Manufacturing
electronic workstations
11000 Seymour Ave.
Franklin Park, IL 60131
800–521–9614
www.bretford.com

Brewster
display panels
Old Saybrook, CT 06475
203–388–4441

Brodart General
equipment and furnishings
100 North Road Clinton County
Industrial Park
Box 300
McElhattan, PA 17748
888–820–4377
www.brodart.com

Checkpoint
theft detection and self serve checkout
101 Wolf Drive Box 188
Thorofare, NJ 08086
800–257–5540
www.checkpointsystems.com/library

Current Designs
audio station
115 West 23 St.
New York, NY 10011
212–463–0795

Darnell-Rose
casters for backtrucks and furniture
17915 Railroad Street
City of Industry, CA 91748
626–912–3765
www.casters.com

Day-o-Lite
library stack light
126 Chestnut St.
Warwick, RI 02888
401–467–8232

Design within Reach
*elegant catalog for mail order of high style
modern furniture*
455 Jackson St.
San Francisco, CA 94111
www.dwr.com

Display Fixtures
*inexpensive painted plywood display
fixtures*
Box 7245
Charlotte, NC 28217
704–588–0880

DuPont Flooring Systems
*electronic floors and Library Liftman stack
moving systems*
1–800–4dupont
www.dupontflooringsystems.com

Electrix
small desk lamps
Stamford, CT 06902
203–359–0230

Elliptipar
asymmetric lights
145 Orange Ave.
West Haven, CT 06516
203–932–4899

Estey div. Tennsco
steel bracket shelving
201 Tennsco Drive
Dickson, TN 37056–1888
800–251–8184

Eustis Enterprises
fine wooden chairs and booktrucks with epoxy-injected joints
Box 842
Ashburnham, MA 01430
978–827–3103

Fetzer
fine wooden furniture
1436 S. West Temple
Box 26706
Salt Lake City, UT 84126–0706
801–484–6103

Fixtures Furniture
office chairs
1642 Crystal
Box 6346
Kansas City, MO 64126–2825
800–821–3500

Franklin Fixtures
display fixtures
20 Patterson Brook Road
West Wareham, MA 02576
508–291–1475

Garcy Studs
steel shelving supports that fit into sheet rock walls
2501 North Elston Ave.
Chicago, IL, 60647
312–235–5600

Gaylord Bros.
furniture and equipment
Box 4901
Syracuse, NY 13221–4901
800–448–6160

Gressco
supplies and equipment (especially children's)
328 Moravian Valley Road
Box 339
Waunakee, WI 53597
800–345–3480

GroupComm System
recessed and semi-recessed Para Vision desks, children's furniture, equipment
237 Riverview Ave.
Newton, MA 02466
800–462–1232

Harris Environmental Systems
archival storage units
11 Connector Road,
Andover, MA 01810
617–475–0104

Haworth Office Systems
One Haworth Center
Holland, MI 49423
800–344–2600

Highsmith
supplies and equipment; children's and schools' office chair with changeable cushions
W5527 Highway 106
Box 800
Fort Atkinson, WI 53638–0800
800–558–2110

Huston and Company
fine wooden chairs and tables
226 Log Cabin Road
Kennebunkport, ME 04046
207–967–2345

International Contract Furnishings
modern chairs and tables
145 E. 57 St
New York, NY 10022
212–752–5870

George Kovacs
lighting
24 West 40th St.
New York, NY 10018
212–944–9606

Krueger International
Perry stacking chair
Box 8100
Green Bay, WI 54308-8100
414–468–8100

LCN
handicapped door closures
Princeton, IL 61356
815–875–3311

Let There Be Neon
lighting
451 W. Broadway
New York, NY 10012
212–473–7370

Library Bureau
wooden furniture
801 Park Ave.
Herkimer, NY 13350
315–866–4430

Library Display Design Systems
Box 8143
Berlin, CT 06037
Karen Ribnicky
203–828–6089

Library Display Shelving
clear acrylic plastic shelving
7 Mile fishcamp Enterprises
173 West Ohio Ave.
Lake Helen, FL 32744
80–762–6209

LIFT
display systems for videos, CDs, and DVDs
115 River Road
Edgewater, NJ 07020
800–543–8269 or 201–945–8700

Lighting by Gregory
table lamps
158 Bowery
New York, NY 10002
212–226–1276

Robert Lord
furniture dealer
36 Commerce St.
Glastonbury, CT 06033
203–633–4655

Luxo Lighting
Box 951
Port Chester, NY 10573
914–937–4433

Herman Miller
Aeron chair manufacturers
Zeeland, MI 49464
616–772–3300

Mitchell Furniture Systems
folding tables
Box 1156
Milwaukee, WI 53201
414–342–3111

MJ Industries
steel bookstacks and multi media display systems
Carleton Drive
PO Box 259
Georgetown, MA 01833
508–352–6190

Thomas Moser
wooden furniture
72 Wright's Landing
PO Box 1237
Auburn, ME 04211
800–708–9710
www.thosmoser.com

Multi-Counter
manual counting devices
Stroud Rd.
North Branford, CT 06471
203–488–1800

Norsk Inc.
Ekornes Norwegian lounge chairs stressless, high back, comfortable leather swivel lounge chairs
114 East 57 St.
New York, NY 10022
212–439–7259

NOVA
electronic workstations; embedded terminals
421 W Industrial Ave.
Effingham, IL 62401
800–730–6682
or
217–342–7070

Nova Tech
stack moving system
1320 6th Ave. So.
Moorhead, MN 56560
218–236–2072

Oblique Filing Systems
newspaper files
Box 987
Irmo, SC 29063
800–845–7068
www.ObliqueFilingSystems.com

Paragon Furniture
embedded terminal electronic workstations
6420 Wuliger Way
Fort Worth, TX 76180
800–451–8546
or
817–581–4045

Peerless Cylinder
library lighting
747 Bancroft Way
Berkeley, CA 94710
415–845–2760

Porta-Structures
buildings
Box 30193

Washington, DC 20014
301–951–0500

Proloc
English audio visual display fixtures
www.proloc-online.com

Rentacart
rentacrate for moving
1–800–427–2832

Rudd International
table systems for meeting rooms
1025 Thomas Jefferson St. NW
Washington, DC 20007
202–333–5600

Sauder
wooden chairs
980 West Barre Road
Archbold, OH 43502–0230
800–537–1530

Scania Integrated
shelving system
150 North Michigan Ave. Suite 1200
Chicago, IL 60611–7590
800–3-SCANIA

Showbest
display fixtures
Box 25336
Richmond, VA 23260
804–643–3600

Skools Inc.
Kin-der-link locking stools and other children's furniture
Suite 15A 40 Fifth Ave
New York, NY 10011
212–674–1150

Steelcase Sensor and Criterion Chairs
Turnstone division UNO chairs
Grand Rapids, MI 49501

Stendig Furniture
classic chairs
410 East 62 St.
New York, NY 10021
212–838–6050

Swivelier
screw-in light fixtures
Nanuet, NY 10954
914–623–3471

James M. Taylor
wooden furniture
39 Frost Hill Road
York, ME 03909
207–439–1176

Technichair
ergonomic adjustable chairs
Office Furniture and Design Center
130 East Route 59
Spring Valley, NY 10977
914–356–6556

Thonet Industries Inc.
wooden chairs
150 East 58 St. #30
New York, NY 10155–0399
212–421–3152

3M
book theft detection
3M Center
Bldg. 225–4N–14
St. Paul, MN 55144–1000
800–447–8826

TSAO Designs
lighting
31 Grove St.
New Canaan, CT 06840
203–966–9559

Tucker Library Interiors
dealer
12 Parmenter Road Box 72
Londonderry, NH 03053
603–434–5574

Tuohy
wooden furniture
42 St. Albans Place
Chatfield, MN 55923
507–867–4280

Virco Manufacturing
Perry chairs, comfortable steel stacking chairs
2027 Harpers Way
Torrance, CA 90501
1–800–488–4758

Visa Lighting
stylish table lamps
8600 West Bradley Road
Milwaukee, WI 53224
414–354–6600

Wieland Furniture
upholstered Loop Searies high density foam covered with velcro fastened slip covers for easy reupholstering.
Box 1000
Grabill, Indiana 46741-1000
888–943–5263
www.wielandfurniture.com

The Worden Co.
furniture
199 E. 17th St.
Box 1227
Holland, MI 49423-4298
800–678–0199

Electronic Workstation Web Sites

www. biomorphdesk.com
www.sitincomfort.com
www.sishft.com
www.laptop-laidback.com
www.haginc.com

Library Equipment by Type

(vendors listed but not necessarily recommended)

Archival Storage

Harris Environmental Systems
archival storage units
11 Connector Road
Andover, MA 01810
617–475–0104

Audio-Visual or Multimedia

Abodia
slide storage system
Elden Enterprises
Box 3201
Charleston, WV 25332-3201
304–344–2335

Current Designs
audio station
115 West 23 St.
New York, NY 10011
212–463–0795

LIFT
display systems for videos, CDs, and DVDs
115 River Road
Edgewater, NJ 07020
800–543–8269
or
201–945–8700

MJ Industries
steel bookstacks and multimedia display systems
Carleton Drive
PO Box 259
Georgetown, MA 01833
508–352–6190

Proloc
English audio-visual display fixtures
www.proloc-online.com

See also General Equipment companies

Casters

Darnell-Rose
casters for booktracks and furniture
17915 Railroad Street,
City of Industry, CA 91748
626–912–3765
www.casters.com

Chairs or Seating Furniture

STEEL CHAIRS

American Seating
stacking chairs
401 American Seating Center
Grand Rapids, MI 49504
800–748–0268

Design within Reach
elegant catalog of high style modern furniture
455 Jackson St.
San Francisco, CA 94111
www.dwr.com

Fixtures Furniture
office chairs
1642 Crystal
Box 6346
Kansas City, MO 64126–2825
800–821–3500

International Contract Furnishings
modern chairs and tables
145 E. 57 St.
New York, NY 10022
212-752-5870

Krueger International
Perry stacking chair
Box 8100
Green Bay, WI 54308-8100
414–468–8100

Herman Miller
Aeron chair manufacturers
Zeeland, MI 49464
616–772–3300

Norsk Inc.
Ekornes Norwegian lounge chairs stressless, high back, chrome frame, comfortable leather swivel lounge chairs
114 East 57 St.
New York, NY 10022
212–439–7259

Charles O. Perry
chair designer
20 Shorehaven Road
Norwalk, CT 06855
203–838–0639

Steelcase Sensor and Criterion chairs
Turnstone division UNO chairs
Grand Rapids, MI 49501

Stendig Furniture
classic chairs
410 East 62 St.
New York, NY 10021
212–838–6050

Technichair
ergonomic adjustable chairs
Office Furniture and Design Center
130 East Route 59
Spring Valley, NY 10977
914–356–6556

Virco Manufacturing
Perry chairs, comfortable steel stacking chairs
2027 Harpers Way
Torrance, CA 90501
800–488–4758

Wieland Furniture
Upholstered Loop Series high density foam covered with velcro fastened slip covers for easy reupholstering
Box 1000
Grabill, Indiana 46741-1000
888–943–5263
www.wielandfurniture.com

WOODEN CHAIRS

Eustis Enterprises
fine wooden chairs and booktrucks with epoxy-injected joints
Box 842
Ashburnham, MA 01430
978–827–3103

Huston and Company
fine wooden chairs and tables
226 Log Cabin Road
Kennebunkport, ME 04046
207–967–2345

Thomas Moser
wooden furniture
72 Wright's Landing
PO Box 1237
Auburn, ME 04211
800–708–9710
www.thosmoser.com

Sauder
wooden chairs
980 West Barre Road
Archbold, OH, 43502–0230
800–537–1530

Thonet Industries Inc.
wooden chairs
491 E. Princess St.
York, PA 17405
717–845–6666

See also General Equipment companies

Children's Furniture and Equipment

Gressco
supplies and equipment (especially children's)
328 Moravian Valley Road
Box 339
Waunakee, WI 53597
800–345–3480

Skools Inc.
Kin-Der-Link linked children's stools and wheelbarrow carrels
40 Fifth Ave., Suite 15A
New York, NY 10011
212–674–1150

See also General Equipment companies

Circulation or Reference Desks

Fetzer
fine wooden furniture
1436 S. West Temple
Box 26706
Salt Lake City, Utah 84126–0706
801–484–6103

See also General Equipment companies

Coffee Carts

Continental Cart division of Kullman Industries
732–636–1500
www.kullman.com

Counters

Multi-Counter
manual counting devices
Stroud Rd.
North Branford, CT 06471
203–488–1800

Displayers

Alpha
display systems
330 South Wood St.
East Canton, OH 44730
800–442–5742

BCI Danish Library Design
multimedia display units
2216 Bisonnet
Houston, TX 77005
713–522–9715
www.bciusa.com

Beemak
plastic displayers
7424 Santa Monica Blvd.
Los Angeles, CA 90046
213–876–1770

Brewster
display panels
Old Saybrook, CT 06475
203–388–4441

Bro-Dart
furniture and equipment
1609 Memorial Ave.
Williamsport, PA 17705
800–233–8467

Display Fixtures
inexpensive painted plywood display fixtures
Box 7245
Charlotte, NC 28217
704–588–0880

Franklin Fixtures
display fixtures
20 Patterson Brook Road
West Wareham, MA 02576
508–291–1475
www.franklinfixtures.com

Garcy Studs
steel shelving supports that fit into sheet rock walls
2501 North Elston Ave.
Chicago, IL, 60647
312–235–5600

Library Display Design Systems
Box 8143
Berlin, CT 06037
203–828–6089

Library Display Shelving
clear acrylic plastic shelving
7 Mile Fishcamp Enterprises
173 West Ohio Ave.
Lake Helen, FL 32744
800–762–6209

LIFT
display systems for videos, CDs, and DVDs
115 River Road
Edgewater, NJ 07020
800–543–8269
or
201–945–8700

MJ Industries
steel bookstacks and multimedia display systems
Georgetown, MA
508–352–6190

Scania Integrated
shelving system
150 North Michigan Ave., Suite 1200
Chicago, IL 60611
800–3-SCANIA

Showbest
display fixtures
Box 25336
Richmond, VA 23260
804–643–3600

See also General Equipment companies

Dealers

BKM Office
furniture dealer
340 Woodmont Road
Milford, CT 06460-3702
800–786–4350

GroupComm System
recessed and semi-recessed Para Vision Desks, children's furniture, equipment
237 Riverview Ave.
Newton, MA 02466
800–462–1232

Kernan Library Office Group
dealer
Box 68
New Hartford, NY 13413
315–732–7373

Tucker Library Interiors
dealer
12 Parmenter Road
Box 72
Londonderry, NH 03053
603–434–5574

The Worden Co.
furniture
199 E. 17th St.
Box 1227
Holland, MI 49423-4298
800–678–0199

Door Closures

LCN
handicapped door closures
Princeton, IL 61356
815–875–3311

Electronic Workstations

Biomorph
electronic workstations
11 Broadway, Space 10
New York, NY 10004
212–809–4323
www.biomorph.com

Bretford Manufacturing
electronic workstations
11000 Seymour Ave.
Franklin Park, IL 60131
800–521–9614
www.bretford.com

NOVA
electronic workstations and embedded terminals
421 W. Industrial Ave.
Effingham, IL 62401
217–342–7070

Paragon Furniture
electronic workstations and embedded terminals
6420 Wuliger Way
Fort Worth, TX 76180
800–451–8546
or
817–581–4045

ELECTRONIC WORKSTATION WEB SITES

www. biomorphdesk.com
www.sitincomfort.com
www.sishft.com
www.laptop-laidback.com
www.haginc.com

See also General Equipment companies

Files

Oblique
newspaper files
800–845–7068

Russ Bassett
files
8189 Byron Rd.
Whittier, CA 90606
800–624–4728

Folding Tables

Mitchell Furniture Systems
folding tables
Box 1156
Milwaukee, WI 53201
414–342–3111

General Library Equipment Companies

Brodart
general equipment and furnishings
100 North Road
Clinton County Industrial Park Box 300
McElhattan, PA 17748
888–820–4377
www.brodart.com

Demco
hi/lo electronic workstations
1–800–356–1200

Gaylord Bros.
general equipment and furnishings
Box 4901
Syracuse, NY 13221–4901
800–448–6160

Gressco
supplies and equipment (especially children's)
328 Moravian Valley Road
Box 339
Waunakee, WI 53597
800–345–3480

Haworth
office systems
One Haworth Center
Holland, MI 49423
800–344–2600

Highsmith
general equipment and furnishings; children's and schools; office chair with changeable cushions
W5527 Highway 106
Box 800
Fort Atkinson, WI 53638–0800
800–558–2110

Steelcase
office landscape systems, chairs and tables
Grand Rapids, MI 49501

Lighting

Art Directions
pendant lighting
6120 Delmar Blvd.
St. Louis, MO 63112–1204
314–863–1895

Day-o-Lite Library
stack light
126 Chestnut St.
Warwick, RI 02888
401–467–8232

Electrix
small desk lamps
Stamford, CT 06902
203–359–0230

Elliptipar
asymmetric lights
145 Orange Ave.
West Haven, CT 06516
203–932–4899

George Kovacs
lighting; small lamps
24 West 40th St.
NY 10018
212–944–9606

Let There Be Neon
lighting
451 W. Broadway
New York, NY 10012
212–473–7370

Lighting by Gregory
table lamps
158 Bowery
New York, NY 10002
212–226–1276

Luxo Lighting
Box 951
Port Chester, NY 10573
914–937–4433

Peerless Cylinder
library lighting
747 Bancroft Way
Berkeley, CA 94710
415–845–2760

Swivelier
screw-in light fixtures
Nanuet, NY 10954
914–623–3471

TSAO Designs
lighting
31 Grove St.
New Canaan, CT 06840
203–966–9559

Visa Lighting
stylish table lamps
8600 West Bradley Road
Milwaukee, WI 53224
414–354–6600

Moving

DuPont flooring systems
electronic floors and Library Liftman stack moving systems
1–800–4dupont
www.dupontflooringsystems.com

Nova Tech
stack moving system
1320 6th Ave. So.
Moorhead, MN 56560
218–236–2072

Rentacart
rentacrate for moving
800–427–2832

Portable Buildings

Porta-Structures
buildings
Box 30193
Washington, DC 20014
301–951–0500

Shelving

Estey div. Tennsco
steel bracket shelving
201 Tennsco Drive
Dickson, TN 37056–1888
800–251–8184

Library Bureau
wooden furniture
801 Park Ave.
Herkimer, NY 13350
315–866–4430

MJ Industries
steel bookstacks and multimedia display systems
Georgetown, MA
508–352–6190

See also General Equipment companies

Tables

John Adden
furniture
10 Thacher St.
Boston, MA 02113
617–227–9120

Huston and Company
fine wooden chairs and tables
226 Log Cabin Road
Kennebunkport, ME 04046
207–967–2345

Mitchell Furniture Systems
folding tables
Box 1156
Milwaukee, WI 53201
414–342–3111

Thomas Moser
wooden furniture
72 Wrights Landing
Auburn, ME 04210
800–708–9710
www.thosmoser.com,

Rudd International
table systems for meeting rooms
1066 31st St. NW 20007-4405
Washington, DC 20007
202–333–5600

James M. Taylor
wooden furniture
39 Frost Hill Road
York, ME 03909
207–439–1176

Tuohy
wooden furniture
42 St. Albans Place
Chatfield, MN 55923
507–867–428

See also General Equipment companies

Theft Detection

Checkpoint
theft detection and self-serve checkout
101 Wolf Drive
Box 188
Thorofare, NJ 08086
800–257–5540
www.checkpointsystems.com/library

3M
book theft detection
3M Center
Bldg. 225–4N–14
St. Paul, MN, 55144–1000
800–447–8826

Source 5

Resources and Further Reading

American Library Association. *Minimum Standards for Public Library Systems, 1966.* Chicago: ALA, 1967. Chapter on physical facilities, pp. 56–64.
This is the last time that the library association issued national standards for public libraries.

American Library Association. *Standards for College Libraries.* Chicago: ALA, 1986.

Baumann, Charles H. *The Influence of Angus Snead Macdonald and the Snead Bookstack on Library Architecture.* Metuchen, N.J.: Scarecrow Press, 1972.
A fascinating account of a visionary pioneer in library design who projected an incredible futuristic library. He was also a pioneer in modular steel stack design.

Beckman, Margaret. *Public Library Buildings for the 21st Century: A Handbook For Architects, Librarians and Trustees.* New York: Bowker, 1993.

Black, J.B., et al. *Surveying Public Libraries for the ADA.* Tallahassee, Fla.: State Library of Florida, 1992.

Brawne, Michael. *Library Builders.* London: Academy Editions, 1997.
A European perspective on library design.

Brawner, Lee B., and Donald Beck, Jr. *Determining Your Public Library's Future Size.* Chicago: American Library Trustee Association, 1996.
A very useful and meticulous treatment for sizing the library.

Breisch, Kenneth A. *Henry Hobson Richardson and the Small Public Library in America: A Study in Typology.* Cambridge, Mass.: MIT Press, 1997.
A beautiful monograph on a much-admired library design that influenced American small public library design in the nineteenth century.

Cohen, Aaron, and Elaine Cohen. *Designing and Space Planning for Libraries, a Behavioral Guide.* New York: Bowker, 1979.
Elaine and Aaron are the most prolific library building consultants in the world.

Dahlgren, Anders. *Planning the Small Library Facility.* Chicago: ALA, 1996.
A thoughtful and careful guide for small library planning.

Dancik, Deborah, and Emelie Shroder, editors. *Building Blocks for Library Space; Functional Guidelines—1995.* Chicago: LAMA, 1995.

De Chiara, Joseph. *Time-Saver Standards for Building Types.* 3rd ed. New York: McGraw-Hill, 1990.
Useful general building planning information.

Dewe, Michael. *Planning and Designing Libraries for Children and Young People.* London: Library Association Publishing, 1995.
Michael's wonderful book is full of useful planning ideas for children's facilities

Hagloch, Susan B. *Library Building Projects: Tips for Survival.* Englewood, Colo.: Libraries Unlimited, 1994.

Hall, Richard B. *Financing Public Library Buildings.* New York: Neal-Schuman, 1994.

Hill, Ann B. *The Small Public Library; Design Guide, Site Selection and Design Case Study.* Milwaukee, Wis.: University of Wisconsin Center for Urban Architecture, 1980.

Himmel, Ethel Eileen. *Planning for Results: A Public Library Transformation Process.* 2 vols. Chicago: ALA, 1998

Holt, Raymond M. *Wisconsin Library Building Handbook.* Madison, Wisc.: Div. of Library Service, Wisconsin Dept. of Public Instruction, 1978.
A classic treatment of the planning process.

Holt, Raymond M. *Planning Library Buildings and Facilities.* Metuchen, N.J.: Scarecrow, 1990.

Jones, Theodore. *Carnegie Libraries Across America.* New York: Preservation Press, John Wiley and Sons, 1997.
An interesting account of the grant history. See especially Chapter 7 on renovations and additions.

Kaser, D.E. "25 Years of Academic Library Building Planning." *College and Research Libraries,* July 1984 (pp. 268–81).

Library of Congress. *Planning Barrier Free Libraries*. Washington, D.C.: National Service for the Blind and Handicapped, 1981.
The handicapped access bible.

Lushington, Nolan. "Getting It Right; Plan Reviews in the Library Planning Process." *LAMA Journal*, Summer 1993.
An attempt to place the plan review process in the overall setting of library planning. Includes a sample review of a small library plan.

Lushington, Nolan, and James Kusack. *The Design and Evaluation of Public Library Buildings*. Hamden, Conn.: Shoestring, 1991.
Designing according to library roles and library building evaluation.

Lushington, Nolan, and Willis N. Mills, Jr. *Libraries Designed for Users: A Planning Handbook*. Hamden, Conn.: Library Professional Publications, 1979.
Planning from the point of view of the library user. A basic planning manual.

McCabe, Gerard B. *Planning for a New Generation of Public Library Buildings*. Westport, Conn.: Greenwood, 2000.

McClure, Charles R., et al. *Planning and Role Setting for Public Libraries: Manual Prepared for the Options and Procedures Project*. Chicago: ALA, 1987

Michaels, David L. "Technology's Impact on Library Interior Planning." *Library Hi-tech*, Winter 1987 (pp. 59–63).

Mohney, Kirk F. *Beautiful In All Its Details, The Architecture of Maine's Public Library Buildings*. Augusta, Maine: Maine Historic Preservation Commission, 1997.

Myller, Rolf. *The Design of the Small Public Library*. New York: Bowker, 1966.
A nicely illustrated basic planning guide.

Nelson, Sandra. *New Planning for Results: A Streamlined Approach*. Chicago: ALA, 2001.

Novak, Gloria, ed. "The Forgiving Building: A Library Consultant's Symposium On the Design, Construction and Remodeling of Libraries To Support a High-Tech Future." *Library Hi-Tech*, Winter 1987 (pp. 77–99).
An innovative first look at the future of libraries, still useful for ergonomic planning.

Oehlerts, Donald E. *Books and Blueprints: Building America's Public Libraries*. New York: Greenwood, 1991.

Petroski, Henry. *The Book on the Bookshelf.* New York: Knopf, 1999.
See especially Chapter 9 on book stack engineering and Chapter 10 on book stacks that move.

Pevsner, Nikolaus. *History of Building Types.* Princeton: Princeton University Press, 1976.
Pevsner's chapter on libraries puts this building type in an overall architectural perspective. Pevsner is a distinguished art historian.

Public Library Association. *Planning and Role Setting for Public Libraries.* Chicago: ALA, 1987.

Public Library Association. *Planning for Results.* Chicago: ALA, 1999

Rochell, Carlton. *Wheeler and Goldhor's Practical Administration of Public Libraries As Completely Revised by Carlton Rochell.* New York: Harper and Row, 1981.

Rohlf, Robert. "Library Design: What NOT To Do." *American Libraries,* February 1986.
Bob Rohlf has been the consultant on dozens of major public libraries and is highly critical of some common design flaws.

Sannwald, William. *Checklist of Library Design Considerations.* Chicago: ALA, 1996.
A useful list of design considerations that is helpful in reviewing plans and visiting libraries.

Schell, Hal B. *Reader on the Library Building.* Englewood, Colo.: Microcard Editions, 1975.

Staff of the Williamsburg Regional Library. *Library Construction from Staff Perspective.* Jefferson, N.C.: McFarland and Co. to be published.
Staff accounts of working with architects, contractors, and project managers on four years of new construction, renovation, and additions. Includes fundraising, celebratory events, team building, and technology upgrades.

Van Syck, Abigail. *Free to All: Carnegie Libraries and American Culture 1890–1920.* Chicago: University of Chicago Press, 1995.
A wonderful account of the evolution of the Carnegie library building type with an interesting account of the debate between librarians and architects in the late nineteenth century. Includes Carnegie's adviser Bertram's design suggestions.

Webb, T.D. *Building Libraries for the 21st Century: The Shape of Information.* Jefferson, N.C.: McFarland and Co.
A series of brief essays on new library buildings including the San Antonio Public Library and several university libraries.

Financing

Hall, Richard B. *Financing Public Library Buildings.* New York: Neal-Schuman, 1994.

Library Furniture

Michaels, Andrea A. "Design Today—Buying Furniture for a High-Tech Library." *Wilson Library Bulletin*, September 1987 (pp. 56–59).
Michaels, Andrea A. "Standard Lines or Custom-Designed?" *American Libraries*, April 1988 (pp. 267–269).
Murphy, Tish. "Some Considerations In Choosing Library Furnishings." *Public Libraries*, July/August 1999 (pp. 244–246).

Building Costs

Library Journal, December issue, 1968-present. Costs reported to *LJ* for the year ending June 30.
Means, R.S. Co., Inc. *Square Foot Costs.* Kingston, Miss.: annual.

Signage

Haskell, Peter C., and Dorothy Pollet. *Sign Systems for Libraries.* New York: Bowker, 1979.
Mallery, Mary S., and Ralph E. DeVore. *A Sign System for Libraries.* Chicago: ALA, 1982.

Non-Standard Storage Solutions

Gorman, Michael. "Movable Compact Shelving: The Current Answer." *Library Hi-tech*, Winter 1987 (pp. 23–26).
Kounz, John. "Industrial Storage Technology Applied to Library Requirements." *Library Hi-tech*, Winter 1987 (pp.13–21).

Customer Behavior

Gladwell, Malcolm. "The Science of Shopping." *The New Yorker*, November 4, 1996 (pp. 66–75).
A fascinating account of Paco Underhill and how he tracks people in retail stores.

Underhill, Paco. *Why We Buy.* New York: Knopf, 1999.
Underhill is the leading researcher in how people behave in buying in stores. He shares his research techniques as well as his knowledge of how people buy.

Helpful Web Sites

Connecticut State Library Home Page
www.cslib.org/libsp99.pdf
Library space planning guide and worksheet.

Wisconsin State Library
www.dpi.state.wi.us/dpi/dltcl/pld/plspace.html
Public library space planning outline and worksheet.

The University of British Columbia—School of Library Archival and Information Studies
www.slais.ubc.ca/resources/architecture/planning.html

Library Land
http://sunsite.berkeley.edu/libraryland/

Index

About the Author

During the past 30 years Nolan Lushington has worked with over 190 public libraries as a library consultant. He has been chairman of the American Library Association Buildings and Equipment section and a juror on the joint ALA/American Institute of Architects Building Awards Program. Mr. Lushington was a Council on Library Resources Fellow and, with Anthony Tappe, he has taught the summer workshop in Public Library Design at the Harvard University Graduate School of Design for the past 12 years. For over two decades Mr. Lushington was the Director of the Greenwich Public Library in Connecticut, and for 11 years was an Associate Professor at the library school at Southern Connecticut State University. He is married to Librarian of the Year Louise Blalock, Chief Librarian of the Hartford Public Library in Connecticut. The 1979 edition of *Libraries Designed for Users* was in print for 20 years.

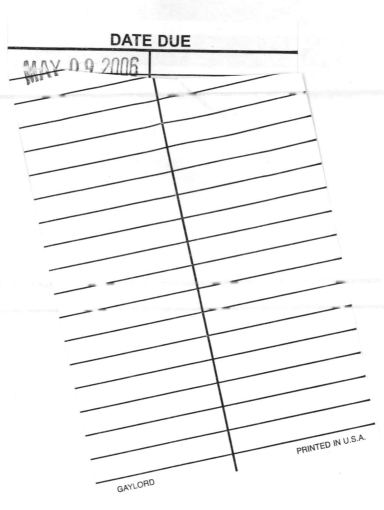